THE GREEN HOUSE

CRE**A**TIVE
HOMEOWNER®

green remodeling

YOUR START TOWARD AN ECO-FRIENDLY HOME

John D. Wagner

CREATIVE HOMEOWNER,® Upper Saddle River, New Jersey

GREEN REMODELING

Produced by Wagner Media; www.JohnDWagner.com

BOOK PACKAGER	John D. Wagner
BOOK DESIGN	Gregory J. Popa
PHOTO EDITOR	John V. Puleio
MANAGING EDITOR	Judy Thurlow
INDEXER	Laura Welcome
FRONT COVER PHOTOGRAPHY	(*right*) courtesy of Neil Kelley Cabinets, (*left, top to bottom*) courtesy of Certainteed, courtesy of Weather Shield Windows and Doors, iStockphoto.com
BACK COVER PHOTOGRAPHY	(*clockwise from top right*) courtesy of Milliken, courtesy of Carrier Corp., courtesy of Weyerhauser, John Puleio

CREATIVE HOMEOWNER

VICE PRESIDENT AND PUBLISHER	Timothy O. Bakke
PRODUCTION DIRECTOR	Kimberly H. Vivas
ART DIRECTOR	David Geer
MANAGING EDITOR	Fran J. Donegan
JUNIOR EDITOR	Jennifer Calvert

Current Printing (last digit)
10 9 8 7 6 5 4 3 2

Green Remodeling, First Edition
Library of Congress Control Number: 2007933862
ISBN 10: 1-58011-396-6
ISBN 13: 978-1-58011-396-0

Printed in the United States of America

CREATIVE HOMEOWNER®
A Division of Federal Marketing Corp.
24 Park Way, Upper Saddle River, NJ 07458
www.creativehomeowner.com

Mixed Sources

Product group from well-managed forests, controlled sources and recycled wood or fiber

www.fsc.org Cert no. SCS-COC-00648
© 1996 Forest Stewardship Council

FSC

safety

Although the methods in this book have been reviewed for safety, it is not possible to overstate the importance of using the safest methods you can. What follows are reminders—some do's and don'ts of work safety—to use along with your common sense.

- Always use caution, care, and good judgment when following the procedures described in this book.
- Always be sure that the electrical setup is safe, that no circuit is overloaded, and that all power tools and outlets are properly grounded. Do not use power tools in wet locations.
- Always read container labels on paints, solvents, and other products; provide ventilation; and observe all other warnings.
- Always read the manufacturer's instructions for using a tool, especially the warnings.
- Use hold-downs and push sticks whenever possible when working on a table saw. Avoid working short pieces if you can.
- Always remove the key from any drill chuck (portable or press) before starting the drill.
- Always pay deliberate attention to how a tool works so that you can avoid being injured.
- Always know the limitations of your tools. Do not try to force them to do what they were not designed to do.
- Always make sure that any adjustment is locked before proceeding. For example, always check the rip fence on a table saw or the bevel adjustment on a portable saw before starting to work.
- Always clamp small pieces to a bench or other work surface when using a power tool.
- Always wear the appropriate rubber gloves or work gloves when handling chemicals, moving or stacking lumber, working with concrete, or doing heavy construction.
- Always wear a disposable face mask when you create dust by sawing or sanding. Use a special filtering respirator when working with toxic substances and solvents.
- Always wear eye protection, especially when using power tools or striking metal on metal or concrete; a chip can fly off, for example, when chiseling concrete.
- Never work while wearing loose clothing, open cuffs, or jewelry; tie back long hair.
- Always be aware that there is seldom enough time for your body's reflexes to save you from injury from a power tool in a dangerous situation; everything happens too fast. Be alert!
- Always keep your hands away from the business ends of blades, cutters, and bits.
- Always hold a circular saw firmly, usually with both hands.
- Always use a drill with an auxiliary handle to control the torque when using large-size bits.
- Always check your local building codes when planning new construction. The codes are intended to protect public safety and should be observed to the letter.
- Never work with power tools when you are tired or when under the influence of alcohol or drugs.
- Never cut tiny pieces of wood or pipe using a power saw. When you need a small piece, saw it from a securely clamped longer piece.
- Never change a saw blade or a drill or router bit unless the power cord is unplugged. Do not depend on the switch being off. You might accidentally hit it.
- Never work in insufficient lighting.
- Never work with dull tools. Have them sharpened, or learn how to sharpen them yourself.
- Never use a power tool on a workpiece—large or small—that is not firmly supported.
- Never saw a workpiece that spans a large distance between horses without close support on each side of the cut; the piece can bend, closing on and jamming the blade, causing saw kickback.
- When sawing, never support a workpiece from underneath with your leg or other part of your body.
- Never carry sharp or pointed tools, such as utility knives, awls, or chisels, in your pocket. If you want to carry any of these tools, use a special-purpose tool belt that has leather pockets and holders.

contents

what does it mean to be green?

Saying you're for green is like saying you're for progress. It can mean many things to many people. Today, the word green is a moving target in a largely unregulated marketplace. A paintbrush manufacturer that uses plastic handles may claim its products are green because the use of plastic avoids the need to harvest wood, while a manufacturer that uses wood handles may claim that its handles avoid the use of non-biodegradable plastic.

Over time, the marketplace will sort out who is greener, and—just as we saw in the organic food industry—government regulators may step in with a unified effort to certify and label products as green. But don't hold your breath waiting for that to happen. The building materials marketplace is so large, multinational, and unwieldy—home building and remodeling combine to create *by far* America's largest industry—that it will be *buyer beware* for years to come.

RIGHT Durable, attractive cabinets can be made with environmentally responsible materials, such as low-VOC finishes and sustainably harvested woods and veneers. For their cores, many green cabinets—like those shown here—use formaldehyde-free wheatboard.

ABOVE Dustless sanding services are now available that link high-efficiency particle accumulator (HEPA) vacuums directly to the floor-sanding head. This eliminates a major source of dust and keeps the air clear.

DEFINING GREEN
CAN ANYTHING DEFINITIVE BE SAID ABOUT GREEN TODAY? YES. HERE ARE SOME BASIC TENETS, AS WELL AS SOME BACKGROUND ON PRODUCTS THAT MAKE YOUR REMODELING PROJECT GREEN.

A GREEN PRODUCT OR PRACTICE IS ONE THAT

→ IMPROVES the indoor air quality of a home, thereby improving the health of the people who live in it.

→ LOWERS pressure on the environment through the use of products that support responsible manufacturing and sustainable harvesting of natural resources, such as lumber, water, and extracted minerals.

→ REDUCES the use of water throughout a home, thereby lowering demands on freshwater sources and the energy-intensive infrastructure required to pipe, store, and purify it.

→ REDUCES the "carbon footprint" of a home—the amount of energy that will be burned to heat and cool a home over its lifetime—which calls for efficient appliances, lighting, windows and doors, and an energy-efficient building envelope.

→ REDUCES the chemical danger and exposure risks to people working on, or eventually living in, the home.

UNDER THESE GUIDELINES, A HIGH-PERFORMANCE caulk would be considered green. It contributes to sealing air infiltration and helps to create a sound building envelope, which will reduce the home's carbon footprint. But there is a distinction between *green* and *sustainable*, and a tube of caulk is a good example. A high-performance, high-VOC (volatile organic compound) caulk that creates toxins during the manufacturing process and poisons the air for workers during application may be green *after* it is applied on-site, but is it sustainable to produce and use if it creates toxic by-products and poisons the air? A high-performance caulk that doesn't give off fumes and is manufactured through a process that has little or no impact on the environment is both green *and* sustainable. For many of the products that are required for practices recommended in this book, you will have three basic choices: (1) products that are not green, because they are environmentally costly to make and use, such as traditional oil-based polyurethane; (2) products that can be considered green because they contribute to the overall quality of your remodeling job, even if the products are environmentally costly to manufacture; and (3) products that are both green *and* sustainable; for example, a no-VOC, water-based polyurethane produced by an environmentally conscious manufacturer. Whenever possible, select products that are both green and sustainable.

Green versus Nongreen

By way of introduction to the green-building process, here's a system-by-system look at various aspects of a typical remodeling job and what can make them green.

 Building Orientation. No single step in the design and remodeling process has more impact on a home than its orientation. A new room addition that contains six large windows, all facing due south, with no soffit to screen out the direct rays of the high summer sun, will act as a heat collector that will drive up air-conditioning bills. Because around 90 percent of electricity in the United States is created by burning fossil fuels, a south-facing home with nothing to mitigate solar heat gain will directly contribute to unnecessary pollution.

When remodeling, be mindful of which way the home is facing. If you must install windows that face south, frustrate their ability to pump heat into the house by choosing high-quality windows with low solar heat gain coefficients (SHGC)—the measure of how much radiant heat passes through the window—and roof soffits, or overhangs, that are designed to

GUIDE TO PROJECTS

🦘 **EASY**
Even for beginners.

🦘🦘 **CHALLENGING**
Can be done by beginners who have the patience and willingness to learn.

🦘🦘🦘 **DIFFICULT**
Can be handled by most experienced do-it-yourselfers who have mastered basic construction skills. Consider consulting a specialist.

Environmentally friendly wood treatments and preservatives can be applied at the factory. These treatments can circumvent the need for mold and termite protection on-site.

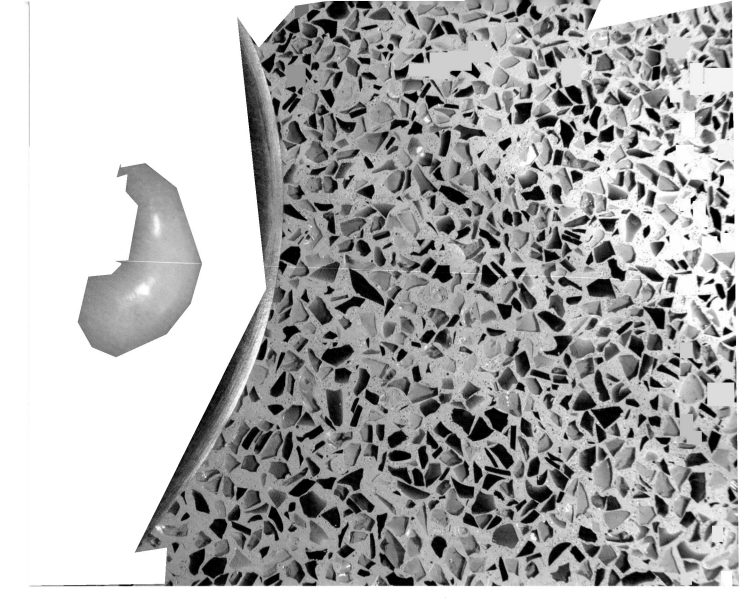

ABOVE Countertops can now be made from multicolored glass chips that come from recycled bottles, mirrors, and plate-glass windows. These attractive countertops can achieve surface hardness that exceeds marble terrazzo, yet they are very green indeed.

the proper length for your latitude to block out the sun during peak heating hours. If you are remodeling a home and you inherited poor orientation that can't be changed, various types of high-performance sheathing and wall systems—even the color of the roof shingles—can help prevent heat from entering the home.

A High-Integrity Building Envelope. After the orientation of the home, the integrity of the building envelope is the next most important attribute of a green remodeling effort. An energy-efficient home that uses wall systems that are designed to reduce air infiltration and suppress mold (thereby improving indoor air quality) is essential. The days are long gone when you could get away with leaky walls or connections between walls and

the roof that lacked proper insulation. Energy is just too expensive and too environmentally costly to produce to heat or cool a house that leaks warm air in the winter or experiences hot-air infiltration in the summer.

A quality building envelope is energy-efficient and allows other green activities, such as active venting of indoor air spaces and the drying out of building components that may get damp during different times of the year—typically, where there are high temperature differentials between the inside and the outside of the home.

A green building is a long-lasting building. Building components should last 100 years or more. That way the home isn't contributing to the waste stream before it has had a long, productive service life.

RIGHT Low-flow technology for toilets, faucets, and showerheads now offers performance that even the pickiest remodeler will be happy with.

BOTTOM RIGHT The integrity of the building envelope is among the most important attributes of any green remodeling project. Housewrap and proper window flashing are essential to any good wall system.

Foundation Systems. Reducing the carbon footprint of the home—which is measured in large part by how much fuel will be consumed to heat and cool the home over its lifetime—can mean reducing the size of your remodeling project. A smaller footprint reduces the amount of air that must be heated or cooled, called "conditioned space." It also reduces the amount of building materials used to create the new space. Most foundation systems use concrete, which is an energy-intensive product to create. Though there are concrete additives that can mitigate the carbon-intensive aspects of the manufacturing process, nothing substitutes for a smaller building footprint and an effort to optimize interior space. You may not want to "think small," but what's wrong with "thinking medium"?

Roofing. It used to be that putting black shingles on a rooftop was standard operating procedure. Unfortunately, a roof with black shingles reflects only about 5 percent of the sun's heat. Black roofs have low *solar reflectance*, whereas gray shingles reflect back about 20 percent, and white shingles around 25 percent. Black roofs get as much as 9 degrees F hotter than white roofs, and if the shingles have low *solar emittance*, the shingles won't radiate that heat back out to the air. The Environmental Protection Agency (EPA) has found that just changing the color of a roof can reduce cooling costs by 10 to 30 percent. EPA figures also show that $40 billion is spent each year in the United States to cool buildings. That's more than 15 percent of all the electricity generated each year. So hot roofs actually drive up the amount of pollution created when electricity is generated to power those air-conditioning units. The solution is reflective granules metal-coating technology that is now available. They can reflect and emit a good deal of the sun's heat.

TOP Kitchen cabinets, notorious for off-gassing because of the adhesives that hold them together, are an easy place to go green with low-VOC adhesives.

ABOVE "Green" doors are now available that use a nonwood core under a hardwood veneer.

Windows and Doors. If you thought windows were just glass, wood, and some putty—or if that's what you have currently protecting your home— you're in for a pleasant, though expensive, surprise. These days, windows are highly engineered building components, and every aspect of a quality window has been tweaked by building scientists. The thermal and water-barrier properties of the frame (wood, fiberglass, vinyl, or aluminum), cladding, dual-pane glass, non-conductive gas between the panes, and even the latches and edge spacers are all subject to engineering studies of how they cumulatively affect the ability of the window to keep heat or cold in or out. When you're looking for a green window, superior energy efficiency, long warranties, and third-party certification from the National Fenestration Rating Council (NFRC) are essential. Moreover, green windows should be part of a total wall system, not just wood-and-glass units plugged into holes in the walls.

RIGHT Though more expensive than traditional batt insulation, blown foam has emerged as a highly efficient way to insulate walls. It creates a consistent, high-integrity layer of insulation that covers every cavity and seam. Plus, it typically doesn't have the moisture problems that can be associated with batts.

Insulation. It's easy to say that a home remodeled in a nongreen way doesn't use enough insulation and therefore costs more in terms of dollars and environmental impact to heat and cool over its lifetime. That's undeniably true. But you can no longer rate the effectiveness of insulation simply by saying more is good and less is bad. Insulation inserted in exterior-facing walls must be part of a wall system that—without depending too much on caulk, which eventually fails—shuns water, dries out, controls moisture, blocks air infiltration, and allows for the insertion of windows and doors through connections that ensure the wall's thermal integrity.

Why have walls gotten so complicated, given the simplicity of the homes in which most of us grew up? After all, those homes seemed simple and were made using plain wood studs and batts of fiberglass insulation that are anything but exotic. Many homes built before the 1970s are not as tight as homes built since then. This is partially because building science, especially when focused on buildings as thermal envelopes, didn't advance very rapidly until the oil shortages of the 1970s. However, since then, the science has advanced dramatically. The main driver is energy costs, followed by comfort, safety, and concerns about health and indoor air quality. In real terms, it costs less to heat and cool a home in 1965 than it did in 2000, and it's only getting more expensive. Given the sustained, upward trend of energy prices, homeowners, contractors, and designers—and the building component manufacturers who serve them—now universally recognize that $1,000 spent on beefed-up insulation will save that amount many times over in fuel costs during the lifetime of the home. Up to a point, people remodeling their homes seem to be willing to make investments in energy efficiency. And, generally speaking, a seven-year payback seems to be the consensus limit of tolerance for spending extra dollars. Coincidentally, that's the number of years the average U.S. homeowner stays in any one residence before moving on.

Siding and Trim. A house built at the turn of the last century, between 1890 to 1910, that has its original siding and trim is relatively rare, unless the siding and trim has been painted every seven to ten years to seal out the weather and mitigate the effects of the sun. Years ago, natural wood was one of the only siding choices. But clearly, natural wood takes a great deal of care to maintain. It is constantly beaten by rain, wind, freeze-thaw cycles, and the sun. Moreover, it has many points of entry for moisture, including knot holes, cracks, and open grain. Even the best paint job can't keep out all the weather.

If the wind, rain, and sun aren't breaking down the wood, it's bugs, such as wood-boring insects, mold, and termites looking at wood siding and thinking it is food. So new generations of pretreated wood, composite wood products, and even nonwood (fiber-cement) siding and trim are available, with expected life spans of 50 years or more. Are they a green choice? Consider the environmental impact of harvesting knot-free spruce or cedar for siding a house, and then add in the environmental impact of painting it time and again. Now, think of what that siding will contribute to the waste stream when it is removed and discarded. You will quickly see that pretreated wood, nonwood, and fiber-cement siding and trim may be the greenest choice, despite the energy-intensive nature of the manufacturing process. What wood manufacturers claim is an "eco choice" or a "green choice" may not be so green when you look at the entire life-cycle impact of that product. You may end up realizing that cementitious siding is your greenest choice.

Lumber. Harvesting lumber, domestically or internationally, can be environmentally costly, especially if the harvested land isn't properly cared for or planted with replacement trees. The environmental and societal damage caused by the harvesting of endangered wood species (typically tropical hardwood) has been well documented.

Today, tropical-lumber markets have responded with plantation-grown alternatives, and many lumber suppliers—on U.S. and international stages—have subjected themselves to voluntary standards set forth by competing "certified lumber" trade associations and nongovernmental organizations. The leading standard-setting organizations—the American Forest & Paper Association's Sustainable Forestry Initiative (SFI) and the Forest Stewardship Council (FSC) Certification System—examine the chain of custody of the lumber and, in some cases, the social impact of its harvest. When buying the dimension lumber that makes up a typical remodeling job—the 2x4s, 2x6s, and the like—the harvesting methods of most of this lumber isn't egregious, but check for a certified label nonetheless. As you get into higher-end finished wood, such as mahogany, redwood, or teak, it's good to be aware of the certification systems and environmentally favorable alternatives like Ipe or Pau Lope, which can ease your conscience while you help relieve pressure on sensitive forests.

RIGHT   Lumber harvests put pressure on forests, but engineered lumber, which can be made from "secondary demand," or less desirable, lumber may hold an answer. Engineered lumber can be used for most framing jobs.

ABOVE   An interior can be green just by being well designed, well lit by natural light, and a pleasure in which to live.

Green Interior Building Components

Wall Systems. What makes an interior wall green? With tighter homes, the inside walls—which are typically uninsulated, unless they have been soundproofed—can act as air barriers that contain moist air or fumes. Ideally, a green home should have a balanced heating, ventilation, and air-conditioning (HVAC) system, where interior air is exchanged with outside makeup air that is conditioned—preheated or precooled by the stale interior air on the way out. Tight interior walls are essential to optimizing a balanced HVAC system. You don't want a kitchen exhaust to suck fumes out of the closet or basement where the gas-fired HVAC unit is working, and you don't want an air-conditioning duct to pump cool air that ends up leaking into spaces that are not meant to be cooled, such as garages or basements. So the integrity and design of interior walls is as important as those of exterior walls.

Indoor Air Quality. As houses have become tighter through better design, there has been increased concern about chemicals that building components contain, such as adhesives in plywood or sheet goods, plastic and vinyl, carpet binders, paints, floor finishes, and wood treatments. Additionally, when remodeling, pay special attention to how air quality is affected by chemicals released when existing building materials—such

as lead, PCBs, and asbestos-are dismantled, stripped, reconditioned, or removed. During construction, pay attention to how common products can affect indoor air quality. Some of these include off-gassing from caulks, adhesives, paints, and various mastics used when building. Last but not least, allergens, dust, and VOCs from cleaning fluids and paints can be released into the indoor air long after you finish your remodeling project.

The levels of these pollutants can be five times higher than pollutants commonly found in outdoor air. Because we spend 90 percent of our time indoors, these are serious concerns that can affect the health of variety of people. The EPA rates indoor pollution a "top five" public health concern.

A green remodeling job is one that keeps the air clean during construction and equips the house with a way to bring fresh air into the living space, while exhausting bad or stale air to the outside. To do that, you have the option of installing e whole-house or room-specific air-filtration systems, or you can address the issue directly by making an effort to reduce or eliminate items that can contaminate the air.

Plumbing. Even in the last decade, there have been great advances in water-saving technology and fixture performance for low-flow toilets, dual-flush toilets, and low-flow showerheads and faucets. Problems that plagued early attempts at low-flow fixtures have been solved, in part through the standardization of testing and rating systems that have established clear performance specifications for which manufacturers can design. These standards are called Maximum Performance (MaP) standards, and they have been incorporated into the broader voluntary Uniform North American Requirements for Toilet Fixtures, which has become the de facto standard for toilet performance. These water-saving components are entirely viable in any bathroom or kitchen for even the most demanding remodeler, and should be a core part of any green bath or kitchen design.

Heating, Ventilation, and Air-Conditioning. Here is an area of remodeling that can combine a number of green features: good indoor air quality, reduced heating and cooling costs, and moisture (mold) control. For heating, cooling, and active ventilation, there are three types of HVAC systems: those that only exhaust air, such as kitchen fans; those that only supply air (outdoor makeup air piped to heating and cooling appliances); and those that do both in a balanced way—hence their name, "bal-

ABOVE Energy Star–qualified appliances incorporate advanced technologies that use 10 to 50 percent less energy and water than standard models.

anced systems." When cost is no object, a balanced system is the way to go because it brings in fresh air and conditions it for you—which can make the system highly efficient—improves indoor air quality, and saves on fuel, which cuts down on pollution. Air filtration is also an option with HVAC systems. Manufacturers have responded to increased attention to asthma and allergies with a variety of whole-house air-filtration systems that range from particulate filters all the way up to virus zappers.

Paints and Finishes. No area of green building has seen such a profusion of new products than that of paints and finishes. When the California Air Resource Board set VOC standards for California markets, the manufacturers that responded with California-specific products found themselves ahead of the curve—green building suddenly became all the rage on a national scale. The EPA also set standards for low- and no-VOC paints and finishes on which manufacturers could set their sights. As a result, high-performance, low- and no-VOC paints and finishes are widely available at prices you used

to pay for more dangerous paints. The benefit is not just to the indoor air quality, but to the overall air quality as well because VOCs contribute to smog. And what could be greener than reducing smog?

Flooring. Green building has brought many products into the mainstream that used to be considered fringe, such as bamboo and cork flooring, tile made of recycled glass, natural linoleum, recycled-content rubber tiles, or chlorine-free polymer resin tiles. Today, even carpets can be entirely recycled ("down cycled"); in fact, some are made out of corn and can be buried in the backyard when they wear out. In every room of your remodel, you can choose from a good variety of high-performance green flooring options, from carpet and tile, which can contain up to 70 percent post-consumer recycled glass, to sustainably harvested wood or recycled lumber. It's easy to go green with flooring. Even the adhesives that are required for proper floor installation are increasingly available in low-VOC formulations that don't compromise strength or durability.

1

how green is different

Green building is nothing new. It started in the 1980s and has continued up to the present. It has always been about good building practices, using quality products, and the creation of a building envelope that reduces heating and cooling costs while providing a safe environment for the occupants and the people who build and remodel the building. But the need for green remodeling is more urgent today than it has been in the past. And with all the attention focused on going green, building-product manufacturers have responded with a wave of new green products. Whether these products are low-VOC (volatile organic compound) adhesives and paints, wood products that make use of every last bit of the tree, or concrete that contains additives to reduce the energy needed during manufacture, they can dramatically accelerate your ability to turn your ordinary remodeling project into a green one. Follow the building recommendations described in this book, and consider the green products highlighted in the "Your Green Choices" sidebars. By combining the two, you'll be well on your way to greening up your remodeling project.

REAL PROBLEMS, REAL SOLUTIONS

GREEN REMODELING EMPLOYS GOOD BUILDING PRACTICES combined with green products and the enhanced construction techniques for which these products call. However, throughout any project, whether you are replacing a single window or tearing out and replacing the whole back of your home, certain core green principles remain constant. These including improving indoor air quality; using products rated for green construction; making the home more comfortable through energy efficiency; lowering pressure on the environment by conserving natural resources; reducing water usage; and orienting the house with respect to the sun.

OPPOSITE Low- and no-VOC paints, caulks, adhesives, and finishes keep some of the ingredients that make up smog out of the air, reducing both indoor and outdoor air pollution.

RIGHT Many paint manufacturers are developing new formulations for paints and other finishes that are nontoxic and environmentally benign.

What Does Green Building Mean in Practice?

Do those principles sound too theoretical and abstract? Let's examine some examples of each of these points, and then look at the categories of products that provide green choices.

Improve Overall Air Quality. Ground-level ozone—also called smog—is created in part because of the VOCs released by paint. Smog results when sunlight reacts with nitrogen oxides from gasoline and VOCs. At 60 parts per billion (ppb)—which is a very small concentration—ozone can damage respiratory and cardiovascular systems. By selecting low- or no-VOC paints, caulks, adhesives, and finishes, you are actually reducing your community's air pollution and potentially affecting in a positive way the respiratory and cardiovascular systems of those around you.

The air-quality issues do not even begin to address the positive environmental aspects of a greener manufacturing process. For example, silica is often contained in nongreen paints, but silica dust at the manufacturing plant can cause a respiratory disease called silicosis. And many nongreen paints add in titanium dioxide for whiteness. Manufacturing titanium dioxide is energy intensive, and as a result, some European markets limit how much can go into paint.

Who Rates the Products? Because the Environmental Protection Agency (EPA) has set national VOC standards, any claims about VOCs should refer to those standards. But also look for Greenguard, Green Seal, or Master Painters Institute's (MPI) Green Performance Standards. Greenguard focuses on indoor air quality, whereas Green Seal and MPI also look at hiding power, durability, and washability.

YOUR GREEN CHOICES

EPA VOC Limits

To achieve an EPA zero-VOC rating, paint must have fewer than 5 grams per liter. For a low-VOC rating, paint must contain 5 to 250 grams per liter for latex paint, or 380 for alkyd (oil-based) paints.

In addition to the federal government, private-sector building and trade groups have started certifying products. For paints, look for materials certified by Greenguard, Green Seal, Scientific Certification Systems, or the Master Painters Institute's Green Performance Standards.

ABOVE Radiant barriers attached to the underside of roof sheathing can block radiant heat from escaping.

LEFT Some building components specialize in stopping heat flow. This housewrap helps stop air and insulates, too.

Make the Home More Comfortable through Energy Efficiency. Heat is transferred through the walls and windows of your home by radiation, convection, and/or conduction. One aim of your green remodeling project should be to stop that heat flow. There are building components and building practices that specialize in doing just that, whether the aim is to keep it from heating up the home in the summer or blocking it from leaving the home in the winter—or both.

A great deal of heat—as much as two-thirds—is lost or gained through radiant heat flow. The other third is attributed to air leakage or air infiltration. To stop air infiltration and defeat radiant heat, combine standard insulation with housewraps (or new thermal-insulating housewraps), radiant barriers that can bar radiant heat, low-E coatings on windows, and windows with low U-factors and low solar heat gain coefficients. (See "How to Read a Window Label," page 103.)

NFRC National Fenestration Rating Council® CERTIFIED	World's Best Window Co. Millennium 2000+ Vinyl-Clad Wood Frame Double Glazing · Argon Fill · Low E Product Type: **Vertical Slider**

ENERGY PERFORMANCE RATINGS	
U-Factor (U.S./I-P)	Solar Heat Gain Coefficient
0.35	**0.32**

ADDITIONAL PERFORMANCE RATINGS	
Visible Transmittance	Air Leakage (U.S./I-P)
0.51	**0.2**

Manufacturer stipulates that these ratings conform to applicable NFRC procedures for determining whole product performance. NFRC ratings are determined for a fixed set of environmental conditions and a specific product size. NFRC does not recommend any product and does not warrant the suitability of any product for any specific use. Consult manufacturer's literature for other product performance information. www.nfrc.org

ABOVE Look for high-performance windows that have low-E coatings, low U-factors, and low solar heat gain coefficients. National Fenestration Rating Council (www.nfrc.org) labels allow you to compare one window with another.

RIGHT Engineered lumber products help optimize lumber resources. Made from small wood chips that are bonded together, this kind of engineered lumber uses 75 percent of a log.

BOTTOM Engineered lumber like these truss floor joists is made from small-diameter trees that, on their own, do not have sufficient structural strength to be made into floor joists.

Conserve Natural Resources. When you use a long piece of dimension lumber, say a 12-foot 2x10 joist or rafter, you are using a "primary demand" natural resource, and the extraction of that 2x10 from a sawlog at the mill may not make optimal use of the tree. Some engineered lumber products are made up of smaller wood chips held together by resins, and though engineered lumber usually costs more, many manufacturing processes can use up to 75 percent of a log. These processes can also use small-diameter (secondary demand) trees that are not large enough or strong enough to be of structural value on their own.

To further optimize lumber resources, select veneer products, especially for cabinets and trim. Valuable, slow-growing hardwood sawlogs, such as oak or cherry, can be cut into thin strands and then glued to particleboard substrates. A block of $^5/_4$, pronounced "five-quarter," solid hardwood can be used to make 50 veneer products—up to 95 percent of the source wood is used. In addition, look for chain-of-custody approval ratings from the Forest Stewardship Council (FSC) and the Sustainable Forestry Initiative (SFI)—which indicate that you are buying sustainably harvested wood.

RIGHT A block of solid hardwood can be used in one finish application, such as a trim board, or 50 veneer products. With veneers, up to 95 percent of the source wood is used. Here, a hardwood veneer covers a softwood substrate.

ABOVE Need a new roof? Think light. Light-color shingles reflect more heat back into the atmosphere than dark colors. The EPA estimates that you can reduce cooling costs by 10 to 30 percent by switching from black asphalt shingles to a lighter color. And while you are saving money, remember: every dime you save means a reduction in the amount of electricity needed and in the pollution often associated with power generation.

Cool Down That Roof! Think of the home as a living, breathing system. It's not a green practice to just stuff walls and ceiling with loads of insulation and assume you've done everything you can to reduce fuel consumption for heating and cooling. It's more complicated than that. A home is made up of wall systems that must be designed to manage moisture and heat transfer, as well as to accommodate windows, doors, and penetrations for utilities, such as ductwork, cables, and pipes. It doesn't take a PhD in heat dynamics to know that a home that consumes a minimum amount of fuel for heating and cooling over its lifetime will have a low carbon footprint. But the green design of a home must go beyond walls and incorporate other aspects of the building envelope, and one of the areas that is often overlooked is the roofing system.

A roof with black shingles reflects about 5 percent of the sun's heat. (Black roofs have low solar reflectance.)

Whereas a roof with gray shingles reflects back about 20 percent of the sun's heat, and white shingles reflect around 25 percent. As a result, black roofs get as much as 9 degrees F hotter than white roofs, and if the shingles have low solar emittance, they won't radiate that heat back out into the air. Instead, the heat is transferred into the building, especially if there is no radiant barrier in place.

Hotter roofs mean hotter buildings and environmental and financial costs to cool them down. The EPA has found that just changing the color of a roof by going from dark to lighter-color shingles can reduce cooling costs by 10 to 30 percent. That is a hefty savings. And because about 15 percent of the electricity generated each year in this country goes to cooling buildings, there is an environmental savings as well. Cool roofs lower the amount of pollution created when electricity is generated by coal, oil, or gas.

LEFT Even with typical usage by a small household, a low-flow toilet can save a large volume of water each day. Manufacturers have addressed performance problems that plagued earlier models.

RIGHT Low-flow showerheads can use less than 2.0 gpm.

Reduce Water Consumption. As a country, the United States uses around 408 billion gallons of water each day. But just 4 percent of that (15 billion gallons per day) is consumed in homes and businesses. Harvesting, purifying, and delivering that water (and taking away the wastewater) is a monumental task. The United States has made real advances in water-saving technology. Total U.S. water use has remained around 400 billion gallons per day over the last 20 years, even as the population has grown. Today, with the EPA's WaterSense, which recognizes and labels water-saving devices, you have a good method for identifying products that can save water.

Long ago, manufacturers responded with such products as high-efficiency toilets (HETs) that use 1.28 gallons per flush—around 20 percent less water than a standard toilet and about 37 percent less water than older 3.5-gallon-per-flush toilets. Low-flow aerators are another technology that has become popular. Aerators let you feel as though you're getting a full burst of water, even though they can limit use to 1.5 gallons per minute (gpm) or less. Low-flow showerheads can use less than 2 gallons per minute and perform well for even the pickiest remodeler.

ABOVE Faucet aerators can limit water use to 1.5 gpm. They also catch sediment, so clean them periodically to keep them operating properly.

ABOVE Choose windows based on your climate. To reduce cooling costs, look for windows with low solar heat gain ratings. For best results, look for a rating of 0.40 or below.

ABOVE A home's roof color, orientation, wall insulation, and types of windows can all have a dramatic effect on cooling costs and energy consumption.

Prevent Your Home from Gaining Solar Heat in Warmer Months. The Department of Energy (DOE) says that just adding effective window shading can save up to 40 percent on energy bills. That's a dramatic number. But when you realize that the heat gain from sunlight streaming through a 6-by-7-foot sliding glass door can require nearly 12,000 Btu of air conditioning to cool the area, it doesn't take long to realize how much a home's orientation affects its heating and cooling load. If you are remodeling, you don't have much control over which way your house faces, but you do have control over the placement and kind of windows you use. If you have a south-facing wall in a hot climate and do not act to block solar gain through landscaping, roof overhangs, high-performance windows, and interior shading, your remodeled home isn't going to be very green. Your heating, ventilating, and air-conditioning unit will have to slave away, consuming gas or electricity to cool the space that is absorbing tens of thousands of Btu per hour.

Don't forget the value of window treatments such as blinds, shades, and curtains. They look great and reduce unwanted solar heat gain.

Curtain dust-containment systems can seal off a room even offer an air-lock-type door for getting in and out

DEMOLITION AND CHEMICALS

FIFTY YEARS FROM NOW WHEN PRODUCTS installed today are removed for a home renovation, there will be health risks due to the demolition process. Though the toxins and health hazards of older building materials are being systematically removed, the asbestos, lead, and polychlorinated biphenyls (PCBs) of yesterday may be replaced by the formaldehyde, mercury, and silica contained in today's products. This underscores the importance of differentiating between *green* and *sustainable* products. Whereas the term "green products" can be widely applied to many building materials, such as compact fluorescent lightbulbs, sustainable products are those that are not toxic when they are manufactured, installed and applied, or discarded. For example, a compact fluorescent lightbulb is very green because it dramatically reduces the electricity required to illuminate a room, but all compact fluorescent lightbulbs contain mercury. When they burn out, they need to be disposed of at designated hazardous-waste sites.

When engaging in demolition, there are hazards no matter what products are involved. Some hazards, such as dust, are simply a nuisance, and some, such as asbestos, are toxic. Here's a look at common hazards. (Also see "How to Deal with Hazards," page 33.)

Asbestos. Asbestos is a mineral commonly found in fire-retardant products. It has since been banned in many applications because it is a health hazard when inhaled. Asbestos is a real danger that can cause lung cancer, mesothelioma (a cancer of the lining of the chest and the abdominal cavity), and asbestosis (where lungs are scarred with fibrous tissue). Many older homes contain asbestos, which can be found in pipe and furnace insulation, asbestos shingles, floor tiles, millboard, textured paints, and some coatings. If left undisturbed, asbestos fibers do not pose a risk. But if they are stirred up and inhaled, they cause real damage.

Vermiculite. Another potentially dangerous insulation material that can contain asbestos is vermiculite. Asbestos wasn't put into the vermiculite, but vermiculite is often found in the same geological areas where asbestos occurs, and the two were mined together. An EPA study found that 15 percent of vermiculite contains asbestos.

smart tip

hire the right pro

REMOVING ASBESTOS FROM PIPES, HEATING SYSTEMS, AND THE LIKE IS NOT A DO-IT-YOURSELF PROJECT. HIRE A LICENSED ASBESTOS ABATEMENT CONTRACTOR WHO WILL EXPLAIN HOW THE WORK WILL BE PERFORMED AND WHAT STEPS HE WILL TAKE TO SEAL OFF THE AREA FROM THE REST OF THE HOUSE.

TOP Many older homes contain asbestos, which can be found in pipe and furnace insulation. It should be removed by a professional.

BOTTOM An EPA study found that 15 percent of vermiculite contains asbestos. Vermiculite was commonly used as loose-fill insulation in walls and attic floors.

Polychlorinated Biphenyls. PCBs cause a variety of adverse health effects, including cancer and serious noncancer conditions in animals, such as disorders of the immune system, reproductive system, nervous system, and endocrine system. PCBs are oily, waxy, and nonflammable, and they insulate well in electrical applications. You'll find them in older electrical equipment (pre-1977, the same year lead was banned in paint), and in plastics, caulking, and paints of that same era. PCBs were used because they are so stable, which means that PCBs in your home are just as stable and, therefore, have not broken down or biodegraded.

Formaldehyde. Formaldehyde is still a widely used industrial chemical, even though it is a known carcinogen. It is also a by-product of combustion and other processes in nature, so there are substantial amounts in the air and inside and outside of your home. Formaldehyde can be found in new building materials, and it is used as a component of glues and adhesives and as a preservative in some paints and coating products. In your home, formaldehyde is likely contained in pressed wood or particleboard products (like oriented strand board—also called OSB) and anything manufactured with adhesives that contain urea-formaldehyde (UF) resins. It can also be found in particleboard that is used for cabinetry and furniture and in hardwood plywood paneling. You'll also find it in medium-density fiberboard (MDF), some plywood, and most fiberglass insulation.

At very low levels (0.1 part per million), formaldehyde can cause watery eyes, burning sensations in the eyes and throat, nausea, and difficulty breathing. When discarding products that may contain formaldehyde, do not burn them. It's inadvisable to burn any building material.

Lead. Lead has long been recognized as a harmful environmental pollutant. The main concern for remodelers is lead in paint or lead in dust that has come from sanding lead paint. Airborne lead gets in your body through your lungs, either as dust or as vapor from paint that is stripped with a torch.

ABOVE PCBs were used as insulators because they are so stable, but that means they haven't broken down over time. Dispose of them properly.

BELOW Lead paint is a dangerous toxin, but it can be removed without sanding or the use of torches through specialty applications that peel away the old paint.

Maximum Acceptable VOC Levels		
Type of Paint	VOCs (grams/liter)	VOCs (pounds/gallon)
Interior Architectural		
Flat	50	0.042
Nonflat	150	1.25
Exterior Architectural		
Flat	100	0.083
Nonflat	200	1.66
Anticorrosive		
Flat	250	2.10
Semigloss	250	2.10
Gloss	250	2.10

Volatile Organic Compounds. Volatile organic compounds (VOCs) are called volatile because they evaporate at room temperature. Concentrations of VOCs can be ten times higher indoors than outdoors. So ideally you don't want VOCs released inside your home, especially a home that you have just tightened up with the latest building-envelope applications. VOCs are emitted by paints, adhesives, paint strippers, cleaning supplies, pesticides, building materials, and even furniture. VOCs not only create ground-level ozone, a.k.a. smog, they are also unhealthy to breathe—a very small concentration of smog can damage respiratory and cardiovascular systems.

Mercury. Even a droplet of mercury can contaminate tens of thousands of gallons of clean water. Health effects of mercury poisoning can include a lifetime of learning disabilities, mental retardation, and liver and kidney damage; it can even be fatal. For remodelers, mercury is found in old switches, thermostats, and regulators on heating systems.

Pesticides. Besides the pesticides you may have in your home, the danger of pesticides when remodeling comes chiefly when you disturb soil that may be contaminated with pesticides. If your home is on the grounds of an old farmer's field or orchard, the soil could have pesticides in it that are released when you excavate for a foundation.

Dust. The bane of any remodeling job is dust. It gets everywhere, not only in other rooms but also on your clothes and in your lungs. If you don't know what's in your walls and you have an older home (especially pre-1977, when lead and PCBs were banned), you have to assume that the dust may be hazardous. Asbestos and lead may be in the walls, and as the walls are pulverized during demolition, you may release those poisons into the air. Your lungs may also be irritated by mold spores in the dust or by just the dust itself.

LEFT Where houses are built on old farmland, soil can contain pesticides.

ABOVE Contact your town or the EPA to find out how to dispose of hazardous items, such as asbestos, batteries, thermostats that contain mercury, and fluorescent bulbs.

smart tip

make a dust buster

To create an opening in plastic that seals a doorway, hang two layers with the second layer perhaps 6 feet wide. Slit an opening on the "clean side" of one plastic sheet. It won't stop all the dust, but it will help.

In addition to personal dust protection, consider installing a dust-containment system. The curtain-type dust-containment systems can seal off a room and even offer an air-lock-type door for getting in and out. Dust-containment systems are often sold by companies that have a variety of dust-containment products, such as contact paper to protect carpets. However, there's no need to go to great expense. A low-tech but very effective approach to keeping adjacent rooms clean is to tape 6-mil plastic over the doorway and seal the edges and seams with duct tape.

Disposal of Toxic Debris. Using a dumpster is a common and convenient way to handle the trash that invariably accumulates during remodeling. With the dumpster right outside the window, it is tempting to just toss everything into it, including potentially hazardous waste. But hazardous items, especially asbestos, batteries, thermostats that contain mercury, and fluorescent bulbs (old and new—they all contain mercury) should not be put into the everyday waste stream. Go to EPA.gov and search "household hazardous waste" to find a collection site and program near you. Americans generate 1.6 million tons of household hazardous waste each year. If you're not disposing of it properly, you are polluting the very air, soil, and water that you, your children, and your neighbors use.

YOUR GREEN CHOICES

How to Deal with Hazards

ASBESTOS. If you find asbestos (most commonly used in pipe insulation) in your home, do not remove it. That job must be done by a licensed asbestos remover or specialist contractor. However, expensive removal isn't always required. Because asbestos is dangerous only when disturbed, the contractor may find that the best alternative is for you to simply seal the asbestos or vermiculite right in place.

DUST. Always wear a dust mask during demolition. Because they are not that expensive, step up from a nuisance mask—the inexpensive, single layer mask—to an N95 dust mask. Often used in medical applications, N95 masks are 95 percent effective in blocking airborne particles from entering your nasal passages and lungs.

FORMALDEHYDE. Look for formaldehyde-free products in every wood product category. Use formaldehyde-free insulation, which is available nationwide. Even inside your home, use exterior-grade pressed-wood products because they contain phenol resins, not urea resins.

LEAD. Test old paint for lead with widely available swab kits. If the test comes back positive, contact a restoration contractor to have it properly removed. Don't sand lead paint. It takes professional-grade equipment to sand or remove it properly, including high-efficiency particulate accumulator (HEPA) vacuums and phosphate washes. Though lead isn't as dangerous for adults, it can have dramatic negative health effects on children.

MERCURY. Avoid building products that contain mercury, such as thermostats and switches. Mercury-free alternatives are widely available. Never throw an old thermostat into the trash; the mercury will eventually end up in the groundwater. Always bring these items to your region's hazardous-waste drop-off day.

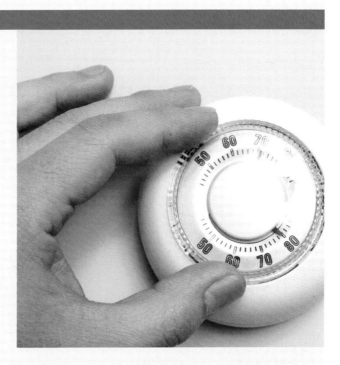

Mercury is found in old switches and thermostats. Do not discard mercury-containing devices into the everyday trash; it is a dangerous toxin.

PCBs. If you think you have PCBs, have the suspect product—paint or caulk—tested before you discard it. Search "testing for PCBs" on the Internet to find a lab. By all means, don't sand it or do anything to turn it into dust or particulate form, and do not discard it in the general waste stream; instead, discard it on hazardous-waste drop-off day.

PESTICIDES. Have soil tested for pesticides and lead. Search "soil test" on the Internet to find a place to send a sample. If it comes back positive, contact the local health department. You may have to scrape and replace the soil. Today, biologically based controls, such as pheromone traps and microbial pesticides, are gaining popularity. These are often safer than chemical pesticides.

VOLATILE ORGANIC COMPOUNDS. Select low- or no-VOC paints, caulks, adhesives, and finishes. Claims of low-VOCs or no-VOCs are actually regulated by EPA standards.

33

ABOVE Check with your town's building inspector to determine whether you need a permit for your project. The inspector may request a set of plans for his review. You or your contractor will need to schedule the necessary building inspections.

Permits and Zoning. Never start a remodeling project of any size without checking with your town's building inspector to see if you need a permit. Building inspectors have remarkably broad powers to shut down a project—or even revoke the occupancy permit for the entire home—if the job doesn't have a permit or if they deem it unsafe. Permits often require that you submit plans and pay a fee that is indexed to the value of the work you plan to do or to the square footage of the project.

You will have to schedule building inspections at various times during the remodeling job, and now, before the job starts, is a good time to determine when those inspections should occur. Inspections are usually triggered by job-site milestones, such as after the utility rough-in is complete (when the first phase of HVAC, plumbing, and electrical is installed), after rough framing (when the studs are still open and exposed), and after the completion of such job stages as electrical rough-in, final drywall, and final-final, when you get your last approval. There can easily be seven or eight inspections for modest-sized jobs, even if you are doing the work yourself.

While you are at the building inspector's office, check across the hall for zoning requirements. In nearly every municipality, zoning approval is required. Never underestimate the importance of a zoning review and preapproval of your project. It is commonplace for zoning boards to require that people tear out remodeling work that wasn't approved by the zoning board.

smart tip

meet the inspector on-site

TRY TO BE THERE WHEN THE INSPECTOR ARRIVES. YOU CAN'T TALK HIM OUT OF A "RED TAG," A.K.A. FAILURE, BUT YOU MAY BE ABLE TO CORRECT THE PROBLEM RIGHT THERE AND SAVE THE FEE FOR A RETURN VISIT.

Look for These Green Product Seals

Carpet and Rug Institute/Green Label. The Carpet and Rug Institute (CRI) is a trade organization run by the carpet industry. Though it is a pro-industry association, it does independent testing of carpets and rugs through the Atlanta-based Air Quality Sciences lab to check for chemical emissions. The Air Quality Sciences lab subscribes to the American Society for Testing and Materials (ASTM) methods, a well-noted national set of testing standards. If you buy national carpet brands (as opposed to boutique carpets that use green adhesives or are woven with no adhesives), look for a CRI Green Label (Carpet-rug.com). It ensures that your carpet will have low emissions of VOCs.

Greenguard. The Greenguard Certification Program (Greenguard.org) is run by the Greenguard Environmental Institute. It certifies low-emitting products for indoor air |quality, focusing on such harmful chemicals as VOCs and formaldehyde in adhesives, appliances, building materials, finishes, and flooring. Testing follows ASTM and EPA standards.

Green Seal. Green Seal (Greenseal.org) is an independent third-party organization that provides environmental testing and certification for a wide range of materials, including building materials. They look at a product's entire life cycle, and manufacturers pay a fee to be evaluated. If the product passes the various certification evaluations, it earns the Green Seal.

Green Certified Lumber. For evaluating the "chain of custody" of lumber (from where it is harvested to where it is sold), there are two leading agencies, one of which—SFI—is viewed as perhaps a little too pro-industry. **Forest Stewardship Council.** The more objective and independent lumber certification organization is the Forest Stewardship Council (FSC) at Fscus.org. The FSC promotes responsible forest-management practices worldwide. FSC sets standards to protect ecosystems, water quality, habitats, and even local communities. They also accredit third-party organizations to help verify its standards. There are two certificates available: a Forest Management Certificate and a Chain-of-Custody Certificate, which tracks lumber from raw materials to the consumer. **Sustainable Forestry Initiative.** The American Forest and Paper Association set up the SFI Program (Aboutsfi.org) to foster the economic benefits of long-term forest management as well as the protection of the environment. SFI also has two certificates: one for producers of wood products and another for processed wood. SFI has been criticized by the Sierra Club, Greenpeace, the National Resources Defense Council, and the National Wildlife Federation for ties that are too close to the lumber industry.

SmartWood. A program of the Rainforest Alliance and accredited by the FSC, SmartWood (Rainforest-alliance.org) certifies all types of forests for FSC Forest Management Certification, FSC Chain-of-Custody Certification, FSC Non-Timber Forest Products Certification, and SmartWood Rediscovered Wood Certification.

ABOVE In addition to checking references and visiting previous jobs as you would when hiring any contractor, find out how green your contractor candidates are by using the checklist, opposite.

SELECTING A CONTRACTOR

ONCE YOU HAVE PLANS FOR A REMODELING PROJECT, you need to find contractors to carry them out—or maybe not. There are no set rules about which jobs to tackle and which to leave to the pros. Do-it-yourself skills, interests, and budgets vary so widely that you might do an excellent job on a part of the project that your neighbor wouldn't touch. But there are sensible guidelines you can apply. Number one is "if in doubt, don't." Don't plunge into a project unless you have a realistic idea of the tools, skills, time, and money involved. Then you can make common-sense decisions, including the most important one: whether or not you can do the work safely.

YOUR GREEN CHOICES

Checklist for Your Contractor

When interviewing contractors, here is a list of questions to ask them to see whether they are attuned to green building. (See the other "Your Green Choices" sidebars in this chapter for a list and description of green-building programs and product-certifying organizations.) If a contractor is well versed in green building, he should be able to answer—or immediately tap into experts and subcontractors who can answer—these questions about green building.

❑ What is the contractor's understanding of green building and what makes a project green? What are his key sources of information?

❑ Is the contractor a recognized Energy Star contractor? If not, what green-building standard does the contractor subscribe to?

❑ Has the contractor built other green projects, and what qualified these projects as green?

❑ Does the contractor's designers or allied architects have training in green-building practices, which can range from knowledge about house orientation and window basics to the ability to specify green products in every part of the home?

❑ Does the contractor have reliable sources for green products, such as Energy Star-qualified HVAC systems; low-VOC caulks, adhesives, and finishes; and sustainably-harvested lumber?

❑ For finished wood applications like trim or shelving, does the contractor have a plan for using composite woods, such as medium-density fiberboard (MDF), and plantation-grown green alternatives to tropical hardwoods, such as bamboo or Pau Lope, that will reduce pressure on forests?

❑ Does the contractor subscribe to any framing optimization system that can reduce job-site waste? This can simply mean that the contractor uses a software system to optimize framing so that his crew uses fewer structural wood components.

❑ Is the contractor aware of advanced insulated foundation, roof, or wall systems that can achieve high R-values, such as insulated concrete forms (ICFs) and structural insulated panels (SIPs)?

❑ Does the contractor have any knowledge of—or subcontractors who have knowledge of—solar electric systems or solar hot-water systems?

❑ Does the contractor employ subcontractors who are aware of green-building techniques, such as floor finishers who use no-VOC water-borne polyurethane?

❑ What systems does the contractor have in place to check on and audit the green practices of the subcontractors who will be working on your job, such as preapproval of materials?

❑ Does the contractor have a waste and recycling plan so that building materials such as metal or useable wood are recycled rather than discarded?

❑ Does the contractor have a toxic-waste disposal plan? Ask the contractor what he plans to do with old thermostats that contain mercury or light ballasts that contain polychlorinated biphenyls (PCBs). If he doesn't have a deliberate plan for disposing of these highly toxic materials, his credentials are suspect.

❑ Does the contractor have a plan for ensuring the indoor air quality (IAQ) of the home before and after construction, even if there is active ventilation when finishes are applied on-site? IAQ is a key component of any green remodeling job.

YOUR GREEN CHOICES

Whole-House Green-Building Standards

Energy Star Homes. How do you determine the green qualities of your home during the planning stages? Except for the Energy Star program, no national green-building organizations certify the builder. Instead, the programs certify the home and its contents, such as appliances, light fixtures, and heating and cooling systems. The Energy Star program—a very effective EPA program—qualifies the home and provides resources for you to find Energy Star-certified builders and testers who will give the home a passing grade (often required to qualify for energy-efficient mortgages). Energy Star has no political agenda—unlike the antiregulatory intention of the National Association of Home Builders (NAHB) or the pro-industry lumber chain-of-custody certification system called Sustainable Forest Initiative (SFI).

Here's how it works. The EPA started rating energy-efficient products in 1992. In 2005, Energy Star issued its Qualified Homes National Performance Path Requirements. For a home to qualify as an Energy Star home, it must meet performance criteria that address the house's building envelop, ductwork, and Energy Star compliance with products such as windows, appliances, and heating and cooling systems. After the home is completed, it must be tested by field representatives accredited by Residential Energy Services Network (RESNET). To earn an Energy Star rating, a home must be at least 15 percent more energy efficient than "benchmark" homes built to the 2004 International Residential Code (IRC). And the home must include additional energy-saving features that achieve 20 to 30 percent efficiency above and beyond standard homes. So, Energy Star is both a building-practices and product-selection approach to building a home. The Energy Star Web site (Energystar.gov) is a gold mine of free information and resources for green building, including lists of qualified products, right down to the lighting fixtures, compact fluorescent bulbs, ventilation fans, and appliances that can help you achieve Energy Star compliance. The site will also link you to Energy Star builders and third-party certifiers.

In addition to Energy Star, there are other programs that can help "green up" your home. Here's a review of the leading programs.

National Association of Home Builders National Green Building Standard. NAHB, a Washington, DC-based, nonprofit organization of more than 800 state and local associations, is one of the largest lobbying organizations in the United States. NAHB also runs the Home Builders Institute and the NAHB Research Center. In an effort to circumvent green-building regulations and to counter the U.S. Green Building Council's (USGBC) Leadership in Energy and Environmental Design (LEED) program, which NAHB views as overly regulatory, NAHB created the Model Green Home Building Guidelines. These lay out a system of voluntary compliance that builders can subscribe to at little or no cost. The Guidelines are so widely accepted that municipalities have started to adopt them as regulations, prompting the NAHB to work with the International Code Council and ANSI (a national standards-setting organization) to codify NAHB's standards. The result is a very informative standard called the National Green Building Standard. It is available for free at NAHB.org and can serve as a practical guide for your contractor.

U.S. Green Building Council's Leadership in Energy and Environmental Design Program. USGBC is a professional organization with thousands of member firms. USGBC set up the LEED Green

LEED for Homes

Building Rating System and in 2006 started pushing a standard for homes called LEED for Homes (LEED-H). LEED is a voluntary program that certifies buildings based on the number of points earned. There are 64 points available in the following categories: sustainable sites (14 points), water efficiency (5 points), energy and atmosphere (17 points), materials and resources (13 points), and indoor environmental quality (15 points). An additional 5 points are available for innovation and design process, for a total of 69 points. All assessment is done by a USGBC-approved third party. There are four levels of LEED certification: Basic LEED Certification (26–32 points), LEED Certified Silver (33–38 points), LEED Certified Gold (39–51 points), and LEED Certified Platinum (52–69 points). The knock on LEED is that it is expensive to pay for the inspections and the materials required to earn a certification; plus, LEED responds punitively if the house exceeds a certain size. To achieve certification for a large house of more than 2,200 square feet, you have to make up points with extraordinary efforts in other categories.

EarthCraft House. The Greater Atlanta Home Builders Association and the Southface Energy Institute, based in Atlanta, have created an admirable program called EarthCraft House. EarthCraft House has a certification process that involves a training course and compliance with the program's standards.

(See Earthcrafthouse.org.) If verified by a third party, homes can achieve up to 150 points, half of them coming from energy efficiency. It's a good voluntary model to subscribe to, even if you don't seek the certification.

2

building basics

To have a green home you need a well-built structure, and that requires you to go back to the basics. All the world's low-VOC paints and soy-based insulation won't green-up a home that's been poorly constructed. Though "green remodeling" may be a new term, the practices it calls on are age-old, tried-and-true building techniques that have been perfected over decades of incremental developments in building science. Though high-tech windows and doors are now available that keep the heat out or in, depending on the season, those windows and doors are worthless if they are improperly inserted in rough openings that bleed heat through gaps in poorly designed walls. The same is true across every aspect of the building. This chapter will look at some basic building practices, from wall construction to finished flooring, and offer you "green choices" along the way to supplement and enhance these building techniques.

CONCRETE & LUMBER BASICS

FRESH CONCRETE IS A SEMIFLUID MIXTURE OF PORTLAND CEMENT, sand (fine aggregate), gravel or crushed stone (coarse aggregate), and water. As the cement chemically reacts with water, a process called hydration, the mix cures to a stone-like consistency. Properly mixed and cured, concrete creates strong structures that will weather the extremes of summer heat and winter cold with little maintenance.

Though concrete can create very green structures that are durable and airtight, it is energy intensive to produce and truck to building sites. As much as 5 percent of U.S. carbon dioxide emissions are created by the manufacturing of concrete. There are efforts by concrete manufacturers to reduce these emissions, but green remodelers can do two things to cut down on the contribution of greenhouse gases from concrete. One is to build with a smaller footprint, and the other is to use concrete with additives that reduce the Portland cement in concrete. (See "Concrete Additives," page 47.)

Mixing Concrete

FOR LARGE-SCALE PROJECTS, such as a patio, concrete is sold by the cubic yard and delivered in a ready-mix truck ready to pour. For smaller jobs—say, steps for the patio—you can mix your own by purchasing dry ingredients in bags and adding water. But don't get too ambitious: one wheelbarrow-size batch is less than 3 cubic feet, around $^1/_9$ of just one cubic yard. A concrete truck containing one cubic yard is a convenience for which it's worth paying.

You may be tempted to adjust the mix proportions—for instance, by adding more water to make the concrete easier to mix and pour. However, as water content can drastically affect strength, the best policy is to order concrete ready-mixed or follow directions on the dry ingredient bags. The concrete needs just enough water to cure properly, and too much will compromise its strength.

The standard proportion of water-to-cement produces concrete with a compressive strength of about 3,000–4,000 pounds per square inch (psi). Adding less water makes mixing more difficult but increases concrete strength. Concrete that dries too quickly can be a problem, however.

Even the best mix may dehydrate in hot weather, robbing the concrete of the water it needs to cure. In extreme cases, a steady hot, dry breeze can even accelerate evaporation so that the masonry surface begins to set before it can flow into the forms and be smoothed on its exposed surfaces. Concrete begins to cure as soon as it is mixed and can support your weight within a few hours. Most of the curing takes place in the first two weeks, but it takes a month to reach maximum hardness.

To eliminate the risk of wasting your efforts on a job that doesn't last, don't pour in temperatures over 90 degrees F; if you must, start very early in the morning to beat the heat. It's also important to remember that hot surfaces contacting the mix can burn off moisture. It's wise to spray some cool water on forms that are sitting in the sun before you start to pour.

Placing Concrete

Steel reinforcement helps control the cracking associated with the natural shrinkage of concrete as it dries. The two basic types are rebar (reinforcing bar) and welded or woven wire mesh. Rebar is ridged for a better bond with the concrete or smooth for nonbonding control joints. Rebar is stronger than wire mesh—use it for concrete that will carry a heavy load, such as footings and piers. Wire mesh is

CONCRETE FINISHES

A WOODEN FLOAT finish is slightly rough, just enough to be slip-resistant and glare-free.

A STEEL TROWEL finish should be perfectly smooth, and is best suited for interior applications.

A BROOMED SURFACE is rough and slip-resistant, ideal for outdoor steps and patios.

EXPOSED AGGREGATE is smoothed into the concrete while drying for an attractive, rough surface.

made from steel wire in a grid of squares and is sold in rolls and mats. Use it in flat slabs on grade, such as patios and walks. Cut wire mesh with fencing pliers, and flatten it out before use. Fill large areas by overlapping sections of mesh by at least three inches and tying them with wire.

Avoiding Problems

Pouring the concrete is a simple matter; the crucial stage begins as the mix sets and begins to cure. If raw concrete is left exposed to the wind and sun, it may dry too quickly and may not attain half its potential strength. You can still walk on it, but the slab will be likely to crack.

Tooling control joints into the surface of concrete slabs helps make settling cracks break at planned locations. Control joints weaken the concrete surface, causing cracks to occur at the bottom of the joints, where they are inconspicuous and will not spread.

pouring a patio

Patios will forever be "on display" because you can't cover them up with framed walls, as you can with a foundation. So take the time to get the form exactly right, keeping in mind that any irregularity in the form will become an irregularity in the concrete.

TOOLS & MATERIALS

- ► Broom
- ► Compactor
- ► Darby
- ► Edging trowel
- ► Float trowel
- ► Jointing trowel
- ► Line level
- ► Mason's hoe
- ► Mason's string
- ► Measuring tape
- ► Rebar chairs
- ► Screed
- ► Shovel
- ► Sledgehammer
- ► Wheelbarrow ► Concrete mix
- ► Double-headed nails
- ► Formboards
- ► Gravel
- ► Stakes
- ► Welded or woven-wire mesh

concrete 101

TO CALL A CONCRETE TRUCK A "CEMENT TRUCK" IS AN ERROR. CEMENT IS JUST ONE ASPECT OF CONCRETE. CONCRETE IS CREATED BY MIXING CEMENT WITH AGGREGATES.

1 Your crew may not bring in one this big, but most jobs begin with a bulldozer to cut away the sod and level the ground.

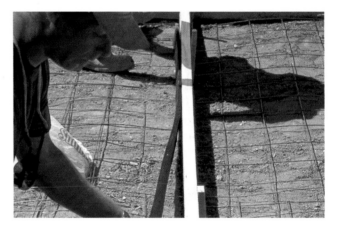

3 To strengthen the concrete, welded wire is laid near the bottom of the slab, generally on short supports, called chairs.

5 The rough surface left by screeding can be smoothed with a float or textured with a broom finish for better traction.

2 Once the perimeter is established and the forms are in place, the ground should be compacted.

4 As concrete pours from the ready-mix truck, a straightedge guided by a screed board on each side levels the mix.

6 Control joints that prevent cracking can be formed into the pour, although some crews cut them after the mix hardens.

TESTING CONCRETE

A TYPICAL MIX is 11% portland cement, 26% sand, and 41% crushed stone, plus 16% water and 6% air.

IF CONCRETE IS TOO WET, ridges made in the mix with a trowel won't hold their shape.

IF CONCRETE IS TOO DRY, you won't be able to make ridges, and it will be difficult to work.

WHEN MIXED CORRECTLY, the ridges will hold most of their shape; only a little water will be visible.

smart tip

ready mix

THERE ARE SEVERAL ADVANTAGES TO ORDERING READY-MIXED CEMENT. THE CHUTE CAN EXTEND AND SWIVEL TO POUR CONCRETE WHERE IT'S NEEDED. READY-MIX TRUCKS CAN DELIVER CONCRETE AT TEMPERATURES THAT MAKE IT POSSIBLE TO POUR DURING A HEAT WAVE. READY-MIX CONCRETE IS AVAILABLE WITH AN ADDITIVE THAT PRODUCES MICROSCOPIC AIR BUBBLES IN THE MIX. AIR-ENTRAINED CONCRETE IS MORE RESISTANT TO CRACKING THAN THE CONCRETE MIXED ON SITE.

forming a curved corner

A poorly formed curve in a concrete slab will always be a distraction to the naked eye, because the eye craves symmetry. Don't guess at the measurements of the curve or use just your eye to set the form. Use artificial measuring and forming aids to establish the curve to keep it consistent.

TOOLS & MATERIALS

- ► C-clamps ► Hammer
- ► Saw ► Screw gun or drill driver
- ► Small sledgehammer ► Common nails
- ► 1x4 or 1x6 boards ► Screws
- ► ¼-in. plywood ► 2x4 stakes

1 To make a curved form, use a flexible material that you can bend in a large radius, such as thin hardboard.

2 Center the hardboard in the corner; clamp the ends in position; and secure them to the forms using screws.

3 A flexible form needs at least one supporting stake to prevent the concrete from distorting the radius.

REINFORCING CONCRETE

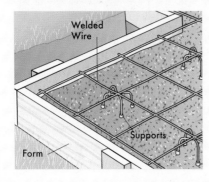

Welded Wire

Supports

Form

◄ **WELDED WIRE MESH** must be fully embedded in concrete for maximum strength. Supports called chairs hold it off the ground.

SECTIONS OF REINFORCING BAR ► turned up into the foundation at each corner will add support to pilasters on a brick or masonry wall.

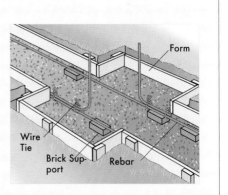

Form

Wire Tie

Brick Support

Rebar

YOUR GREEN CHOICES

Concrete Additives

As much as 5 percent of U.S. carbon dioxide emissions are created by the manufacture of concrete. To help green up concrete, start by reducing how much Portland cement is in concrete. There is a whole family of additives that can replace Portland cement. These additives work as binding agents that can strengthen concrete and even make it more workable. Let's look at these additives after looking at how concrete works.

Cement is made of oxides of calcium, silica, and aluminum; these are mixed with water to create calcium silicate hydrate. Cement (and therefore concrete) doesn't harden, it cures. As it cures, cement binds with the aggregates to create concrete. Additives that replace cement must be a source of silica that reacts with lime. This way the additives can work as binding agents. You can ask for concrete with additives when you order your mix. Some of those additives include the following:

Coal Fly Ash. This ash is really tiny glass spheres whose ingredients include silica, alumina, calcium, and iron.

Blast Furnace Slag. When iron ore is melted, impurities will be cooked off and, if cooled properly, the impurities actually become granules that act like cement.

Microsilica. These particles are extremely small and can reduce concrete's permeability: ideal for walkways and driveways where you want water to flow through to the ground beneath.

Can these additives really make an environmental difference? Here are some fascinating statistics from Building Green. Each ton of cement produces a ton of CO_2, and there are around 100 million tons of cement produced in the United States each year, representing about 1.6 percent of global greenhouse gas emissions. If a car that gets 25 miles per gallon travels 12,500 miles a year, it will emit about 5 tons of CO_2. So, cement consumed in the United States each year represents the equivalent emissions of 22 million passenger cars. Reducing the cement content of concrete by 15 percent with additives saves 1 ton of CO_2 emissions for each 11.4 cubic yards of concrete.

EDGING & JOINING

Edging is tooled into fresh concrete as soon as the water sheen disappears after the first floating. Run an edging trowel along the entire perimeter of a slab. Control joints can be hand-tooled into fresh concrete with a jointing trowel, cut into cured concrete with a circular saw fitted with a masonry blade, or (usually with isolation joints) preformed with fixed divider strips of hardboard, cork, rubber, plastic, or felt paper.

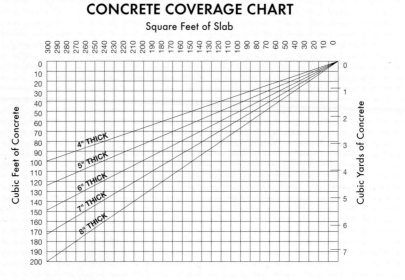

ESTIMATING

To figure out how much concrete to mix or order, use the chart at left or total up the volume inside the forms in cubic feet (length x height x width); then divide this figure by 27 to convert into the ordering standard of cubic yards. Some contractors build in a reasonable excess factor of about 8 percent by changing the conversion factor to 25.

CONCRETE COVERAGE CHART
Square Feet of Slab

Chart showing Cubic Feet of Concrete (left axis) and Cubic Yards of Concrete (right axis) versus Square Feet of Slab, with lines for 4" THICK, 5" THICK, 6" THICK, 7" THICK, and 8" THICK.

Insulated Concrete Forms

Stay-in-place insulated concrete forms (ICFs) are gaining in popularity for good reason: they create walls with high R value, sometimes as high as R-50, which is extraordinary. They are great for sound attenuation as well. ICFs are made of polystyrene foam that is often reinforced with plastic spanners that keep the polystyrene foam from blowing out under the weight of the wet concrete as it is poured between the polystyrene forms. Even so, pour carefully, working the form tier by tier and slowly adding concrete layer by layer. The forms are left in place, and wall treatments are attached directly to them.

Plywood

Plywood is generally an environmentally responsible material for decking and sheathing. It comprises an odd number of thin veneer layers of wood, called plies. The veneers are cross-laminated so that the grains of each ply run perpendicular to one another, then are glued and sandwiched together and heated to over 300°F under 200 pounds per square inch (psi) of pressure. Standard plywood thicknesses are $5/16$, $3/8$, $7/16$, $15/32$, $1/2$, $5/8$, $23/32$, $3/4$, and $1\frac{1}{8}$ inches. If you order $1/2$- and $3/4$-inch plywood for your job, you'll most likely get $15/32$- and $23/32$-inch plywood, respectively. Panels are almost invariably 4 x 8 feet after factory trimming. Corner to corner, panels can be off square by $3/32$ inch. Be sure the plywood contains no formaldehyde.

Every piece of plywood has a face veneer and a back veneer. These are the outside plies. The plies under the face and back veneers are called crossbands, and the center ply is called the core. The core can be either veneer or solid lumber. Some plywoods even have fiberglass or particleboard at their cores, but you won't be using these kinds of plywood for sheathing. Veneer-core lumber is stronger than lumber-core plywood, but lumber-core plywood can hold a screw better at its edge.

Used in the right applications, plywood is strong and adds stiffness to walls and strength to floors. As wall sheathing, plywood is a vast improvement over the old style of wall sheathing, nailing 1-inch boards diagonally across the wall. A relatively thin $5/16$-inch plywood-sheathed wall has twice the stiffness of a wall sheathed with 1-inch diagonal boards. Besides conventional sheathing plywood, you can buy treated, fire-retardant, and waterproof plywood for special applications.

Other Panel Products

Panel products other than plywood, called nonveneer or reconstituted wood-product panels, are sometimes used for sheathing. Some of these panels are just as strong—and cheaper—than plywood. There are four types: structural particleboard, waferboard, oriented-strand board (OSB), and composite board. These products are called reconstituted because they're made from wood particles or wood strands that are bonded together with adhesive into 4-by-8-foot sheets.

The smooth-faced structural particleboard (also called flakeboard or chipboard) is simply a panel of

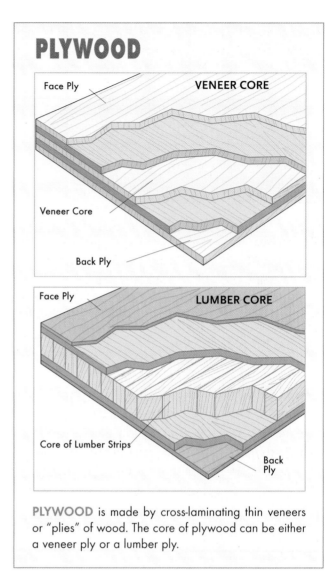

PLYWOOD is made by cross-laminating thin veneers or "plies" of wood. The core of plywood can be either a veneer ply or a lumber ply.

wood particles held together by hot-pressed resin. Some exterior-rated products have a layer of resin or wax on the outside to repel water. The glue used in these products is urea-formaldehyde or phenol-formaldehyde adhesive. Don't use these for a green remodel. (See page 54.) Some building-code organizations now allow you to use structural particleboard as an underlayment, a subfloor, or a roof deck.

Waferboard is just like structural particleboard, except that the wood particles in these boards are all $1\frac{1}{2}$ inches long. An exterior-grade phenolic resin glues the particles together. Where codes allow, you can also use these panels for subflooring, sheathing, and roofs.

Another panel material, OSB, also uses strands of wood, but the layers are crossed layer for layer, just as plywood is cross-laminated, to give it strength. The three to five layers of strands in OSB are bonded together with phenolic resin. These panels have a smooth face and are often rated for structural applications.

Composite board, which is basically a hybrid of plywood and particleboard, has a reconstituted wood center but a face and back of plywood veneer. Where codes allow, you can use composite-board wall sheathing and floor underlayments.

Rating Panel Products

When you purchase structural panels, a grading label tells you what you're buying. The leading grading association is the APA—The Engineered Wood Association and it's their stamp you're most likely to see.

Panel Grade. Panel products are also rated in a number of other categories. If you look at a typical APA grade stamp, you'll see the panel grade on the top line. This entry designates the proper application for the panel—rated sheathing, rated flooring, rated underlayment, and the like.

Span Rating. Next you'll see a large number or numbers, indicating the span rating. This rating is the recommended center-to-center spacing in inches of studs/joists/rafters over which you can place the panel. If you see numbers like $^{32}/_{16}$, the left number gives the maximum spacing in inches of the panel when used in roofing (32 inches of allowable span along the side of the panel with three or more supports), and the right number gives the maximum spacing when the panel is

used as subflooring (16 inches of allowable span along the side of the panel with three or more supports).

Thickness. In addition, the grade stamp identifies the actual thickness of the panel, often in thirty-seconds of an inch—$^3/_8$ inch, $^7/_{16}$ inch, $^{15}/_{32}$ inch, $^{23}/_{32}$ inch, and so on.

PLYWOOD VENEER GRADES (4-by-8-foot panels)

A	**SMOOTH, PAINTABLE.** Not more than 18 neatly made repairs, boat, sled, or router type, and parallel to grain, permitted. May be used for natural finish in less-demanding applications.
B	**SOLID SURFACE.** Shims, circular repair plugs, and tight knots to 1 inch across grain permitted. Some minor splits permitted.
C Plugged	**IMPROVED C VENEER** with splits limited to ⅛-inch and knotholes and borer holes limited to ¼ x ½ inch. Admits some broken grain. Synthetic repairs permitted.
C	**TIGHT KNOTS** to 1½ inches. Knotholes to 1 inch across grain and some to 1½ inches if total width of knots and knotholes is within specified limits. Synthetic or wood repairs. Discoloration and sanding defects that do not impair strength permitted. Limited splits allowed. Stitching permitted.
D	**KNOTS AND KNOTHOLES** to 2¹⁄₂₂-inch width across grain and ½ inch larger within specified limits. Limited splits are permitted. Stitching permitted. Limited to Interior and Exposure 1 panels.

Source: APA—The Engineered Wood Association

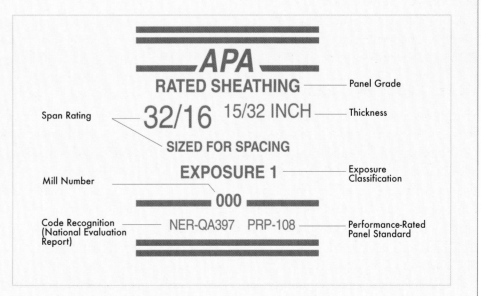

RATING PANEL PRODUCTS

A TYPICAL PLYWOOD GRADE STAMP indicates the panel grade, thickness, and span rating; assures the buyer of code compliance; and identifies the grading body and the mill. Certified green plywood will be stamped "FSC" for the Forest Stewardship Council.

APA
RATED SHEATHING —— Panel Grade
32/16 15/32 INCH —— Thickness
Span Rating
SIZED FOR SPACING
EXPOSURE 1 —— Exposure Classification
Mill Number
000
Code Recognition (National Evaluation Report) —— NER-QA397 PRP-108 —— Performance-Rated Panel Standard

GLUE-LAMINATED LUMBER

GLUE-LAMINATED LUMBER is built up of finger-jointed dimensional lumber that must be engineered (sized) for your application. It can be assembled in two configurations, depending on the span and load of the application.

Exposure. The stamp also lists the exposure and durability classification for plywood: Exterior indicates exposure to weather is possible; Exposure 1 designates suitability for wall and roof sheathing; Exposure 2, for applications that will have low moisture exposure, such as subfloors.

Mill and Standards Numbers. The mill number simply identifies the manufacturer. The remaining numbers on the label—national evaluation report (NER), and performance-rated panel standard (PRP)—indicate that the panel meets all construction requirements and requisite codes.

Veneer Grades. Plywood is also rated for veneer grades, and that rating appears on the edge of the plywood, using combinations of letters. There are six categories in veneer ratings: N, A, B, C Plugged, C, and D, indicating descending order of quality. N is a smooth surface of select woods with no defects, but you won't be using N in framing. It's for use in cabinetry. For construction-grade plywood, the face-and-back-veneer grades are combinations of letters. B-C, for example, is suitable for sheathing, whereas you'd use A-B when both the face and back veneers will show. A-C or A-D is suitable when only the A side will show, and C-D is used for concrete forms.

Engineered Lumber

Engineered lumber can be seen as a green product because it saves having to use large-dimension lumber, which would normally come from old-growth trees. There are a number of engineered, nonwood, and steel products that you can successfully use in place of traditional timber when framing a house. They were created to respond to the span requirements of changing house designs that include open floor plans, cantilevered decks and lofts, and overhanging roofs. The engineered-wood products include glue-laminated lumber, laminated-veneer-lumber, and parallel-strand beams. Be aware that you must use these products in strict accordance with manufacturers' span specifications. In addition, you must install them with special connectors and specified techniques. (See also pages 54 and 59.)

Glue-Laminated Lumber

A glue-laminated beam is a built-up product, a beam made up of smaller pieces of wood glued together lengthwise with waterproof glue. For example, six 2x4s, each measuring $1\frac{1}{2}$ x $3\frac{1}{2}$ inches, will create a 9 x $3\frac{1}{2}$-

inch beam. To make a beam, high-quality lumber is finger-jointed together and stacked. Finger-jointing is a technique used to join wood end to end into a single member. The ends of component wood pieces are cut to look like fingers and glued together.

Glue-laminated lumber can be as long as you like—25 feet or longer. Each beam is specifically engineered to support the intended building load: for heavier loads, the beam may use a more supportive component configuration, heavier component pieces, or more boards glued together.

Appearance Grades. You can use glue-laminated lumber, hidden or exposed, as ridge beams, purlins, headers, floor girders, and garage-door headers. It comes in three appearance grades, which have nothing to do with strength: industrial, architectural, and premium. Industrial-grade beams are simply planed to a uniform dimension. The wood may have checks and knotholes. Architectural-grade beams have been sanded on all four sides, and blemishes have been filled. Premium-grade beams have had all defects and blemishes fixed. All three kinds of lumber are dried, then wrapped in watertight wrapping.

Residential Grade. Residential-sized, glue-laminated lumber is a similar product made to replace headers, the horizontal structural supports above doors and windows. These beams are made to standard framing widths and are designed to bear residential loads. They also have a slight bow, called a crown, which you must install upward. The top side is labeled on the wrapper.

Connectors. No matter what kind of glue-laminated lumber you install, you can't just nail it in place. You may be required to use framing connectors, shear plates, threaded rods, nail-on clips, or hangers. Be sure to double-check the manufacturers' installation requirements and span ratings.

Cost. Glue-laminated beams are 30 to 50 percent more expensive than beams built up out of framing lumber. For shorter length applications, like headers, you'll find that a beam made of face-nailed conventional lumber is more economical. For longer spans, such as garage door headers or the structural ridge beams for large open rooms, however, glue-laminated beams offer a price advantage and dramatic labor savings. If you frame a span of 30 feet with a glue-laminated beam, you'll surely save money on labor and materials over comparable "stick-built" framing systems. You'll also

VENEERED BEAMS

LAMINATED-VENEER LUMBER (LVL) is a beam composed of plywood-like pieces of lumber glued together side by side, as seen in this header above the window openings.

PARALLEL-STRAND LUMBER is made from strands of softwood lumber. These engineered beams may be up to 7 in. thick.

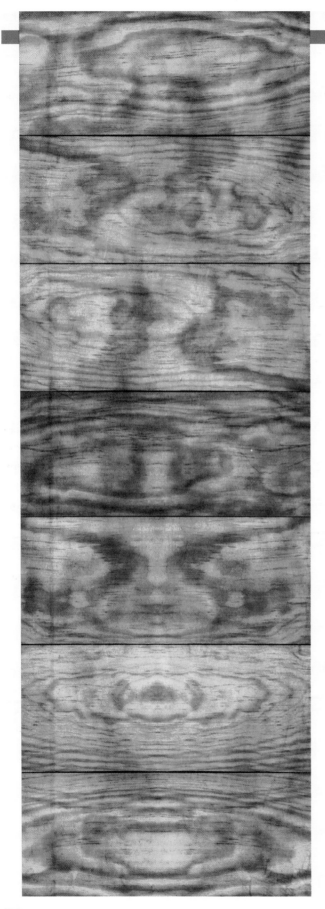

Is There Such a Thing as Green Lumber?

There's nothing really green about cutting down trees, but trees are a renewable resource and, responsibly harvested, can represent a green source of material to build homes. You can, however, pay a slight premium to obtain wood whose chain of custody has been scrutinized. (See "Green Product Organizations" in Chapter 1.) The certifying organizations do not verify the quality of the lumber, only that it wasn't harvested in a destructive way. So just because you get green certified lumber, don't expect it to be better lumber than what you'd otherwise find in a lumberyard.

The leading certifying agencies are the Forest Stewardship Council (FSC) and the Sustainable Forest Initiative (SFI). Although SFI is sponsored by lumber industry dollars, it does establish some lumber harvesting guidelines that are better than none at all. On the other hand, FSC is a truly independent agency that looks closely at the lumber custody and supply chain, starting with the effect logging has on certain communities, before it bestows a certification.

In addition to the lumber certifications, there are green features to look for in any wood product. The principle concern centers around the adhesive used for plywood and oriented strand board (OSB). Almost all adhesives in sheet lumber use formaldehyde, a known carcinogen. There are, however, formaldehyde-free sources, which are easy to find through the Internet. But remember, you are not just looking for formaldehyde-free plywood, but formaldehyde-free sheet goods for the underlayments of cabinets and floors as well. If you buy cabinets made from a very green product like bamboo, which is a grass and not a wood, you haven't really gone green unless the OSB that makes up all the other aspects of the cabinets is entirely formaldehyde-free.

WOOD I-BEAMS

WOOD I-BEAMS. Made with fir rails and ½-in. plywood or OSB webs, wood I-beams can take the place of costly lumber beams. Web stiffeners and framing connectors may be required.

gain design versatility, on which you can't always put a price. A stick-built framing system in a 30-foot-wide room will not allow for wide-open spaces, as you would have to divide the room up with partition walls to support the roof. With a glue-laminated beam, which can span 30 feet, you can keep that space open.

Laminated-Veneer Lumber

Another commonly available engineered wood material is laminated-veneer lumber (LVL). You'll use these beams where you would have used steel or an oversize glue-laminated beam. They are made, as their name implies, by laminating $^1/_4$-inch-thick plies together to a thickness of $4^1/_2$ inches. You'll have to consult with the manufacturers' span charts to determine the size LVL to use on your job. Even when you get the span rating down, be careful, because you can't notch or drill LVLs for pipes, wires, and heating or air-conditioning ducts, and you have to use the proper framing connectors.

Parallel-Strand Lumber

Parallel-strand lumber is a kind of engineered beam that can be between $1^3/_4$ and 7 inches thick. The beams are made of matchstick-like strands of Douglas fir and/or southern yellow pine. The strands are glued together

running parallel with one another—hence the name parallel-strand lumber. These beams are more dimensionally stable than LVLs or glue-laminated lumber beams, and they serve in the same framing applications. Parallel-strand lumber tends not to cup or twist when it is stored, which is a potential problem with some glue-laminated beams and LVLs.

Wood I-Beams

Another popular engineered product, wood I-beams are dead-straight, dimensionally stable, and ideal for longer spans, say 24 feet. Wood I-beams are light and can be installed by just two people. The web, or center, of a wood I-beam is typically $^1/_2$-inch plywood or OSB, and the 2-inch rails at the top and bottom are fir. Wood I-beams come in four sizes: $9^1/_2$, $11^7/_8$, 14, and 16 inches deep. You can simply nail them in place in many applications, or use commonly available connectors and hangers in others. The manufacturers of these products will provide design help and technical support.

Roof Trusses

If you're nervous about cutting rafters from scratch and you don't mind losing the open attic space, roof trusses are a good option. On small sheds, trusses are usually 2x4s held together by gussets, which are flat

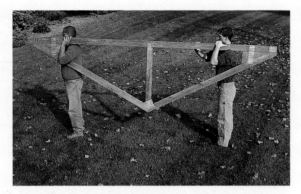

TRUSSES for small buildings, such as this 12-ft. truss for a 4-in-12 gable-roofed shed, can easily be carried and raised into position by two strong people.

Trusses

Trusses are engineered configurations of dimension lumber that frame a roof or floor. Because they rely on carefully engineered opposing and supporting forces among their chords, they can use lumber that has smaller dimensions to achieve the strength offered by framing lumber. You can avoid the use of 2x10 or 2x12 rafters and longer large joists by using 2x3s or 2x4s arranged in a gable formation. What's more, because trusses use smaller-dimension lumber, often in short lengths, they require "secondary demand" lumber and not the big, long pieces needed to make rafters. In this way, more of the tree is used, and the trees used can be smaller.

Roof trusses come in stock configurations—with various pitches and lengths—but they can be custom made at reasonable costs. They are typically delivered on a scissor truck that can lift its bed so that the trusses can slide onto the wall's top plate. They can also be swung in by crane, which is a very convenient way to set them. Properly sheathed, they perform just like dimension lumber rafters, and they are indeed a greener way to frame roofs. Floor trusses are also available, and they take the place of solid lumber joists made from larger pieces of dimension lumber.

BASIC TRUSS TYPES

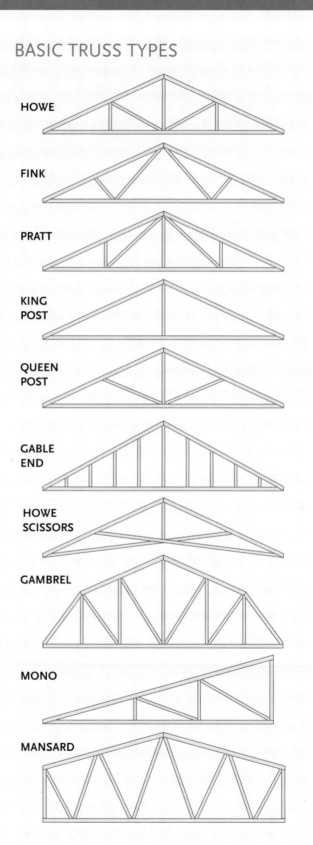

HOWE

FINK

PRATT

KING POST

QUEEN POST

GABLE END

HOWE SCISSORS

GAMBREL

MONO

MANSARD

erecting trusses

Trusses must be erected with the right spacing or the thin chords of the truss can become overstressed by wind and snow loading. Be sure to use the manufacturer's design specification for your truss and for the wall-to-wall distance over which the truss spans.

TOOLS & MATERIALS
- Hammer ► Stepladders or scaffolding
- 4-ft. spirit level ► Measuring tape
- Trusses ► 16d nails
- 2x4s for braces, blocking & strapping

1 Place the first truss on one end of the building and its ends on the cap plate with the top pointing downward. Two or more people will be needed to raise it upright depending on its size.

2 Fasten the truss to the cap plate using 16d nails or metal anchor brackets. Plumb the truss with a level, and nail it off to 2x4 braces that run to the ground.

3 Mark the positions of all the trusses on the cap plates. Nailing 2x4 spacer blocks between the truss locations will stabilize a truss while it is toenailed into place.

4 Set the second truss in place against its spacer, and toe-nail it to the cap plate using four 16d nails or fasteners specified by the truss manufacturer.

5 With three trusses installed, tack strapping across the top on each side. Nail strapping on additional trusses as you set them in position to tie the trusses together.

metal or plywood plates that cover and reinforce the joints. The two top chords and one long bottom chord form the shape of a gable roof. Internal framing members, called webs, tie the chords together. Cutting any one of the members compromises the structural integrity of the entire truss.

Roof trusses commonly come in two forms, the Fink and Howe truss. But there are many different configurations and sizes. End trusses often don't have the same webs as the trusses for the interior of the roof. Instead, the webs are vertical two-by studs installed at 16 or 24 inches on center.

Order trusses from a truss manufacturer by specifying the length of the bottom chord, which should include the span, wall thicknesses, and soffits. Trusses tend to come in low-angle pitches.

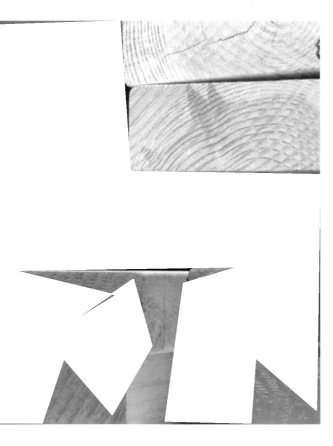

ABOVE Not all lumber is equal. The SFI and FSC are two organizations that certify wood products after examining the supply chain of lumber to ensure that is was not harvested in a destructive way.

Setting Trusses

Lightweight 2x4 trusses for a small shed are easy to set up. (See "Erecting Trusses," page 57.) The key is to add braces and strap them to trusses as you set them in position. But the only way to erect large trusses is with a crane and best left to a professional.

The First Truss. Before lifting up the first truss, nail short two-by boards on the gable ends of the structure to act as stops so that the truss doesn't slip off the end of the plate. These can be removed when the sheathing is in place. The best approach is to set the truss upside down, hanging from the wall plates peak down. Then walk it into place and turn it upright after calculating where the bottom chord will land on the plate. You need to work carefully.

Bracing the First Truss. Positioning the first truss is relatively easy on a small shed; however, it's important to brace it securely, which can be more time consuming. You'll need several long 2x4s that reach down to the ground and lateral braces that pin the truss in place on the gable-end wall. Because the rest of the trusses will depend on the stability of this first truss, you should include at least two braces running from the truss down to cleats on the floor.

Adding Strapping. With strapping passed up from below, tie trusses together with at least one line of strapping on each side of the ridge. Use a strong material, such as 2x4 boards or $^5/_4$ furring. You can stagger the strapping temporarily and use short boards in a pinch to secure the next truss in line. Another option is to leave some strapping extended into the next bay before you tip up the truss. But after several trusses are installed, you should go back to the end wall, double check for plumb, and install a continuous strip of strapping on each side of the ridge.

The Last Truss. Setting the last few trusses in place can be difficult if you do not have a crane because there isn't much room to maneuver them. You often have to raise them peak up. Set the last truss against two-by stops on the gable-end plate to keep it from slipping off during positioning. Check all trusses for plumb. Attach trusses to the top plate using 16d nails.

Where Does Engineered Lumber Make Sense?

As forests come under increasing pressure, you will see more and more engineered lumber for sale. Engineered lumber is typically made by gluing or bonding together wood strands or wood fiber to create a beam or sheet product that is as strong as or stronger than dimension lumber. Another way to put it: it's structural lumber that has been fabricated.

Engineered lumber can actually be stronger and higher performing than "stick" lumber of the same dimension. Cross-laminated plywood and OSB has good weight-distribution characteristics. Glulam beams and wood I-joists can span greater distances and carry greater loads than dimension lumber of the same size.

Plus, engineered lumber is consistent. It's ideal for the framing behind cabinets where even $^1/_8$ inch variance can show up in the finished product. When you buy stick 2x4s, you will note that they are not all the same quality, but engineered framing lumber is remarkably consistent because it's made in a factory to tight tolerances, and the component materials are always dry.

Additionally, engineered lumber uses more of the tree and can use smaller trees. Wood I-joists (laminated webbing with wood flanges, shaped like a steel I-beam) can be made 40 feet long yet use 60 percent less wood than stick lumber. Because of their I-flange, they can weigh up to 60 percent less than stick lumber joists. A single person can easily carry a wood I-joist that is 25 feet long.

Engineered lumber makes financial sense when replacing long runs of rafters and joists for roofs and floors. It also makes great sense for structural beams, but review the manufacturer's span tables, and be sure that you have a structural engineer review your plans.

INSULATION

THE EFFICIENCY WITH WHICH WE KEEP HEAT in during winter or out during summer has implications that reach far beyond monthly fuel bills. Just cooling U.S. homes costs $40 billion each year and consumes 15 percent of all U.S. power—90 percent of which is created with coal and fossil fuels. So insulating a home is a good investment environmentally. Proper new insulation or retrofits can easily save 20 percent of fuel costs. But insulating a home has gotten a little complicated lately. Here's why: when energy was less expensive, and structures were not built as tightly as today's homes, moisture and mold weren't a problem. That's because air flowed—or was drawn or forced—through walls, drying them out naturally. Contractors could pack a wall with fiberglass or cellulose insulation (forget about vapor barriers), button up the walls, and never worry about a callback or lawsuit. Mold oozing out of switch plates was practically unheard of, unless the house flooded. Choosing insulation was simple: most of it came in batts, and products differed only in color.

The Green Building Envelope

WITH TIGHTER HOUSES, greater mold risks, indoor-air-quality concerns, and a much greater understanding of the dynamics of heat flow, insulation has become a highly specialized industry. Today, you can still buy a standard batt of fiberglass. But for a slight premium, you can get batts with smart paper facing that changes its molecular configuration to allow moisture out or in, or blown foam that produces tiny chemical reactions that link cells to keep air and moisture entirely out of walls.

Formaldehyde-Free, Mold-Resistant. Formaldehyde is a known carcinogen, yet it is widely used in binders and adhesives sold in the United States. When a traditional fiberglass batt is manufactured, the spun glass needs something to hold the thin glass strands together, and that's the job of a binder. Batts and rolls that use binders are referred to as "bonded" fiberglass insulation. For people who are concerned about formaldehyde off-gassing into their homes—a major indoor-air-quality issue for green builders—there are lines of formaldehyde-free insulation. Even better, some of this insulation line is treated for mold resistance.

Blown Foams. Of all the recent insulation innovations, the one with the greatest positive impact on the building envelope is blown foam. Though it is relatively costly and has to be applied by a specialty contractor, it offers near-zero air permeability and great insulation properties; therefore, the resulting building envelope has a high R-value and high integrity, two very green features. Moreover, these foams are self-adhering to walls, and they can be sprayed into the tightest spaces. Blown foam can prevent warm, moist air from entering the building, which is important, because when warm moist air meets cold or air-conditioned air, it condenses out as moisture. If that moisture happens to be within the wall, you have the potential for mold, rot, and indoor air-quality problems. So blown foam serves as insulation, plus it can boost indoor air quality and prevent mold.

Insulating Housewraps. A great deal of heat, as much as 60 percent, can be lost or gained as radiant heat—one of three kinds of heat (the others types are conduction and convection). Some housewraps can offer an additional R-2 and still allow walls to breathe.

INSULATION TERMS

- **BATT OR BLANKET INSULATION** is usually made from fiberglass cut to fit into framing cavities. Batts are provided in sheets, while blankets come in rolls.

- **BRITISH THERMAL UNIT** (Btu) is a measurement of heat. One Btu is the heat required to raise the temperature of 1 pound of water 1°F.

- **RIGID BOARD INSULATION** is manufactured in panels that make it easy to clad a large area. Different types provide a range of R-values, although rigid foam generally is highly rated. It also resists water and rot in locations near the ground.

- **R-VALUE** is the standard measure of resistance to heat flow. Every type of insulation has an R-value per inch. The higher the value, the greater the resistance.

- **THERMAL ENVELOPE** describes the sum total of a home's insulation systems: walls, ceilings, foundation, floors, windows, and doors.

Solutions Abound. There are a number of other insulation choices, of course, like rigid foam boards, stay-in-place insulated concrete forms (ICFs), and sheet goods that combine insulation with a radiant barrier. Search "insulation" on Epa.gov, and you'll get a wealth of informative articles.

Insulation Basics

Like clothing, insulation comes in all shapes and sizes, but each has an R-value, the measure of its resistance to heat flow. In general, lightweight, air-filled materials such as fiberglass insulation batts have high R-values per inch of thickness and are good insulators. Standard fiberglass is rated at about R-3.5 per inch. Heavy, dense materials such as brick (R-0.2) and gypsum plaster (R-0.2) have R-values so low it's difficult even to think of them as insulators. R-values are stamped on the insulation itself and displayed in all insulation advertising. It is the only reliable way to determine how effective the insulation will be, and the only way to compare one type with another.

Comparing R-Values

Thicker is not necessarily better when it comes to insulation. That sometimes confusing subject becomes clear when you compare materials. For example, these three alternatives are rated at R-11 and offer the same thermal protection: $1^1/_2$-inch-thick polyurethane board, $3^1/_2$-inch-thick fiberglass batts, or 4 inches of loose-fill vermiculite. That means you can't pick one insulation over another based only on thickness. A full 5 inches of a traditional, poured-in insulation such as perlite rated at about R-13 would provide only about 60 percent of the thermal protection offered by an inch less (4 inches) of polyurethane board rated at about R-23. So to reach an insulation rating of R-11 in walls, R-19 in floors, and R-30 in ceilings, you would need different thicknesses of commonly used insulation materials.

Comparing R-values without splitting hairs should show which one of several alternatives will provide the most resistance to heat loss. But some insulation materials are better suited to certain kinds of installations. That means you must consider other insulation characteristics in addition to the R-value.

Also bear in mind the law of diminishing returns as it applies to insulation. This means that the first inch in an uninsulated wall offers the greatest benefit, while the second inch offers a bit less, and so on, even though the last inch costs as much as the first.

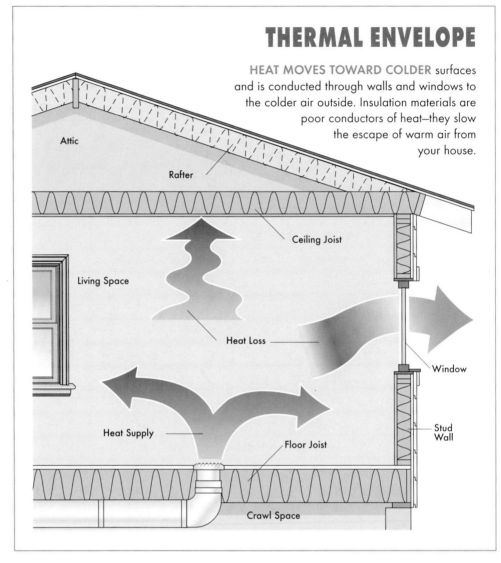

THERMAL ENVELOPE

HEAT MOVES TOWARD COLDER surfaces and is conducted through walls and windows to the colder air outside. Insulation materials are poor conductors of heat—they slow the escape of warm air from your house.

Attic

Rafter

Ceiling Joist

Living Space

Heat Loss

Window

Heat Supply

Floor Joist

Stud Wall

Crawl Space

Choosing Insulation

Two main factors affect your choice of insulation: the configuration (for instance, loose fill or rigid foam board) and the R-value. Some do-it-yourselfers also may consider ease of application, how the material is packaged, and potential drawbacks, such as possible skin irritation. But many lumberyards and home centers stock only fiberglass and a few types of foam boards.

Basic Configurations

Insulation is commonly available in five forms: batts to fit between 16- or 24-inch-wide framing, either paper or foil-faced; loose fill to blow or pour into structural cavities; and foam boards, used mainly on roofs and on the outside of walls and foundations. The two other types, sprayed-in-place cellulose foams and foamed-in-place urethanes, are more expensive and not used as widely.

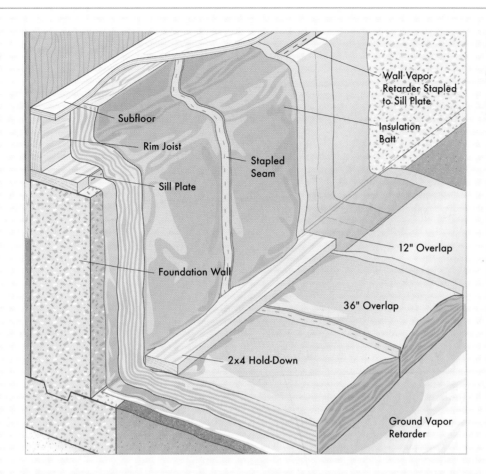

Labels on the illustration: Subfloor; Rim Joist; Sill Plate; Foundation Wall; 2x4 Hold-Down; Wall Vapor Retarder Stapled to Sill Plate; Insulation Batt; Stapled Seam; 12" Overlap; 36" Overlap; Ground Vapor Retarder

INSULATING CRAWL SPACES

IF YOUR KITCHEN sits above a crawl space, prevent cold feet by making sure there is enough insulation in either the floor or on the surrounding foundation. If you insulate the floor by installing fiberglass batts between the joists, be sure to wrap water pipes and ductwork in the crawl space with insulation. An alternative is to insulate the foundation walls and install a continuous vapor retarder as shown at left.

Rooms located over crawl spaces or uninsulated basements often feel uncomfortable because the floor may be cold. Solve the problem by adding fiberglass batts between the floor joists or insulating the foundation walls.

INSULATING THE FLOOR

Cut sections of unfaced insulation to fit snugly between the floor joists. Keep them in place by stapling sheets of house wrap or polyethylene plastic to keep the material from falling down. Protect pipes from freezing and ductwork from losing energy by wrapping them in insulation. Buy insulation designed for these jobs, and seal all joints with duct tape. If the ducts also serve the air-conditioning system, the insulation will help save energy during the summer as well.

INSULATING THE FOUNDATION

The most important part of this project is to keep moisture vapor generated in the ground from migrating into the house and the house framing. Spread a 6-mil sheet of polyethylene plastic over the exposed ground in the crawl space. Staple sheets of polyethylene to the sill plate, and let the plastic drape down the wall and overlap the sheet on the ground by about 12 inches. (See the drawing above.) Each sheet of plastic attached to the rim joists should overlap the one next to it by 12 inches. Measure the distance from the top of the rim joist to the ground, and add 36 inches. Cut insulation to this length. Push the cut batts against the rim joist and between the floor joists. Staple the batts in place with the kraft-paper covering facing into the crawl space. The batts should overlap the ground by about 36 inches. Hold them in place with 2x4s. Connect the batts together, creating a good seal, by stapling the seams together every 8 inches.

Fiberglass

Mineral Wool

Cellulose Loose Fill

Extruded Polystyrene

Polyurethane

Polyisocyanurate

COMMON TYPES OF INSULATION

▉ FIBERGLASS

The most common of wall and ceiling insulation materials, fiberglass insulation is installed in 80 percent of new homes. R-values available in a variety of different thicknesses range from R-11 to R-38. Unfaced batts can be laid on top of themselves to create super-insulated attics. Most residential applications use either rolls or precut batts.

▉ MINERAL WOOL

Like fiberglass, mineral wool is made from a hard mineral slag and spun into a soft material. Mineral wool gets clumpy when wet and will lose R-value. When dry, mineral wool has the same R-value as fiberglass.

▉ CELLULOSE LOOSE FILL

Cellulose is made from shredded newspapers that have been chemically treated with a fire retardant. It is sold in large bags and can be easily poured in between attic floor joists or professionally blown into wall cavities. When it is blown into walls, some settling can occur, creating under-insulated slices along the ceiling line.

▉ EXTRUDED POLYSTYRENE

This form of rigid board insulation has an R-value of about 5.0 per inch. The extruding production process creates a denser layer of polystyrene than expanded polystyrene. Boards are usually pink or blue in color. A similar material, called expanded polystyrene (EPS) has many tiny foam beads pressed together, like a styrene foam coffee cup or cooler. EPS is commonly called "beadboard" and has an R-value of about 3.5 per inch of thickness.

▉ POLYURETHANE

This versatile type of foam has a white or yellowish color and an R-value of about 6.0 per inch. Rigid panels can be faced with foil for radiant heat deflection. Used on a large scale on exposed framing, the material can also be mixed on-site and sprayed into place as a dense liquid that fills both large areas and small spaces in irregular framing bays. The material bubbles up after application, and is later trimmed flush with the framing.

▉ POLYISOCYANURATE

This plastic has an R-value of approximately 6.0 per inch. It has a white or yellowish appearance and is usually backed with foil for radiant heat reflection.

Recommended R-values

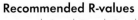

	A	B	C	D
	38	11	11	11
	38	11	11	19
	38	25	11	19
	38	25	11	19
	38	25	11	19
	38	25	18	19
	49	25	18	19
	49	25	18	19
	49	25	18	19
	55	25	18	19

A=Ceilings below ventilated attics
B=Floors over unheated basements
C=Exterior walls (wood frame)
D=Crawl space walls

Be sure to check general R-value recommendations against the requirements of local energy codes.

R-VALUE ZONE MAP

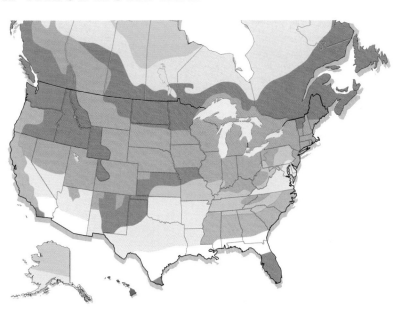

AVERAGE R-VALUE RECOMMENDATIONS FOR U.S./CANADIAN CLIMATE ZONES

INSULATION PERFORMANCE

R-Value Comparisons

The most common type of insulation is fiberglass, which has R-values ranging from R-11 to R-38, depending on thickness. Other types of materials include blown cellulose, several varieties of rigid boards, sprayed foams, and many less common materials, such as cotton fiber and aluminum foil bonded to plastic bubble pack.

The table at left compares approximate R-values for different types of common insulation. Each material is evaluated on how much resistance to heat change it offers. Values can be slightly different for very similar materials. To be certain of the value—and that you meet local energy codes—check product labels. All are required to list the R-value per inch. Generally, extruded plastic boards like polystyrene and polyisocyanurate offer the highest R-values.

FIBERGLASS BATTS

3¹/₂"	R-11
6¹/₂"	R-19
7"	R-22
9"	R-30
13"	R-38

LOOSE FILL (per inch)

Cellulose	R-3
Perlite	R-3
Vermiculite	R-2

RIGID BOARD (per inch)

Expanded Polystyrene	R-4
Dense Polystyrene	R-4
Extruded Polystyrene	R-5
Polyurethane	R-6
Polyisocyanurate	R-6–7

SPRAYED OR FOAMED FILL (per inch)

Cellulose	R-3–4.0
Polyurethane	R-5.5–6.5

Some materials come in only one configuration, others in several. You can get by using scraps of one material in spaces where another product would offer more protection. But to do a thorough job of creating a thermal envelope around your living space, particularly in the framing compartments of an existing building, you may want to use more than one type of insulator.

Materials

Cellulose fiber is a paper-based product and has roughly the same R-value as fiberglass, about R-3.5 per inch. Typically, it is made from shredded recycled paper combined with a fire retardant. Loose fill can be blown in using a pressurized air hose. Several newer insulating materials use a mix of about 75 percent recycled cotton fiber (even scraps of old blue jeans) with 25 percent polyester to bind the fibers together. The material comes in batts and as loose fill. Its R-value is generally about the same as cellulose.

Polyurethane foam can be sprayed by contractors into open framing cavities where it provides a thorough seal against air leaks and a thermal rating of about R-6.0 per inch. It also comes in pint-sized quantities—in a can with a nozzle so you can use foam to fill small openings in the building envelope.

Cementitious foam is made from magnesium oxide compounds extracted from seawater—a natural alternative to synthetic foams. This material (rated at about R-2–3 per inch) will not burn and does not shrink, but like polyurethane, is relatively expensive.

Expanded polystyrene board (beadboard) is similar to the material used in disposable coffee cups and is the first in a line of foam boards. Each offers a step up in quality, R-value, and of course, cost. All are highly resistant to moisture and water damage. Expanded board is crumbly but can add R-4.0 per inch under new roofing and siding or over foundation walls when covered with an exterior finish. Extruded polystyrene board is a more expensive, somewhat denser board that offers R-5 per inch for more insulating value. Polyisocyanurate board is a more rigid foam board that carries a very high rating of about R-6.3 per inch. In one inch of space you get almost double the thermal resistance provided by fiberglass.

Bubble pack is a flexible, foil-backed sheet of plastic with air-filled bubbles. It looks like packing material. Use it where there isn't room for batts or foam boards. You can wrap the $\frac{1}{4}$- or $\frac{5}{16}$-inch-thick sheeting around ducts and even use it under new drywall, say, between the house and garage.

TOOLS & SPECIAL HANDLING EQUIPMENT

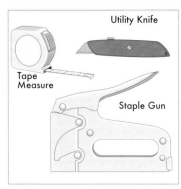

INSULATION can be installed with simple tools that are probably already in your garage or workshop.

Tape Measure, Utility Knife, Staple Gun

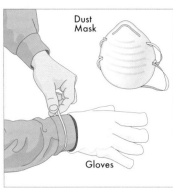

PROTECTIVE gear for installing insulation includes gloves, a dust mask, and a shirt with long sleeves secured with rubber bands.

Dust Mask, Gloves

An advantage that rigid board and foil bubble pack have over fiberglass is that they require no protection against airborne particles. You can easily cut rigid boards using a utility knife, and you don't need to wear gloves and a dust mask. With fiberglass insulation, however, you must take care to protect your eyes and lungs from glass fibers that can become lodged in your skin or breathed into your lungs.

WARNING: If you encounter asbestos insulation on old pipes, do not attempt to remove it yourself—call in a professional.

Foundations

Foundations can be insulated in two ways: from the inside and from the outside. Attaching insulation on the inside is much easier, but over the long term, insulating outside is more effective. Ideally, foundations should be insulated and waterproofed from the outside before they are backfilled during construction. But if your foundation is not insulated, and you are thinking about fixing base-

Spot-Application Spray Foams

Most spot-application spray foams are designed to be used when installing doors and windows or when sealing utility penetrations in walls and framing members. Spray foams should be used when the gap to be filled can't be sealed with caulk. Look for foams that are paintable and "toolable" (so they can be worked when wet). Foams that are water-based (that clean up with water) are easier to manage. Finally, look for foams that claim they don't overexpand. Many foams expand to 120 percent of their application dimension, which can pinch windows and doors if too much foam is applied.

ment leaks—which will require digging out around the foundation anyway—this may be the time to consider it.

From the Outside

An outside foundation insulation project requires digging out the backfill from the entire perimeter of your house—not an easy job. But if you go that route, remember to repair cracks with cement and check the overall foundation for signs of deterioration. Once the foundation is exposed, trowel a liberal layer of liquid asphalt on the outer surface for waterproofing; then attach rigid insulating board, and backfill the foundation. The backfill should consist of mainly gravel for the below-grade level and at least $1^1/_2$ feet of topsoil for plantings and shrubbery.

If your house is built on a perimeter foundation with a shallow crawl space instead of a full basement, digging from the outside to expose the wall surface may be easier than trying to apply insulation from inside the foundation.

From the Inside

First, clean and paint the walls with a masonry paint. If efflorescence (white, powdery spots) occurs anywhere, then water is coming from the outside into the basement and should be addressed as a separate problem. If your basement is dry year-round and you want to add insulation, you can apply rigid foam board or batts and a modular system of furring strips or studs to hold a finishing layer of paneling or drywall.

You can stuff fiberglass insulation around openings in the foundation, for instance, where plumbing pipes exit the house, and then seal the opening with caulk or cement. Another option is to spray foam around the hole, and trim the expanded material flush with the wall.

Adding Insulation

If adding some insulation is a good idea, more must be better—but only up to a point. With insulation there is a law of diminishing returns: the first inch offers the greatest benefit and makes the most noticeable difference in comfort. But layer upon layer provides less and less benefit—even though the last one costs as much as the first.

So when is enough insulation enough? One sensible guideline is to fill the space between framing members. For instance, you can add $3^1/_2$ inches of insulation to wall cavities framed with 2x4s, but trying to cram in 7 inches of insulation is counterproductive.

Interior Coverage

If you do decide to add to existing insulation, be sure to install only insulation, not a vapor barrier. A layer of plastic or foil buried between layers of insulation can cause condensation problems, decay surrounding wood, and greatly reduce the insulation's effectiveness.

For example, if you have only a few inches of cellulose between floor joists in the attic, you could add unfaced batts, rolls, or loose fill. You could build up the insulation depth between joists, and if you don't need the storage space, spread rolls of insulation above the joists at right angles to the framing.

This top layer insulates the attic floor framing as well as the spaces between joists, which are in direct contact with the ceiling of the living space below and act as heat conductors. Because heat rises, extra ceiling insulation is often a cost-effective improvement.

Exterior Coverage

You can gain the same frame-covering benefits outside the house, too, and eliminate thermal weak links, such as the seam between foundation and framing, by cladding walls with a layer of rigid foam board. It can run from underneath the siding, down the exposed foundation wall, and into the ground because foam board won't rot.

Even with a layer of foam, it's important to fill spaces that don't match the size of standard insulation, such as openings between unevenly spaced framing members and gaps around window and door frames.

Blowing in Insulation

Blowing in insulation makes the most sense when the framing cavity is empty. New material won't be blocked by old batts and thermal improvement will be dramatic, even though the dead air trapped in an empty wall cavity does provide some insulation. A contractor can fill the empty space by cutting small holes through the drywall, inserting a hose, and pumping insulation into the bay between each pair of framing members. You do wind up with a row of little cutouts, but they can be patched, sanded, and painted.

Access from the Outside

It may be easier for the contractor to gain access from the outside, by removing a course of clapboards and cutting a channel in the sheathing over the studs. It depends on which way into the wall cavity causes the least damage while providing the best access. In most cases, it's simpler to remove and replace exterior siding than it is to patch and repaint dozens of small holes in an interior wall. But even working blind with a hose through a hole, experienced contractors should be able to gauge how much insulation the cavity should take and know when the flow of loose fill has been blocked—say, by a construction brace or plumbing. In those cases, they may have to make a second hole to be sure that the bay is completely filled.

You might want to make a thermographic or thermometer test when the job is done to confirm results—although to be completely fair, you would have to duplicate weather conditions of the first test.

Insulating the Attic

Unlike wall cavities, you can't just fill all the empty spaces in the attic with blown-in insulation. You might find that there is room for a lot of new insulation—under the roof edges, for example—but you have to leave at least 1½ inches of air space under the roof for ventilation. Why? Because even when the ceiling insulation is protected with a vapor

(*Continued on page 70.*)

insulating foundation exteriors

TOOLS & MATERIALS
- ► Shovel
- ► Chalk-line box with plumb bob
- ► Hammer
- ► Trowel ► Hose
- ► Straightedge
- ► Rigid insulation
- ► Stucco ► Masonry nails

insulating foundation interiors

TOOLS & MATERIALS
- ► 4-ft. level
- ► Hammer
- ► Wood shims ► Work gloves
- ► Rigid insulation
- ► Drywall ► Masonry nails
- ► 6-mil polyethylene vapor barrier

FOIL INSULATORS

Foil-covered bubble pack sheets are thinner and more flexible than rigid boards, which makes them more versatile in their insulating applications. Foils are also impermeable to vapor, which allows them to double as a vapor barrier. Cold, sweaty pipes and air-conditioning vents benefit most from vapor-resistant insulation. Foil's flexibility makes it very useful in wrapping pipes and ductwork, and no safety precautions against airborne fiberglass particles or skin irritation are needed.

Foil also can be draped underneath plywood roof sheathing to improve energy efficiency. Laboratory testing of foil has shown that 90 percent of radiant heat can be reflected from a foil's surface. Depending on how and where the material is applied, the R-values can range from R-6 to R-18 or more in highly controlled and stable environments.

ABOVE New wall spaces can also be insulated with foil-backed bubble pack, which has an R-value around R-18.

OPPOSITE Foil sheeting installed under the roof deck between rafters can cut air-conditioning bills by reflecting radiant heat.

1 Excavate the dirt around the foundation. Check for cracks and holes; clean with a garden hose; and let dry.

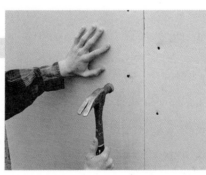

2 Nail rigid foam board insulation directly into the concrete or block foundation using masonry nails.

3 Apply cement plaster to protect the above-ground insulation from the weather and present a finished surface.

1 Install furring strips to support rigid foam panels. Use wood shims and a spirit level to plumb the strips.

2 Nail the strips in place with concrete nails once you have shimmed them the correct distance out from the wall.

3 Attach the foam between or on top of the furring, or both, to increase the R-rating. Then cover with drywall to finish.

LOOSE FILL IN ATTICS

SPRAYING LOOSE FILL is a great way to add insulation in your attic and cut your heating bills.

You should keep loose fill away from recessed light fixtures in ceilings, which need air flow to prevent overheating. Also keep loose fill blown into attics away from eaves vents. It's pointless to continue insulating out onto the roof overhang. Install some form of dam above the exterior stud wall to hold back the loose fill, preserve its loft, and prevent it from retarding ventilation by spilling onto the soffit vents.

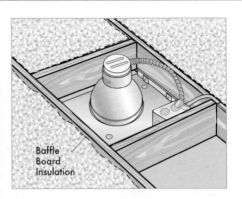

KEEP LOOSE INSULATION away from recessed ceiling light fixtures. Heat from the lamp could start a fire.

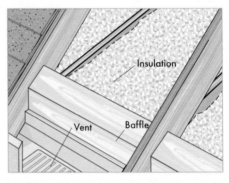

WOOD DAMS between the joists help keep loose fill insulation from spilling onto soffit vents and blocking air flow.

barrier, some moisture from the living space below gets through. Water vapor simply seeps through the insulation, rises against the cold roof, condenses, and drips back into the fiberglass or cellulose. This reduces the insulation's effectiveness and causes mildew, wood rot, and water "leaks" that, in the rooms below, will seem to be substantial enough to have come through the roof, not just from condensation beneath it.

Forming Dams

You need insulation directly over the exterior wall frame, but loose fill won't stay in neat piles along the wall until you close up the roof. And even if it did, over time the loose fill would spill down onto the soffit (the plywood running parallel with the ground on the underside of the overhang) and block the vents.

One way to solve this problem is by stapling foot-long batts of foil-backed fiberglass on the edges between the

joists to form a dam running from the exterior wall back up and into the bays. Air coming up through the soffit vents can flow freely over the short batts and across the loose fill, which can't spill out onto the soffit.

Obstructions

Blown-in insulation works best on walls where the wall cavities are empty. You won't gain much insulating value if existing insulation already fills most of the cavity. Another potential problem is that even if there is no insulation in the wall, some cavities will always be partly blocked by pipes, wires, and built-in obstructions such as horizontal fire-stops. Sometimes, the blown-in insulation will fill around the blockage. Usually, however, a new hole will have to be drilled higher on the wall to feed insulation into the blocked section.

INSULATED HEADERS

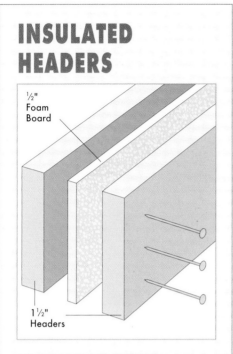

½"
Foam
Board

1½"
Headers

HEADERS THAT BRIDGE openings over windows and doors normally have two timbers, a plywood core, and low insulation value. Where codes permit, raise the value by replacing the plywood with ½-inch foam board.

AIR-SPACE BAFFLES

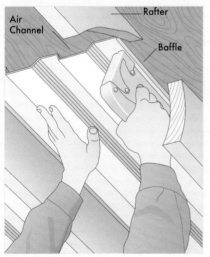

Rafter

Air
Channel

Baffle

AIR BAFFLES stapled to the roof decking moderate roof temperature and protect against damage due to condensation problems. Air can travel beneath insulating batts from vents in the overhang to the ridge.

DIAGNOSING WALL INSULATION

Cool [   ] Hot

A THERMOGRAPHIC PICTURE of your house can reveal where energy is escaping. This temperature-sensitive photograph highlights heat leaks in bright colors, typically at windows and doors. Also notice heat leaks under the double garage doors.

TO STOP AIR AND WATER infiltration on the outside apply a bead of flexible caulking, such as silicone, to exterior seams.

TO REDUCE DRAFTS and cut energy loss around windows, fill narrow gaps around the frame with loose-fill insulation.

To rate the energy efficiency of your house, conduct an energy audit. The most thorough version, handled by professional testing firms, checks air leaks, insulation values, the efficiency of glazing, and more. Many utility companies provide this service free. Some also recommend specific improvements and estimate the expected return on your investment in the form of lower utility bills. One easy way to discover if your home needs an audit is to conduct an insulation test with two thermometers. Tape one on an exterior wall; set the other in the middle of the room—off the floor and away from direct sunlight or heat registers that could skew the results. If the wall surface is within 5 degrees F of the ambient room temperature, the wall is adequately insulated.

insulating walls

TOOLS & MATERIALS
- Staple gun
- Dust or respirator mask
- Work gloves
- Batt or blanket insulation
- Heavy-duty staples
- 6-mil polyethylene vapor barrier

1 Wear gloves and a long-sleeved shirt when you unroll fiberglass. Cut it to length using a sharp bread or paring knife.

2 Fit the batt between framing members by hand. Wear a dust or respirator mask and gloves for protection.

insulating ceilings

TOOLS & MATERIALS
- Utility knife
- Batt, blanket, or loose-fill insulation
- Plywood baffles

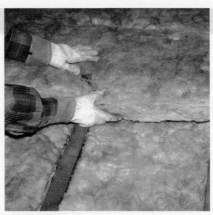

1 To avoid condensation, slit the facing of new batts or use unfaced blankets over existing insulation.

2 For maximum thermal effectiveness, run new insulation over both the old insulation and the framing members.

insulating roofs

TOOLS & MATERIALS
- Staple gun
- Respirator mask
- Work gloves
- Batt insulation
- Air baffles
- Heavy-duty staples
- 6-mil polyethylene vapor barrier

1 Staple air-chamber baffles to the underside of the roof sheathing before installing batts between rafters.

2 Because air can circulate through the baffles, you can fill the remaining space between rafters with batts.

3 Run the insulation behind outlet boxes and other obstacles to reduce thermal loss and prevent pipe freezing.

4 Flatten out the flanges extending from each side of the batt, and then staple them to the wall studs.

3 Pour loose fill into the spaces between joists. Keep it a few inches away from obstructions, such as recessed lights.

4 Install plywood baffles above exterior walls to prevent loose fill from blocking vents in the roof overhang.

3 Position and flatten the insulation as you would between wall studs. Batts should not compress the air baffles.

4 Trim and fit insulation in irregular openings and around obstructions to create a complete thermal barrier.

YOUR GREEN CHOICES

Closed-Cell versus Open-Cell Foam

There are two kinds of foam: open-cell and closed-cell. There are substantial differences in cost, application methods, and performance. With open-cell foam, tiny cells of the foam are not completely closed, so air fills all of the open space inside the material; this foam feels softer than closed-cell foam. With closed-cell foam, the tiny foam cells are closed and packed together. Each cell is filled with a gas that helps the foam rise and expand, which can lead to greater R-value. Various foams are engineered for cell size and density.

Density is measured by weighing one solid cubic foot of foam material. Open-cell foams weigh 0.4 pounds per cubic foot to 0.5 pounds per cubic foot. Closed-cell foams weigh 1.7 pounds per cubic foot to 2.0 pounds per cubic foot. The higher the density, the heavier and stronger the foam.

Closed-cell foam generally has more strength, higher R-value, and greater resistance to air leakage than open-cell. Closed-cell foam is also denser and more expensive. Open-cell foam has an R-value around R-3.5 per inch and typically uses water as the blowing agent. Closed-cell has an R-value of around 6.0 per inch (aged R-value) and uses various blowing agents, some of which can be selected for their ability to preserve the ozone. Look for zero-ozone-depleting propellants. Ideally, use closed-cell foam where small framing sizes need the greatest possible R-value per inch.

Spray-on Fiberglass Insulation

A product line that has positioned itself between fiberglass batts, cellulose, and blown foam is spray-on fiberglass insulation. Handled by a professional, it can be applied almost dry, and it completely fills gaps and voids around electrical fixtures, pipes, and other obstructions to give you continuous insulation coverage. Unlike cellulose, it will not settle or shrink, plus it's inorganic and naturally mold-resistant. What's more, excess insulation can be vacuumed up and reused, so there is no waste.

ABOVE Spray-on fiberglass can fill in hard-to-get places.

RIGHT Excess can be easily removed with a specialty tool (*top right*) and vacuumed up for reuse (*right*).

insulating existing walls

project

TOOLS & MATERIALS
- ► Blower equipment
- ► Blower hose with nozzle
- ► Drill/driver with hole saw attachment (optional)
- ► Pry bar (for wood siding)
- ► Zip tool (for vinyl siding)
- ► Cork or plastic plug ► Stud finder
- ► Loose-fill insulation ► Saber saw
- ► Yellow wood glue

1 Remove vinyl siding using a zip tool. Once the seam is separated, slide the zip tool along to free the panels.

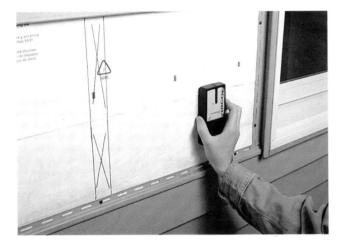

2 Use a stud finder to locate the studs beneath the sheathing. A hole will be drilled into each stud bay.

3 After you've shut off the power to the circuits in that wall, drill a hole using a saber saw or hole saw chucked into a power drill.

4 Place the nozzle in the hole; load the hopper; and operate the blowing machinery per the manufacturer's instructions.

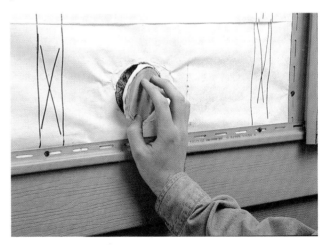

5 After a bay is filled, plug the hole with a cork or plastic plug; replace the siding; and move about 4 ft. up the wall; then repeat.

DRYWALL

DRYWALL IS NOTHING MORE THAN PAPER-FACED GYPSUM. Like other building products that look simple—such as insulation and paint—drywall has been remarkably improved since it first rolled onto the market decades ago to replace plaster and lath. Today's drywall choices are expanding. What used to be a simple product you screwed onto stud walls is now an integral part of indoor air quality and sound attenuation. Even drywall joint compound has improved and a new version has been engineered to produce dust that is heavier than the dust found in traditional joint compound. This cuts down on airborne dust during sanding.

DRYWALL PLAYS A ROLE IN THE INDOOR AIR quality of a home. Here's why: mold is a huge concern now with tighter homes, and the paper face on drywall offers mold spores a source of food. Mold eats rotten trees, so it makes sense that it would like the same food source in the form of paper. As the mold grows, it contributes to poor indoor air quality. So, in this section we cover paperless drywall products that are engineered to prevent mold by depriving it of food.

Additionally, the quality of life inside a finished home is an important aspect of green building. A quiet home that is a pleasure to live in is a healthy home. Therefore, drywall that deadens sound is a green product in many respects, and we will look at this as one more option to green up your home.

Let's look at the basics of hanging drywall and—as we have done in other chapters—review Your Green Choices, where appropriate, because even the purchase of something as simple as drywall can be a step toward achieving a green home.

Thickness

Gypsum drywall comes in $1/4$-, $3/8$-, $1/2$-, and $5/8$-inch thicknesses. Here's a look at common applications for each thickness.

$1/4$-**Inch-Thick Drywall.** Available in 8- and 10-foot panels, this stock is used for curved walls and sometimes for resurfacing over plaster or other solid-surface walls. Handle these panels carefully; because of their thinness, they can easily whip like sheet metal while being carried and can break apart. On curved walls, even a short length of $1/4$-inch-thick drywall requires a maximum stud spacing of 16 inches on center; it will noticeably bow on 24-inch on-center studs. When installing over a solid surface, use adhesive to help hold the panels in place. At $1\,1/5$ pounds per square foot, a 4-by-8-foot sheet of $1/4$-inch-thick drywall weighs about 38 pounds.

$3/8$-**Inch-Thick Drywall.** Available in 8-, 9-, 10-, 12-, and 14-foot lengths, this material is ideal for remodeling partition walls and for patching areas where old plaster has been removed. A $3/8$-inch thickness requires a maximum stud spacing of 16 inches on center. At $1\,2/5$ pounds per square foot, a 4-by-8-foot panel weighs about 45 pounds.

Paperless Drywall

Indoor air quality is a very green feature for homes because it improves the health of the occupants; mold is one reason for poor indoor air quality. Mold is fueled by what it eats, and the paper face of drywall is ideal food for mold. So, to hit mold where it lives, some manufacturers, notably Georgia Pacific, offer paperless gypsum board products. These offer excellent mold resistance because the facing is fiberglass, not paper, and that means there is no potential food source for mold or termites. The gypsum itself is reinforced with glass fiber to add to its moisture resistance. Long used as underlayment for tile, this paperless technology has been adapted for walls and can be finished and painted like traditional drywall.

$1/_2$-**Inch-Thick Drywall.** Available in 8-, 9-, 10-, 12-, 14-, and 16-foot lengths, this most common thickness works well for both walls and ceilings. Stud spacing can be 24 inches on center, unless the panels are hung with their long edges parallel to the ceiling joints. In this case, stick with 16-inch on-center framing to prevent sagging. At $1\,^7/_{10}$ pounds per square foot, a 4-by-8-foot sheet weighs about 54 pounds.

$5/_8$-**Inch-Thick Drywall.** Available in 8-, 9-, 10-, 12-, and 14-foot lengths, this stock, sometimes called firewall drywall, can be used in walls and ceilings. Like $1/_2$-inch, it can be hung on 24-inch on-center framing unless it is hung horizontally. The extra thickness improves sound dampening and resistance to sagging. In many areas, $5/_8$-inch drywall is required by code because of its superior fire resistance. At $2\,^3/_{10}$ pounds per square foot, a 4-by-8-foot panel weighs about 73 pounds.

Double-Layer Systems. To increase a wall's fire resistance and sound-dampening qualities, you can apply a double layer of drywall. A double-layer application also offers superior resistance to sagging and cracking especially when adhesives are used. The bottom, or base, layer is covered by a top, or face, layer. Typically, adhesive is used between layers to add even more wall strength.

Width

Common gypsum drywall panels measure 48 inches wide. Two stacked horizontal pieces or one vertical 96-inch length will span 8 feet, the height of a common ceiling. With some ceiling heights now measuring $8^1/_2$ or 9 feet high, manufacturers have started producing 54-inch-wide panels. Two of these will cover a 9-foot wall.

Selecting Drywall

Drywall panels are available in a variety of sizes. The standard for most residential work is the $1/_2$-inch-thick panel. Larger $5/_8$-inch panels are not usually used in houses because of the extra weight and cost. It may not seem like much, but that extra $1/_8$ inch makes the larger panels much heavier and harder to handle, especially for someone working alone. The lighter $3/_8$-inch-thick panels are good for resurfacing work when a wall is so scarred that spackling cannot save it. The $1/_4$-inch-thick panel is the most economical, but most people,

YOUR GREEN CHOICES

Gasketed or Sealed Drywall

A wall covered with drywall can be made airtight if gaskets are installed behind the drywall around its perimeter and around the perimeters of any rough openings. Gaskets are stapled in place directly to the framing before the drywall is installed. Though gaskets are preferable, silicon caulk can serve as a substitute and achieve similar airtight qualities.

Why would you want to do this? A couple of reasons. First, if your garage is attached to the house, there is a natural airflow dynamic that will pull the cooler air from the garage into the warmer air of the house. It's called "stack affect." If the garage air contains carbon monoxide or fumes, they could be drawn into the living area. Gaskets around the perimeter of the drywall and around rough openings can help prevent this.

Where should you ideally install the gaskets? Staple them in place so they sit between the edges of the drywall all around the two-by framing for all exterior walls. Also, staple them so they sit between the frames of windows and doors and the drywall. You also want to seal around utility penetrations or any other location where it's obvious that air could enter.

including most pros, don't like to use them because the sheets are very whippy and snap too easily during handling. Of course, be sure to check local building codes when planning a large-scale new construction or remodeling project.

As is the case with plywood and other construction sheet goods, the standard size for drywall panels is 4-by-8 feet, although other sizes are available. (See "Gypsum Drywall Sizes and Types," opposite.) The standard size works well with both 16-inch and 24-inch on-center framing.

Two common variations of standard panels are manufactured with qualities that improve drywall performance in key areas: panels impregnated with fire

Soundproofing Drywall

A healthy house is also a quiet house, and the quality of life of the occupants is certainly a green attribute. There are sound-deadening drywall products on the market; you can tell them by their Sound Transmission Class (STC)—Look for an STC in the 70s. (Search "sound-deadening drywall" on the Internet.)

Some of the products offer the noise reduction capability of eight sheets of traditional drywall. If you live near a highway or are bothered by outdoor noises from lawnmowers or leaf blowers, or just neighborhood noise, consider installing sound-deadening drywall. It is installed, taped, and finished as traditional drywall, and panels weigh about the same.

retardants, referred to as FC or fire code panels, and drywall panels that are treated to resist moisture.

From the standpoint of handling, smaller sheets are best—easier to carry and install. But from the standpoint of taping and finishing joints, larger sheets are better because they cover more wall area. The best approach is to use the largest sheets practicable—large enough to eliminate some seams and taping time but not large enough to create major handling problems.

GYPSUM DRYWALL SIZES & TYPES

Gypsum drywall comes in 8-, 9-, 10-, 12-, 14-, and 16-foot lengths. It's best to use longer panels where possible to minimize the number of seams. Fewer seams mean less taping and less chance that irregular seams will show through the finished wall.

Dust Control

Look for "dust control" joint compound. It is a product that will keep the dust down during sanding, a notoriously messy part of any remodeling job. This type of joint compound can reduce airborne dust because it produces "heavy dust" particles that bind together and drop straight to the floor, ready to be vacuumed up. Oddly, this kind of joint compound typically weighs 35 percent less than conventional joint compounds, but it has bonding power equal to or better than traditional joint compound.

installing drywall

Drywall, also called wallboard, has a gypsum plaster core that is sandwiched between two layers of heavy paper. It usually comes in sheets that are 4-feet wide and from 8- to 16-feet long in 2-foot increments. Common thicknesses are $1/4$, $3/8$, $1/2$, and $5/8$ inches.

You can install these panels either horizontally or vertically. Horizontal installations are easier, particularly during the finishing stages. But vertical installations are easier if you are working alone. To prevent cracks, avoid making joints next to doors and windows.

Cutting and Hanging Drywall

Begin by cutting though the surface paper using a sharp utility knife and a straightedge guide. Break the panel against your knee or over a scrap board placed on the floor. Bend back the broken panel and cut the back paper with a utility knife. Smooth cuts with a file or sandpaper. Then cut any openings needed for electrical outlets or other obstructions. Nail or screw the panels in place, spaced every 6 inches around the edge and every 12 inches in the panel field. To butt one panel tightly against the one above, lift the panels using a site-made lever made of scrap lumber.

TOOLS & MATERIALS

► Basic carpentry tools
► Drywall panels
► Drywall saw
► 48-in. aluminum drywall T-square
  (or straightedge)
► Utility knife
► Power drill with drywall screw clutch
► Drywall hammer
► Drywall nails or galvanized drywall screws
  long enough to penetrate at least 1 in.
  into the framing
► Panel lifter

1 To make straight cuts on a drywall panel, first mark the sheet to proper size. Then score the surface paper using a utility knife and a metal straightedge. Always use a sharp blade in the knife and cut only through the paper. Use a drywall saw to make jogged or curved cuts.

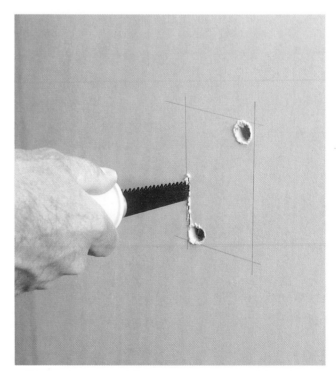

4 To make a cutout for a receptacle or switch box, lay out the box position on the panel. Then drill a hole at opposing corners and cut along the layout lines using a drywall or keyhole saw.

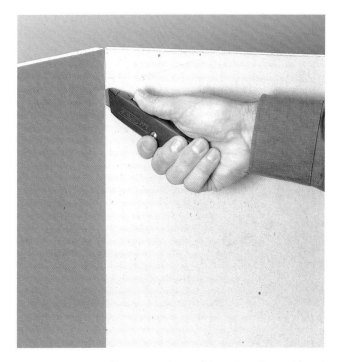

2 Once the paper is scored, the panels are easy to break. Just put your knee behind the cut on the back of the panel and pull both sides toward you. Or, place a piece of scrap lumber under the cut and push down on one side until the panel snaps.

3 After the panel is snapped, stand it on its edge and bend it slightly at the break. Then cut through the paper backing using a sharp utility knife. If the cut edge is too rough to fit, don't recut the panel. Just sand down the edge with coarse sandpaper.

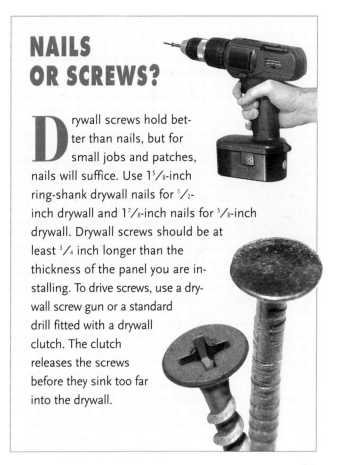

NAILS OR SCREWS?

Drywall screws hold better than nails, but for small jobs and patches, nails will suffice. Use 1⅝-inch ring-shank drywall nails for ½-inch drywall and 1⅞-inch nails for ⅝-inch drywall. Drywall screws should be at least ¾ inch longer than the thickness of the panel you are installing. To drive screws, use a drywall screw gun or a standard drill fitted with a drywall clutch. The clutch releases the screws before they sink too far into the drywall.

5 When you need to lift a panel off the floor so it fits tight to the one above, use a simple site-made lever. Put a wide board under the panel, then another smaller board under the wide board. Step on the end of the lever and the panel will move up.

taping drywall

If you plan to paint your finished walls, the quality of your drywall finishing job is crucial. The smallest dents and ridges will show through paint, especially high gloss products. Wallpaper hides more, and ceramic tile or wood paneling require only one coat of compound and tape on the drywall.

For a top-notch job, begin by filling the screw and nail dimples with joint compound. Then start taping the joints between panels. There are two types of drywall tape: paper tape and self-sticking fiberglass mesh tape. Generally speaking, fiberglass tape works well on tapered joints along the long edges of the panels but doesn't work as well in corners and butt joints across the ends of the panels. If you want to keep things simple, just use paper tape for everything.

First apply a thin coat of compound across a joint; embed a piece of tape in this compound; smooth the tape in place; and cover it with another thin coat of compound. Use tape on inside corners and metal corner bead on outside corners. When joints are dry, sand them smooth and apply the last two coats of compound.

TOOLS & MATERIALS
- Utility knife
- 6-in.-wide drywall knife
- 12-in.-wide drywall knife
- Sanding block
- Tin snips (if you need to cut metal cornerbead)
- Ready-mix joint compound
- Perforated paper tape or fiberglass mesh tape
- Metal corner bead (only if outside corners are present)
- Pole sander with swivel head and 120-grit sandpaper inserts or sanding screen (optional)
- Dust mask

1 Begin the finishing process by filling the nail and screw dimples with joint compound. Use premixed compound instead of the type you mix yourself. And use a 6-in.-wide flexible taping knife. A flexible knife works better for pressing the compound into the depressions.

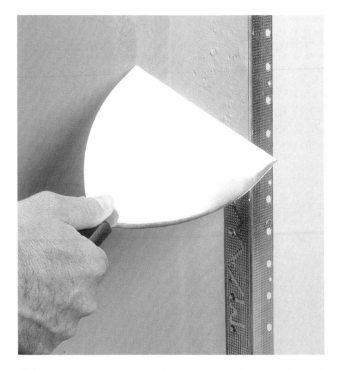

5 On outside corners, nail metal corner bead to the wall framing; then apply joint compound to both sides of the bead, using the raised corner as a guide.

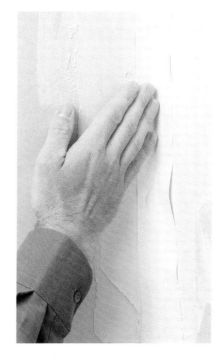

2 All joints must be covered with compound and tape. First, spread a thin coat of compound across the joint; then embed a piece of tape.

3 Once the tape is smooth, cover it with a thin coat of joint compound. Smooth the surface and remove extra compound using a 6-in. knife.

4 On inside corners, apply compound to both sides of the corner. Then place a folded piece of paper tape over the joint and embed it in the compound.

6 Once the first coats of compound and tape are dry, sand all joints with a pole sander and 120-grit sandpaper. Smooth the rough spots and feather the edges. Make sure to wear eye protection and a heavy-duty dust mask.

7 Plan on applying at least two additional coats of compound, with each coat covering a wider area than the one before. Use a large, 10- or 12-in.-wide, taping knife for the final coat. The smoother you apply the compound, the less sanding you'll need to do.

FLOORING

FLOORING IS ONE AREA WHERE YOU CAN REALLY GO GREEN with just a little effort. That's because so many nongreen products have historically gone into floors: carpets, sheetgood flooring (like vinyl), and the underlayment. Let's start from the bottom up. Underlayment is normally just sheets of plywood. But most plywood is made with formaldehyde adhesive, so an immediate green choice is to use formaldehyde-free plywood. Some formaldehyde-free plywood is available today, though efforts to go green have initially focused on hardwood plywood. More formaldehyde-free plywood will become available over time, and that will be driven by the California Air Resources Board (CARB). CARB has been the motivating force behind the development of many green products that are now sold on a national scale. CARB sets air standards for the state of California, and

Carpet Chemistry

Synthetic carpeting is made of petroleum-based products, such as nylon, polyester, and acrylic. These fibers tend to be stable once manufactured; the culprit for the smell and off-gassing from carpet is the backing. Specifically, styrene butadiene rubber—the chemical that gives the backing flexibility—can emit volatile organic compounds (VOCs) that can make you sick and cause irritation in your throat, nose, and eyes. Another chemical, 4-phenylcyclohexene (4-PC) is what you probably associate with that "new carpet smell." A known carcinogen, formaldehyde, is used widely in glue, and that glue is used in carpet. Even a tiny amount of formaldehyde (>0.1 part per million) can cause breathing difficulty in sensitive people. Styrene, also known as vinyl benzene, is another chemical commonly found in carpets. Breathing high levels of styrene can cause effects such as depression, concentration problems, muscle weakness, tiredness, and nausea, and eye, nose, and throat irritation. Perfluorooctanoic Acid (PFOA), 2-Ethyl-1-Hexanol (a plasticizer), Naphthalene, and Polybrominated Diphenyls (a flame retardant) can all cause health problems.

Because the off-gassing originates in the adhesive and backer, the greenest choice is to use a carpet that doesn't use any adhesives.

Carpet Rating Organization. The Carpet and Rug Institute offers its Green Label Plus label, and products that earn this label are in compliance for acceptable levels of more than two

dozen chemicals found in carpets and adhesives. Another rating agency, Scientific Certification Systems—typically associated with the state of California but a truly independent agency—also rates carpets that are green choices.

manufacturers have developed products in compliance with CARB standards so that they can continue to have access to California markets. CARB has now set formaldehyde standards that will change national plywood markets.

Even as CARB may have changed flooring markets, many flooring companies, especially carpet companies,

now offer green flooring choices that use green adhesives (or no adhesives at all) and products made from renewable or recyclable components. "Your Green Choices" sidebars throughout this chapter will examine various options in wood flooring, sheet vinyl, and carpets, while looking at new choices, such as bamboo.

installing plywood underlayment

The correct underlayment will make your new flooring stay flat and resist water for many years. But it needs to be installed properly. First prepare the existing floor so that it provides a solid base. Then select an underlayment thickness that will make the new floor match the height of floors in adjoining rooms. Cut the panels to size, and place them on the floor so the joints are staggered. Then attach the panels with screws driven through the underlayment and subfloor, and into the floor joists.

TOOLS & MATERIALS

- Basic carpentry tools
- Wood filler
- 1-in. ring-shank nails or galvanized screws
- Circular saw with blade for cutting plywood
- Underlayment
- Power drill/driver

1 To cut plywood underlayment, place the panel on scrap boards; mark the length on both edges; and snap a chalk line between the two marks. Make the cut using a circular saw. Be sure to set the blade depth so that the saw cuts through the panel but doesn't hit the floor.

2 Start the second course of underlayment with a sheet that's shorter than the first so that the joints in the underlayment will be staggered. Maintain a uniform 1/8 in. expansion joint between sheets and along the room walls.

3 Underlayment panels should be attached to the floor joists, not just the flooring. Lay out where the joists fall, and snap chalk lines above each. Drive screws that are long enough to reach through all the layers of the flooring and at least 1 in. into the joists.

CREATING LAYOUT LINES

When installing any type of tile floor, it is best to create layout lines to guide the installation. For a standard layout, snap chalk lines in the middle of opposite walls.

To create diagonal layout lines, measure out an equal distance along any two of the original perpendicular lines, and drive a nail at these points (marked A and B in the drawing). Hook the end of a measuring tape to each of the nails, and hold a pencil against the tape at a distance equal to that between the nails and the center point. Use the tape and pencil as a compass to scribe two sets of arcs on the floor. The arcs will intersect at point C.

Snap a diagonal line between the center and point C, extending the lines in each direction. Repeat the process for the other corners.

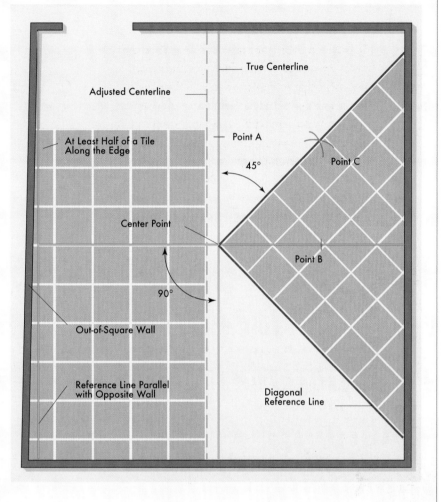

Types of Underlayment

Underlayment-grade plywood made from fir or pine is available in 4x8-foot sheets in thicknesses of $\frac{1}{4}$, $\frac{3}{8}$, $\frac{1}{2}$, $\frac{5}{8}$, and $\frac{3}{4}$ inch. Because it can expand when damp, plywood is not as good a choice for ceramic tiles as cement board.

Lauan plywood, a species of mahogany, is often used under resilient flooring. It is available in 4x8-foot sheets. The usual thickness for underlayment is $\frac{1}{4}$ inch.

Cement board is also called tile backer board. It is made of a sand-and-cement matrix reinforced with fiberglass mesh. It is usually available in 3x5-foot sheets in a thickness of $\frac{1}{2}$ inch. This is the preferred base for ceramic tile and stone floors in wet areas.

If the old flooring is not in good condition, remove it and smooth down the old underlayment before installing the new floor covering. If you can't remove the old floor covering, just apply the new underlayment over it.

UNDERLAYMENT OPTIONS

FLOOR COVERING	ACCEPTABLE UNDERLAYMENTS
Resilient floor coverings	▪ Old vinyl or linoleum flooring in sound condition ▪ Underlayment-grade plywood ▪ Lauan plywood
Wood parquet flooring	▪ Old vinyl or linoleum floor in sound condition ▪ Underlayment-grade plywood ▪ Lauan plywood ▪ Hardboard
Laminate flooring	▪ Any sound surface
Solid wood flooring	▪ Underlayment-grade plywood
Ceramic tile and stone	▪ Old ceramic tiles, if sound ▪ Concrete slab ▪ Cement board ▪ Underlayment-grade plywood

installing vinyl sheet flooring

Unlike laying vinyl tiles, installing vinyl sheet flooring requires some manipulation of large rolls of material. If you can find a big open place to work, the job will be easier. Many people use the garage floor.

Before you begin the installation process, create a scale drawing of the room on a piece of graph paper showing the exact outline of the flooring. A day or two before you begin laying the floor, cut the roll to approximate size, and put the cut section in the kitchen so it can acclimate to the room's temperature and humidity. Also, remove any shoe molding from around the kitchen baseboards. If you are careful removing it, you may be able to reuse it. Otherwise, plan on buying and installing new molding when the floor is done.

Some sheet-vinyl products require no adhesive, some call for adhesive just around the perimeter, while still others demand spreading adhesive over the whole floor. The last method is the one shown here.

TOOLS & MATERIALS

- ► Linoleum roller (from your flooring supplier)
- ► 6- or 12-ft.-wide roll of resilient flooring
- ► Notched trowel ► Framing square
- ► Chalk-line box ► Tape measure
- ► Marker ► Utility knife ► Solvent
- ► Straightedge ► Seam roller
- ► Rolling pin ► Adhesive

change blades frequently

UTILITY KNIFE BLADES DON'T COST VERY MUCH, ABOUT $1 FOR A PACKAGE OF FIVE. THIS MEANS THERE'S NO EXCUSE FOR NOT CHANGING BLADES FREQUENTLY WHEN CUTTING VINYL FLOORING. IF YOU TRY TO FORCE A DULL BLADE, IT CAN EASILY VEER OFF AND CUT VINYL YOU DON'T WANT CUT. CHANGE BLADES AFTER SIX CUTS.

1 Begin installing sheet vinyl by rough cutting the roll to the approximate size. Use a sharp utility knife and a metal straightedge to make the cut. If you can find a place to work where you can roll all of the sheet flat, all of your cuts will be easier.

5 To apply vinyl-sheet adhesive, roll half the flooring back to the center of the room, spread the adhesive on the bare section of floor, and then roll the flooring back to its original place. Repeat the same procedure for the other half of the floor.

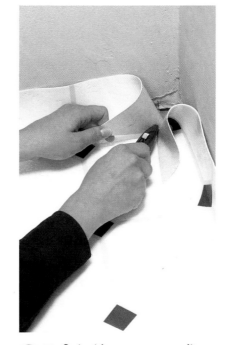

2 To cut around outside corners, slit the sheet margin down to the floor using a sharp utility knife. Be careful not to cut too far, or the cut mark will be visible on the finished floor.

3 To fit inside corners, cut diagonally through the sheet margin until you can get the vinyl to lie flat. Press the sheet gently down onto the floor on both sides of the cut.

4 To trim the vinyl along a wall, use a framing square to guide your cut. Leave $\frac{1}{8}$-in.-wide gap between the flooring and the wall.

6 To make a seam cut, apply adhesive up to 2 in. from the edge of the bottom sheet; then overlap the second sheet on top of the first by 2 in. Cut through both pieces, and remove the waste. Install the second sheet in adhesive, making sure to keep the seam between sheets tight.

7 Use a rented floor roller to force out any air bubbles that might have formed while the flooring was being installed. Work out from the center of the room toward the edges.

Green Carpet Alternatives

Tiles. Natural fiber carpet tiles are a green choice. Some of today's choices are made with green materials, such as wool, and nontoxic backers. Equally important, tiles can be replaced in sections, so the entire carpet does not have to be discarded if a high-traffic area wears out.

WOOL

Wool Carpet. Wool is a very green carpet material because of its natural attributes: it's renewable, biodegradable, and naturally resistant to mildew. There is nothing greener than a woven wool carpet that doesn't use synthetics or toxic chemicals in its underlayment. Look for jute backing. Jute is a natural vegetable fiber made from plants that grow in warm climates.

Vegetable and Natural-Fiber Carpets. Vegetable-fiber carpets are available today that offer you a truly green flooring choice. When these carpets wear out—some are made with corn fiber—they can actually be buried harmlessly in your garden.

Other choices include the following:

Silk. Produced by silkworms, silk is naturally nonflammable, strong, and not affected by static-charge problems.

Cotton. A vegetable seed fiber, cotton can be woven into carpets that actually become stronger when wet. However, it is an absorbent fiber and requires long dry times if wet cleaned. It can also be easily stained and is subject to mold and mildew.

Jute. Grown in South America, Pakistan, and India, jute can be woven into backing or carpets. But the fiber is weak when wet and can suffer dry rot, shrinkage, and mildew.

Sisal. Produced by the agave plant, sisal is very strong but stains easily and is tough to clean.

Rayon. Rayon is a synthetic fiber, but it is produced from natural fibers (cellulose wood pulp and cotton). It looks and acts like silk but has low resistance to abrasion.

Certified Alternatives. Look for carpet certified by GreenGuard Environmental Institute (Greenguard.org), Scientific Certification Systems (Scscertified.com), or the Carpet and Rug Institute (Carpet-rug.org).

Dustless Sanding

Refinishing floors always raises cleanup concerns because it is so dusty. That dust is very hard to contain, and try as you might—with plastic barriers and masking tape—it's hard to keep it within the work area. Increasingly available today is a process called "dustless sanding." It is simply the use of traditional floor sanding machines that are attached to high-efficiency particle accumulator (HEPA) vacuums.

The same amount of dust is created during the sanding process, but it is sucked up into a multi-layer set of filters that doesn't let anything escape into the air. The dust bags can be emptied later—far from the job site.

It's hard to find dustless-sanding machines for rent, but you can find a dustless-sanding company in your area through an Internet search. Floor finishing companies that have upgraded to dustless sanding machinery also tend to carry low-VOC floor finishes among their choices of polyurethane.

Vinyl and Alternatives

Vinyl is not a very green material, though a life-cycle analysis can justify its use. Vinyl flooring is very durable and won't have to be replaced very often. So you can argue—and proponents of vinyl often argue loudly—that a durable floor is a green floor, even if the manufacturing process is one that produces toxins. However, there are sheetgood floor products that can replace vinyl, and these choices—the old standby linoleum, for example—are very green indeed. Combine linoleum with a cork backing (cork is a tree bark), and you are getting even greener.

Linoleum is made of linseed oil (from flax), gums, cork, or wood dust, and pigments. It is a very durable and viable flooring product that can be shined and cleans like any vinyl product. Today, major manufacturers are offering linoleum flooring again, and it is also available in tiles.

Ceramic Tile

CERAMIC AND STONE FLOOR TILES are installed much the same way as vinyl tile. But there are differences, and it's the differences that make tiling more difficult than setting a vinyl floor. Tile is set in thinset adhesive, and cutting tiles is more difficult than trimming vinyl products with a utility knife. (See "Cutting Tiles," opposite.)

You must also grout the spaces between tiles—a step that takes some time and practice to get right. However, the results are well worth the extra effort.

You can start your tile installation in a corner or from the center of the floor, using chalk lines, as described on page 87. In either case, it is best to lay out the tiles in a dry run. Use tile spacers to indicate the width of the grout joint. If using mesh-backed tile sheets, you don't have to worry about joint spacing. Try to lay out the tiles to avoid narrow pieces (less than 1 inch) abutting a wall. If this happens, adjust the layout.

If the corners in the room are not square, or if you must install cut tiles around the perimeter of the room, make guide strips by temporarily nailing 1x2 or 1x4 battens to the underlayment. If you are tiling on concrete, weigh down the ends of the guides with heavy weights, such as a few stacked bricks. Place a strip parallel with each of two adjacent walls, with their leading edges positioned on the first joint line. Begin your installation here, and then go back and fill in the space between the first full row of tiles and the wall by cutting each tile to fit.

To make sure the strips are at right angles, use the 3-4-5 method. Measure 3 units—3 feet, if the room is big enough—from the corner along the guideline or strip, and mark the spot. Measure out 4 units (4 feet) along the long guideline, and mark the spot. Now measure the diagonal line between the two points. If the diagonal measures 5 units (5 feet), then the two guides are at right angles.

YOUR GREEN CHOICES
Ceramic Tile

In addition to providing countless styles and designs, ceramic tile also provides a good green choice when selecting flooring. Ceramic tiles are made from natural materials that are durable, and if installed properly, the tiles themselves will last for years. Best of all, unlike wood and paper products, tile will not provide food for mold. However, the mastics and adhesives used to hold tiles in place are another story. Some contain VOCs that can be harmful when installed. When planning a tiling project, be sure to look for low-VOC mastics.

LEFT Ceramic tiles provide beautiful, long-lasting floors. Notice how the counter material complements the tiles.

CUTTING TILES

A SNAP CUTTER consists of a metal frame that holds the tile in position, a carbide blade or wheel to score the tile, and a lever to snap the tile along the score line. You can buy or rent snap cutters, but many tile dealers loan these tools to their customers for the duration of the project. If you do buy or rent one, make sure that it can handle the tiles with which you will be working. Some models will not cut thick, unglazed quarry tiles or pavers.

TILE NIPPERS take small bites out of tiles. They are good for cutting out curves and other irregular shapes to fit tiles around pipes or openings. The cuts will not be as smooth as cuts produced by the other tools, so plan on hiding the edges of these tiles under molding or some other type of trim.

A WET SAW is a step up from both the tile nippers and the snap cutter. This rental tool is a stationary circular saw with a water-cooled carbide-grit blade. Don't use this tool on floor tiles coated with a slip-resistant abrasive grit because the grit will dull the blade.

BASIC TILE SHAPES & PATTERNS

The basic floor tile measures 12x12 in. with ⅛-in. to ¼-in. grout joint.

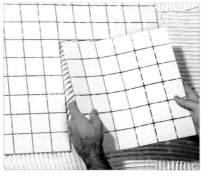

Sheet-mounted tile will look like individual mosaic tiles when installed.

Rectangular tiles can be used to create basket-weave patterns.

Combining different shapes allows you to create a variety of patterns.

Hexagon-shaped tiles create an interlocked pattern.

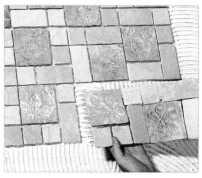

Multicolor and multisize tiles are available in sheets.

laying ceramic floor tile

Ceramic floor tiles come in a wide variety of shapes and colors. One of the primary differences is whether the tile is glazed or unglazed. The unglazed type shown here is a common choice for both bathrooms and kitchens. The reason is simple: most unglazed tiles provide better traction in wet conditions. To protect them from staining, a sealer is applied every year or two.

TOOLS & MATERIALS

- ► Rubber float ► Notched trowel ► Pail
- ► Sponge ► Soft cloths ► Hammer
- ► Tile cutter ► Tile nippers ► Small brush
- ► Jointing tool or toothbrush
- ► Roller and pan ► Tiles ► Grout
- ► Adhesive ► Solvent ► Sealant
- ► 12-in. piece of 2x4 wrapped with carpet

1 Begin by laying out the floor and snapping chalk lines to guide your work. Then spread only as much adhesive as you can cover with tile before it dries. The container will specify the open time of the adhesive inside. Use a notched trowel held at a 45-deg. angle.

4 After the tile adhesive has cured, clean out the grout joints between all the tiles using a soft broom or a shop vac. Then mix the grout, and spread it into the joints using a float tool. Make sure the grout completely fills all the joints.

5 To remove the excess grout, drag the rubber float across the joints at a 45-deg. angle. Do not press too hard because this can pull grout out of the joint, requiring you to apply a second coat.

2 Press individual tiles into the adhesive, giving each a slight twist to make sure the back of the tile is completely covered with adhesive. Keep tiles and grout lines aligned as you work.

3 Make sure all the tiles are embedded completely in the adhesive by tapping them with a padded board and a hammer. Use the block every couple of courses, and make sure the block spans several tiles every time you strike it.

6 Clean off any remaining grout with a sponge and clean water. Work in a circular motion, and clean the sponge frequently. Also change the water as soon as it becomes completely cloudy. When the tiles are as clean as you can make them, let the surface dry. Then buff the tiles using a clean, soft cloth.

7 Seal unglazed tiles and grout with a transparent sealer. Use a roller to apply it, according to the manufacturer's instructions printed on the product container. Diagonal strokes force the sealer into the grout joints better. If your tiles are glazed, apply sealer only to the grout using a brush.

installing a laminate floor

Laminate can be considered a green alternative to solid-wood flooring. A typical laminate floor is installed as a floating system. The boards or tiles are glued to one another but not attached to the floor. To "float" without buckling or cracking as they expand and contract with changes in temperature and humidity. To create a barrier between the floating floor and the immobile subfloor, you install a foam pad that is about ¼-in. thick.

TOOLS & MATERIALS
- Laminate flooring ▸ Spacers
- Foam underlayment padding ▸ Glue
- Hammer ▸ Installation block
- Plastic putty knife ▸ Strap clamps
- Circular saw or handsaw
- Chalk-line box

1 Make sure the existing flooring is in sound condition; then roll out the foam padding starting at one corner. If you are covering a concrete slab, most manufacturers require you to lay a polyethylene vapor barrier underneath the foam.

4 After you've installed three or four rows of boards, hold them with strap clamps, and let the glue set up for about an hour before continuing. As you progress across the floor, just lengthen the strap clamps.

5 To measure the perimeter boards that need cutting, first lay a full plank over the last installed board. Use a third board, pushed against the wall, to scribe the board that needs cutting. Make the cut using a circular saw and a fine-tooth blade.

2 Assemble the first two or three rows of boards by spreading glue along the tongues (inset) and pushing the boards together. Install plastic spacers between the boards and the edges of the floor. The gaps created by these spacers give the floor room to expand with increases in temperature and humidity without buckling.

3 If you can't push a board in place using only your hands, then gently drive the boards together using a softwood block. Don't strike the block too hard because this might cause damage to the tongue on the board. Remove any excess glue using a plastic putty knife.

LAMINATE LAYERS

Laminate flooring has two things going for it: it is easy to install and it can be made to look like anything, including wood, stone, ceramic tile, or any color of the rainbow. The inner fiberboard core provides dimensional stability and water resistance that make these products suitable for installation in a kitchen; the wear layers protect a decorative image. You can install laminate flooring over any substrate except carpeting. Simply make sure that the original flooring is clean and level. Most manufacturers require a foam padding under the floor. A glue-type installation is shown opposite, but some manufacturers also offer a glueless version where the individual components snap together.

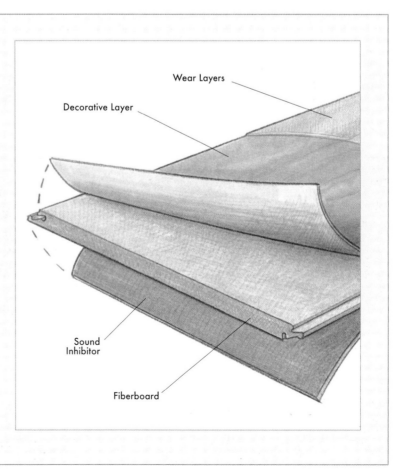

Wear Layers

Decorative Layer

Sound Inhibitor

Fiberboard

installing wood strip flooring

These days many different wood species are used for flooring, generally as veneers glued over plywood panels. But traditionally, solid maple and oak were used for floors. (If you decide to use such flooring, be sure it is FSC certified.) Solid-wood floors may be difficult and time-consuming to install, but they look wonderful and are very durable, often outliving the houses where they were installed.

TOOLS & MATERIALS

- 15-lb. felt building paper ► Backsaw
- Chalk-line box ► Basic carpentry tools
- Electric drill with assorted bits
- Flooring and finishing nails ► Pry bar
- Wood flooring ► Dust mask
- Nail set ► Rented nailing machine
- Circular saw or handsaw

1 Start the job by removing the moldings along the floor. If you want to reuse these boards, then carefully pry them from the wall, and pull the nails out from the back side using locking pliers. Also be sure to label them on the back so you'll know where each came from.

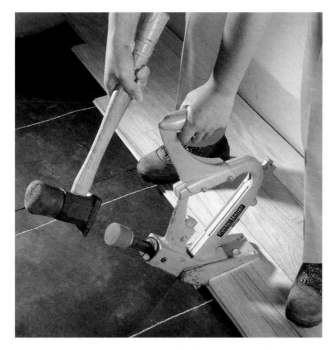

5 Drive each board into the last row until the joint is tight. Then use a rented floor nailer to edge-nail the board. Place the tool over the tongue, and strike the plunger with a mallet. Nail the flooring at the frequency recommended by the manufacturer.

6 Some boards are warped and won't fit easily into the previous row. If these boards are very distorted, set them aside and cut shorter boards out of them later. But for modest problems, you can drive the board in place by tapping a wedge between the board and a block that's screwed to the floor.

2 Use a piece of scrap flooring as a guide to undercut doorway casing boards. Then lay 15-lb. felt paper across the entire floor, and staple it in place.

3 Snap a chalk line for the first board; then push the board against the perimeter spacer blocks. Drill pilot holes along the back edge, and face-nail the board.

4 Test fit several rows of boards. This allows you to plan for staggered joints as well as matching variations in the color between the boards.

7 To fit boards that finish a row, hold the board up to the gap and put a spacer at the end next to the wall. Mark the board, and cut it to length using a miter saw or a circular saw.

8 To close up the joint between the last board and the wall, use a pry bar against a wood block to protect the wall. Hold the joint tight, using the pry bar if necessary, and drive nails along the back edge of the board. Cover the gap with baseboard and shoe moldings.

FLOORING OPTIONS

Wood, above and right, can be a very green product if it is harvested in an environmentally safe way. Among floor choices, it is probably the greenest and most renewable. In fact, many manufacturers today offer floors from lumber sources that are certified for green and sustainable logging practices. Because all floor systems—wood, carpet, ceramic tile, and sheet vinyl—use adhesives and finishes, look for floor systems that contain no- or low-VOC adhesives and finishes, far right.

Bamboo Flooring

Bamboo is a grass, not a wood. It is as strong and durable as wood, and because bamboo is fast-growing, it can provide raw material for extremely durable and very green flooring, depending on the adhesive used to construct the floor. It takes just about 6 years to grow bamboo that is adequate for flooring. The resulting product has a very distinct striped look that is reminiscent of quartersawn lumber.

If the raw material is so green, what are the possible nongreen risks of this product? Like carpet and plywood, it's the adhesive and the preservative. Though urea-formaldehyde (UF) adhesive is common, look for products that offer nonformaldehyde isocyanate resin or phenolic resin. Even if you can't find a nonformaldehyde product, note that the formaldehyde off-gassing from bamboo flooring is relatively less than off-gassing from particleboard products containing formaldehyde. If the bamboo is treated with a wood preservative, look for a nontoxic wood treatment, such as boric acid or borate.

When installing bamboo, note that it is very hard and that traditional floor nailers might not be able to drive your nails. You may have to switch over to a more powerful pneumatic finishing nailer. However, before you rent a floor nailer, test it out at the store to make sure it works.

If you choose a bamboo floor that is treated with a boric acid preservative, has a nonformaldehyde adhesive, and is finished with a water-based polyurethane, it is about as green a floor as you can achieve.

WINDOWS & DOORS

THE ABILITY OF WINDOWS AND DOORS TO BLOCK THE TRANSFER OF HEAT in any form, including radiant heat from the sun, is a key indicator of how green you've made your remodeling project. After all, when remodeling, you are going to build a wall that creates a high-integrity thermal envelope. But then you're going to punch large openings in it for your windows and doors. So, you'd better have quality units to insert in those openings, or all the work you've done on your wall will have been wasted.

Because doors contain so little glazing (glass), and the glazing is usually housed in a thick frame with wide borders, doors do not require the same scrutiny as windows in terms of energy performance. But windows are mostly glass, and if the relatively thin window frames are not engineered for energy performance, they will bleed heat—out during winter and in during summer—costing you money and needlessly burning up fuel. Installing windows is a fairly simple process. Even with basic building skills, it's easy to get a quality thermal connection between the house and the window frame. So most often, the quality of the window will be the single greatest variable in the wall's overall performance. Here is a close look at best-practice installation methods and what to look for in high-quality windows.

How to Read a Window Label

Fenestration is the arrangement of windows in a wall, and sometimes the term more broadly refers to the windows themselves. The National Fenestration Rating Council (NFRC)—an industry group that tests windows and provides standardized information about window performance—has created a performance label for windows to guide your choice. The label rates the windows for energy performance and for such things as wind and impact resistance.

Depending on your location and your local weather, you will want to adjust your window's performance to your environment and surroundings, especially heat gain from sunlight in summer and heat loss through the window in winter.

Each NFRC label contains ratings that are easy to read, once you have some guidance. First, the presence of the NFRC Certified label indicates that the NFRC has licensed the manufacturer and certified the window's performance. In the upper right part of every label, you will find the manufacturer, model, style, and the materials used in its construction (such as "aluminum-clad") to indicate the outward-facing and inward-facing component that make up the window. How the window opens is also indicated, for example, "vertical slider." That information isn't as important as the characteristics that can affect performance, so take a close look at the information below. For target numbers, a quality window will have a U-factor of around 0.32, a SHGC of around 0.27, and a visible transmittance of around 0.46. Look for a 20-year warranty (or more) on the window. Anything less is a signal that the window isn't of the highest quality.

U-Factor. The U-factor is the rate at which the window will lose heat as it passes from the building out into the air—for example, when it's relatively hotter inside the house during the winter. Think of the U-factor as the reverse of an R-value in insulation. The lower the U-factor, the greater resistance the window will offer to heat flow. In other words, the lower the U-factor, the better the window is as an insulator. In areas where you spend most of your energy dollars on heat, the U-factor is the number to which you should pay most attention.

Visible Transmittance (VT). The VT rating tells you how much visible light will be transmitted through the glass. Visible transmittance is a number between 0 and 1. A higher number is better. The higher the visible transmittance, the more light will come through the glass.

Air Leakage (AL). This is a rating of the window's ability to resist heat loss or gain through cracks in the window assembly. The measurement is expressed as cubic feet of air passing through a square foot of window area. The lower the AL, the tighter the window construction.

Impact-Resistant Glass. Just like the glass in your car windshield, impact-resistant glass is created by placing plastic film between pieces of glass. That same film can also block UV light.

World's Best Window Co.

Millennium 2000+
Vinyl-Clad Wood Frame
Double Glazing • Argon Fill • Low E
Product Type: **Vertical Slider**

ENERGY PERFORMANCE RATINGS

U-Factor (U.S./I-P)	Solar Heat Gain Coefficient
0.35	**0.32**

ADDITIONAL PERFORMANCE RATINGS

Visible Transmittance	Air Leakage (U.S./I-P)
0.51	**0.2**

Condensation Resistance	
51	**—**

Manufacturer stipulates that these ratings conform to applicable NFRC procedures for determining whole product performance. NFRC ratings are determined for a fixed set of environmental conditions and a specific product size. NFRC does not recommend any product and does not warrant the suitability of any product for any specific use. Consult manufacturer's literature for other product performance information. www.nfrc.org

Solar Heat Gain Coefficient (SHGC). The solar heat gain coefficient tells you how well the window will block heat from the sun. SHGC ranges from 0 to 1, and the lower the number, the better. A window with a low SHGC will transmit less heat than a window with a high SHGC. In areas where you spend most of your energy dollars on cooling, the SHGC number is the one that is most important to you.

replacing a worn sash

You can replace a worn sash without replacing the entire window. The first steps are to measure the window openings carefully and order your new sash. Then remove the old ones, and fill the window-weight cavities with insulation. Cut the liners to size and install them. Then slide the sash into the liners. Finish up by installing window stops to hold the sash in place.

TOOLS & MATERIALS

- ► Wood chisel or pry bar ► Utility knife
- ► Hacksaw ► Sash-replacement kit
- ► 8d (2½-inch) finishing nails
- ► Loose-fill (vermiculite) and spray-foam insulation
- ► Cup and cardboard guide for insulation

1 Using a sharp utility knife, cut the paint seal that runs along the sash stop boards and the window jambs. Then carefully push a flat pry bar under the stops and pry them off. Pull the nails from the backside of these trim boards.

4 Carefully measure the jamb opening, and cut the new jamb liners to fit, using a hacksaw or a power miter box. Then attach them to the old jambs following the directions that came with the kit. In many cases, you simply screw the liners to the jambs.

5 Install the top sash first by angling one corner of it into the outermost track on one of the liners. Make sure the pin on the corner of the sash (inset) engages in the track channel.

2 Pull the bottom sash away from the window opening, and remove the cords or chains that are connected to the sash weights. Set the bottom sash aside, and pry away the parting strips that separate the top and bottom sash from the grooves in the side jambs.

3 Remove the sash weights, cords, and pulleys from the side jambs; then enlarge the pulley opening using a drill and spade bit. Using a piece of cardboard and a cup, pour loose-fill insulation into the weight cavities; fill the upper cavity with spray foam insulation.

6 Slide the other sash corner into its channel, and push the sash down to the sill. Then lift the sash, and push the bottom into place.

7 Install the bottom sash in the inside liner tracks. Push the bottom against the sill, and then force the top into place.

8 Finish up the job by installing window stop trim boards. If you removed the old ones carefully, you can reuse them.

removing old windows

To remove the old window unit entirely, take off the inside and outside trim. If you work carefully, you may be able to use them for the new window. Once the trim is removed, cut or pull the nails that hold the jambs in place. At this point, loose-fitting units will slide out easily. Tighter units may have to be pried out. If the rough opening is too big for the new window, add boards to the jambs to close it in.

TOOLS & MATERIALS

- Pry bar ► Pliers ► Wood chisel
- Hammer ► Wood shims (as needed)
- Reciprocating saw with metal-cutting blade
- Lumber (for packing out the rough opening, as needed)
- Work gloves and safety goggles

1 To replace an entire window, start by ordering new units that are the same size as the old windows. Then remove the window by prying off the exterior trim using a flat pry bar. Be careful with the trim. You may be able to use it on the new window.

3 Once the trim is off, check to see how the window is attached to the wall. Older windows are nailed through the jambs, so cut these nails using a reciprocating saw. New windows have a nailing flange, so just pull the nails from this flange.

4 After the installation nails are gone, some loose-fitting windows can just be pushed out of the opening. Tighter fits will need to be pried out. Removing the unit from the outside reduces the mess on the inside of the house.

2 Move inside and pry off the interior trim. Again, if you work carefully, you may be able to reuse these boards. Once they are free, pull the nails from the backside of the board using locking pliers.

5 The new window will specify what the rough opening should be. If yours is too wide, fill in the opening by nailing lumber to the jambs. Add the same amount to both sides so the new window will stay centered in the opening.

MAKING A NEW HEADER

If you're putting in a larger window, you'll need to install a new header—the built-up framing member that spans the top of the rough opening. The header will be strong enough if you make it simply by doubling two pieces of two-by lumber of the appropriate width. However, because two-by lumber is actually $1\frac{1}{2}$ inches thick, a doubled two-by will be only 3 inches thick. Because 2x4 studs are actually $3\frac{1}{2}$ inches wide, you need another half-inch of thickness so that the header will be flush with the inside and outside of the stud wall.

The answer is a piece of $\frac{1}{2}$-inch plywood cut to the width and height of the header and sand-wiched between the two-bys, as shown in the photo. Assemble the header with 12d nails.

$\frac{1}{2}$"
Plywood
Spacer
or Foam
Insulation

Two-by
Lumber
(Width
per Local
Code)

12d Nail

cutting an opening through the outside wall

FIRST MARK THE DIMENSIONS ON THE SIDING. THEN CUT THROUGH THE SIDING AND THE SHEATHING USING A CIRCULAR SAW. TACK ON A GUIDE BOARD TO KEEP THE SAW STRAIGHT.

Guide Board

smart tip

ENLARGING A WINDOW OPENING

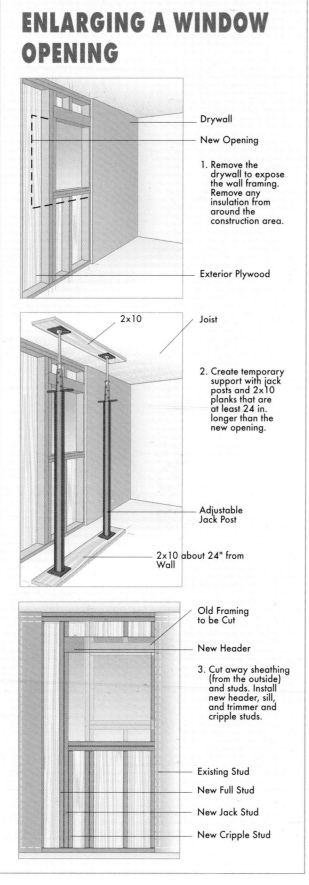

Drywall

New Opening

1. Remove the drywall to expose the wall framing. Remove any insulation from around the construction area.

Exterior Plywood

2x10

Joist

2. Create temporary support with jack posts and 2x10 planks that are at least 24 in. longer than the new opening.

Adjustable Jack Post

2x10 about 24" from Wall

Old Framing to be Cut

New Header

3. Cut away sheathing (from the outside) and studs. Install new header, sill, and trimmer and cripple studs.

Existing Stud

New Full Stud

New Jack Stud

New Cripple Stud

installing new windows

A major remodel is a good time to increase the size of small windows. But you must take care to support the ceiling above when enlarging any window opening. The drawings at left show how to do this.

Once the opening is ready to go, slide the new window into the opening from the outside. Have an inside helper guide the window into position. Center the window in the opening, and make it level and plumb using shims driven between the window unit and the surrounding framing. When you're satisfied with the window position, nail the flange to the sheathing. Then nail the exterior casing boards over the nailing flange. Finish up the outside chores by caulking around the perimeter of the window and the trim with exterior-grade caulk. Clean up any excess caulk, and touch up the paint as required.

Move inside, and fill the gap between the window unit and the rough opening with fiberglass or low-expanding foam insulation. Don't overfill the gap, or you risk distorting the side jambs and making the sash difficult to operate.

TOOLS & MATERIALS
- Window unit
- Pry bar
- Shims
- Level
- Hammer
- Roofing nails
- Exterior casing
- Casing nails
- Caulk
- Fiberglass insulation or low-expanding foam insulation
- Work gloves
- Interior casing

1 Once the opening is prepared, slide the new window in place from outside. Have an inside helper center the unit from side to side; then check for level and plumb. Wedge cedar shims between the window and the framing to keep the window properly aligned.

2 Most new windows have a flange that must be nailed to the wall with galvanized roofing nails. Drive these nails every 4 or 5 in. on the sides and top. The bottom of the window usually has flexible flashing instead of a nailing flange.

3 Cut trim boards to fit the space between the window frame and the siding on all four sides. Nail them using galvanized casing nails.

4 Once the casing boards are installed, caulk the perimeter of the window frame and the casing boards with exterior-grade caulk.

5 Move to the inside and fill the space between the window and the framing with fiberglass or low-expanding foam insulation.

Door Basics

Doors, like windows, serve various purposes. On the functional side, they provide a way into and out of the house, give us privacy when we want it, and keep out unwanted noise, cold drafts, bugs, and people who bug us. But doors (and doorways) also figure in home design. The front door is an important architectural focal point, and interior doors help express the style of the house or complement a room's decor.

A new front door with sidelights can make your entry hall seem brighter and more inviting, while switching from a painted to a wood-finish door adds a touch of elegance. You can improve traffic flow between parts of the house by installing a new door or two, but it comes at a cost. The more doors a room has, the smaller it seems, and every door needs enough space to swing open and closed.

Don't count on adding or moving a door in just one afternoon, because there is a lot to the job. You have to locate and cut a hole through an existing wall, remove the old wall framing, frame the rough opening, and install the door itself. You'll need good carpentry skills and a building permit in many locales, but the job is within the range of many do-it-yourselfers.

Buying Doors

The wood doors you'll find at building-supply centers are either panel doors, which have anywhere from one to ten panels set in a solid wood frame, or flush doors, formed by covering a solid wood core or a lightweight hollow core with thin sheets of wood veneer. While panel doors come in a wide range of wood types, flush doors usually are faced with lauan mahogany or birch, and they are less expensive.

Doors are sold prehung (where the door is mounted in a frame, sometimes with holes for the lockset predrilled) or as individual components. Unless you have hung a door before, spend the extra money for a prehung unit. It's not that the skills required to assemble a

DOOR TYPES

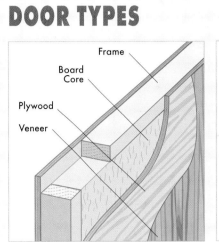

SOLID-CORE DOORS are used on exterior openings for security and durability. They often need three hinges due to their weight.

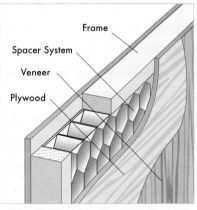

HOLLOW-CORE DOORS are used on interior openings. They are much lighter because the core is an air-filled spacer system.

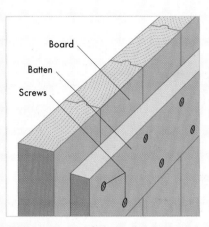

BOARD-AND-BATTEN DOORS generally are used on sheds and other outbuildings. The batten ties together several boards.

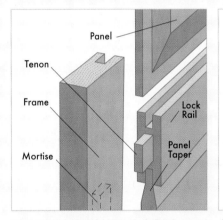

FRAME-AND-PANEL DOORS typically are used on cabinets. Interlocked rails are permanently fixed, and the panel floats inside.

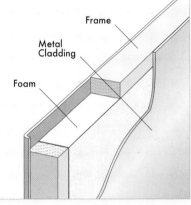

METAL-CLAD DOORS are increasingly popular because the metal needs little maintenance, and the foam core is energy efficient.

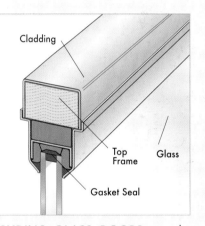

SLIDING GLASS DOORS may be wood- or metal-framed. One panel is fixed with hardware; the other slides in a track.

GLASS VS. SECURITY

Glass will let in light, but a large panel makes an exterior door vulnerable to break-ins. To minimize your risk, you can use tempered or safety glazing that is harder to break. (Double glazing is also more resistant than single glazing.) The problem is that by breaking the glass, a burglar can simply reach inside to undo the locks. To prevent that easy entry, use glass panels on top of the door or small panes that don't allow access to the locks.

EXTERIOR DETAILS

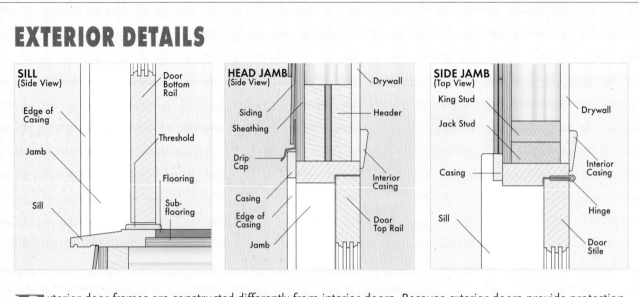

Exterior door frames are constructed differently from interior doors. Because exterior doors provide protection from rain and seal out drafts, the perimeter must be weatherstripped, even at the sill. The sill must slope down away from the house so that water runs off. It should also have a drip edge to prevent water from seeping underneath. A drip cap above the door and caulk around the casing completes the weather protection.

frame and hinge a door are all that difficult, it's the time you'll save. On an exterior door, you will also be assured of a tight weather seal. If you want to replace or upgrade an old door, just buy the door alone and use the original as a template for mounting hinges and the lockset.

More than a Door

Doors don't just hang by themselves, other structural pieces surround the door and provide support. Buried beneath drywall and trim is the door frame, which forms the door's rough opening. It is composed of vertical 2x4s and a horizontal piece called a header. The header is needed for extra support over doorways in load-bearing walls, because some wall studs have been removed to make room for the door.

The doorjambs—two side jambs and the head jamb across the top—form the finished opening for the door itself, as well as the mounting point for the hinges and the lockset. The door sill, or threshold, lies below the door, and the door stops—narrow strips of wood nailed to the jambs—keep the door from swinging beyond the closed position. Trim, also called casing, covers gaps between the rough opening and the jambs. The gaps provide room to level and plumb the door and jambs.

Installing a Prehung Door

To start, don't remove shipping braces from the door—they keep the frame square. If the floor is not level, cut one leg of the frame. Prehung doors are built to allow for thick carpeting, so you may need to cut both legs if the bottom of the door is too high off an uncarpeted floor.

Center the unit in the opening, and check that the top is level. Insert shims in the gaps between the doorjambs and rough framing to square and plumb the door opening. Use prepackaged shims sold for this purpose, tapered wood shingles, or homemade shims.

Remove the stops, and set a pair of shims with tapers opposing between the frame and stud at each hinge location—and if there are only two hinges, in the middle. Increase or decrease the overlap of the shims to adjust the frame until it is plumb. Drive a finishing nail through the jamb, each shim set, and partially into the stud. Then install three sets of shims on the other side jamb and one set above the head jamb. When all shims are in place, the frame is plumb and square, and there is a uniform gap between the door and the jamb, add a second nail at each shim and drive all nails home.

On an exterior door, stuff insulation behind and above the jamb before installing the casing.

project

install a prehung outer door

To install a prehung door, your challenge is simply to make sure it is hung plumb, square, and level, which can be accomplished by even a beginning carpenter.

TOOLS & MATERIALS

- Utility knife ► Staple gun
- Drill ► Hammer ► Putty knife
- Prehung door & lockset ► Level
- Caulk or flashing ► 2x4 brace
- Shims ► Nails ► Wood

1 Cut the felt paper or housewrap across the door opening, and staple back the excess against the sides of the framing.

2 You can install flashing under the sill, although many manufacturers suggest using a waterproof caulk instead.

3 Set a prehung exterior door from the outside of the house. The door already has exterior molding attached to the frame.

4 Working from the inside, use a level to plumb the door. Put a brace across the outside to keep the door in the opening.

5 As you check for level, insert shingle shims in the gaps between the door frame and the 2x4 wall studs.

6 When the door is correctly positioned, predrill and nail through the frame (and hidden shims) into the wall framing.

7 Also drive finishing nails through the face of the exterior molding into the wall framing. Set the heads, and fill with putty.

8 You can order most prehung doors with locks already installed or with the holes predrilled so that you can install your own.

DOOR ACTIONS

SWINGING

BYPASS

POCKET

BIFOLD

MULTIFOLD

ACCORDION

DOOR ANATOMY

DOOR FRAME

Cripple Stud

King Stud

Plywood Spacer

Header

Jack Stud

Shims

Drywall

Door Frame

Trim

Core Material

Stop

Plywood

Paint or Veneer

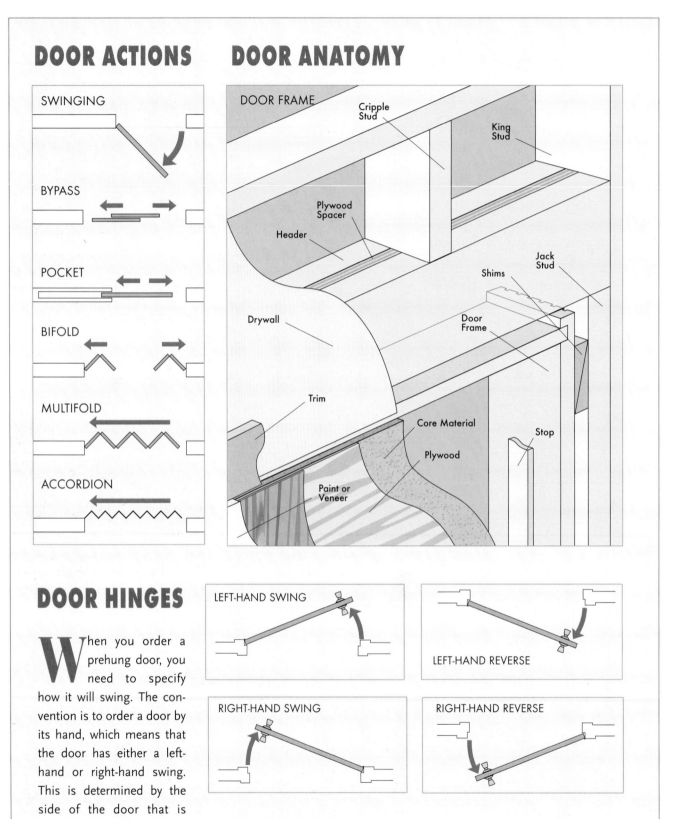

DOOR HINGES

When you order a prehung door, you need to specify how it will swing. The convention is to order a door by its hand, which means that the door has either a left-hand or right-hand swing. This is determined by the side of the door that is hinged when you stand on the outside of the room or street side of an exterior door. When you open the door away from you, right-hand doors will swing to the right, left-hand doors will swing to the left. Reverse models are available for doors that swing toward you.

LEFT-HAND SWING

LEFT-HAND REVERSE

RIGHT-HAND SWING

RIGHT-HAND REVERSE

installing an interior door

Interior doors must be installed properly—make sure they are plumb, square, and level—so, take the time to exactly align the door before driving nails and screws home.

TOOLS & MATERIALS

- ► Power drill/driver ► Hammer
- ► Framing square ► Level
- ► Prehung interior door ► shims
- ► Two-by lumber for header ► Nails
- ► Cross brace ► 2x4s ► Trim

1 To fit an interior door into a non-load-bearing partition, lay out the rough opening, allowing for two jack studs.

2 A jack stud nailed onto a full-height stud helps to support the header. Pack out vertically set headers with $1/2$-in. plywood.

3 With the door framing in place, install drywall panels (typically $1/2$ in. thick) using wide-threaded drywall screws.

4 Although this prehung door is hinged in its frame, it pays to check for square and lock the position with a cross brace.

5 Tip the door into place and hold it temporarily with shingle shims. The cross-brace keeps the frame flush with the drywall.

6 Working from the inside of the wall, use more shingle shims and a level to plumb the door in the framed opening.

7 When the door is plumb, drive 10d finishing nails through the jamb and shingle shims into the 2x4 wall framing.

8 Select trim for the outside face that matches other trim in the room. Cut mitered corners; add glue; and nail.

lighting & plumbing

What could be green about lighting and plumbing? Lots. That's because these systems help us consume electricity or water—two resources that are costly (environmentally and financially) to produce and deliver to our homes.

For electricity, there are power-saving devices and switching systems that can be installed to cut down on electric bills. But lower bills are only part of the payoff. Most power in North America is produced by coal, so saving power saves the planet by directly reducing pollution.

There is nothing more green than saving water. What's more, it's increasingly easier to do so without any inconvenience. Some options include low-flow fixtures and toilets, which have come a long way from those that first came onto the market 30 years ago. This chapter covers a number of water-saving features, such as tankless water heaters and programmable systems. There is also some basic instruction for working with plastic and copper pipe.

Lighting Alternatives:

Compact Fluorescent Bulbs and Light-Emitting Diodes

The vast majority of electrical energy used to create light in incandescent lightbulbs is dissipated in the form of heat. Because the majority of U.S. electricity is generated through burning coal, incandescent lightbulbs directly contribute to the wasteful use of electricity, pollution, and global warming. But there are lighting alternatives that are far more efficient, namely compact fluorescent lightbulbs (CFLs) and light-emitting diodes (LEDs).

Compact Fluorescent Lightbulbs. CFLs earn some black marks for containing mercury, and they must be disposed of properly as hazardous waste, not just tossed in the trash, but they earn high green marks for their efficiency. CFLs can provide as much light as an incandescent bulb but require just a fraction of the power to do so. When shopping for CFLs look for an Energy Star rating. Energy Star CFL bulbs use about 75 percent less energy than incandescent bulbs and last as much as 10 times longer. Each bulb will save more than $30 in electricity costs before it needs to be replaced.

Keep in mind that the wattage on a CFL is not the comparable wattage for an incandescent bulb. Instead, check the lumens or look for labels that say such things as "60-Watt Replacement." You are getting the same lumens as a 60-watt incandescent bulb, which means it is just as bright, but the bulb is not consuming the same wattage to produce those lumens.

Light-Emitting Diodes. LEDs turn electricity into light when excited electrons emit photons. It is an extremely efficient way to create light, and the bulbs do not use mercury, as CFLs do. But it's been historically hard to create white light with LEDs, because LEDs are more apt to emit blue light, which then must be filtered and blended to look white to the human eye.

The light from LEDs is highly concentrated and therefore easy to focus, and many manufacturers are now offering LEDs in architectural lighting lines that achieve brightness by collecting multiple LEDs into a single fixture. Today's LEDs will produce around 30 to 40 lumens per watt, but research at the U.S. Department of Energy is pointing to LEDs that can drive that up by 400 percent.

Besides their efficiency, LEDs have very long lives. An LED can last up to 50,000 hours, whereas CFLs last up to 10,000 hours, and incandescent lightbulbs last up to 2,000 hours.

One thing that is pushing the development of LEDs and CFLs is that manufacturers are eager to sell their products into California markets. Under California's Title 24, lights must perform at 40 lumens per watt or higher for residential applications. But California law considers fluorescent lamps and CFLs as hazardous waste. Because LEDs do not contain mercury, they look to be the most viable long-term green lighting solution.

Daylighting Tubes

Daylighting is a strategy that uses reflective tubing to deliver natural sunlight through your roof to remote locations (interior rooms). These reflective tubes require no framing or specialty wall construction. Where the tube penetrates the roof, the rooftop collector is flashed in place on the roof just the way any penetration, such as a skylight or vent stack, is flashed. There have been terrific advances in these systems, and they now come with light diffusers that attach to interior room ceilings to distribute light evenly. Some diffusers can even serve a dual purpose as the lens for an electric light for nighttime use.

BEFORE AFTER

FROM LEFT This ceiling diffuser is a lens that distributes the sunlight evenly throughout the living area. This tube can deliver sunlight even when installed at an angle. That's because it is treated on the inside with a reflective coating. On the roof, the daylighting device captures light throughout the day.

Occupancy Sensors

Why leave lights on when there is no one in the room? Consider installing occupancy sensors that detect motion or infrared heat. These switches can trigger a switch that turns the lights on instantly when someone enters a room.

PLUMBING BASICS

PLUMBING DELIVERS A PRECIOUS RESOURCE that we all need to consume in pure form: water. Though relatively clean water is delivered to your home through municipal sources, you can contribute to your family's well-being by filtering the water further. Take good care of the resource at points of use by installing low-flow fixtures that use only the water that's required for the task.

Low-Flow Toilets:
New Standards, Improved Performance

Toilets consume more water than any other household fixture. Toilets in the house that you grew up in were probably high-flow fixtures that used between 3 and 7 gallons per flush— much more water than is needed to adequately flush a toilet. By 1992, federal law required that toilets use 1.6 gallons per flush, a dramatic reduction from the standards at the time. But manufacturers didn't respond with a wholesale revamping of production lines, and many of the low-flow toilets that were sold were just high-flow units that were engineered to use less water. The result was poor performance; worse, low-flow toilets got a bad name that would last for years.

U.S. manufacturers changed designs as standardized tests for toilets came into play, such as the Maximum Performance (MaP) testing. MaP rates the mass that a toilet will successfully flush. The MaP tests were remarkably successful in predicting toilet performance, and MaP testing has been folded into the Uniform North American Requirements (UNAR) for Toilet Fixtures. Today, UNAR is the standard for toilet performance, and you can look for the UNAR rating on the various toilets on today's market.

Low-flow toilets come in various styles. Here are the basic types.

Pressure-Assisted Toilets. Some manufacturers have used pressure-assist technology to achieve desirable performance for low-flow toilets. In pressure assisted fixtures, there is a pressure tank inside the water reservoir; water charges out of that tank at high velocity during flushing. These units can be noisy, however, so test them at the store to see if you can live with them.

High-Efficiency Toilets. High-efficiency toilets (HETs) use 20 percent less water (1.28 gallons) than the standard 1.6 gallons per flush (gpf), and this will save the average family of four around 1,000 gallons per year per person.

Dual-Flush Toilets. Dual-flush toilets let you alter the amount of water you are flushing to correspond with the task at hand. For solids, there is a handle for a full flush (1.6 gallons), and for liquids and paper, there is another handle or button that flushes 0.8 to 1.1 gallons, saving a family of four as much as 1,500 gallons per person per year. (See "Installing a Toilet," page 176.)

PLUMBING SYSTEMS

House plumbing has to do three things:

▌ Deliver hot and cold water to the fixtures

▌ Remove waste to the sewer or septic system

▌ Vent the waste pipes to the outside

To conserve water, make sure your system is free of leaks and equipped with low-flow fixtures.

Getting Water to the Fixtures

Every fixture except the toilet requires separate hot- and cold-water supply pipes. Locate a shutoff valve in a convenient place below the fixture. This way, you can make repairs without shutting down the water to the entire

house. By shutting off the main valve, not only will every fixture be out of commission for hours, or even days, but you'll have to run back and forth during repairs.

Hot- and cold-water pipes were previously made of galvanized steel joined with threaded connectors. Cutting and threading pipes was difficult and required specialized tools. Today, do-it-yourselfers can install their own hot- and cold-water pipes, thanks to rigid and flexible copper pipe alternatives, which are far simpler to work with and more economical to install and rework when mistakes are made. Chlorinated polyvinyl chloride (CPVC) plastic is also used for supply pipes. The material is popular because it is easy to work with, but some municipalities may not sanction its use.

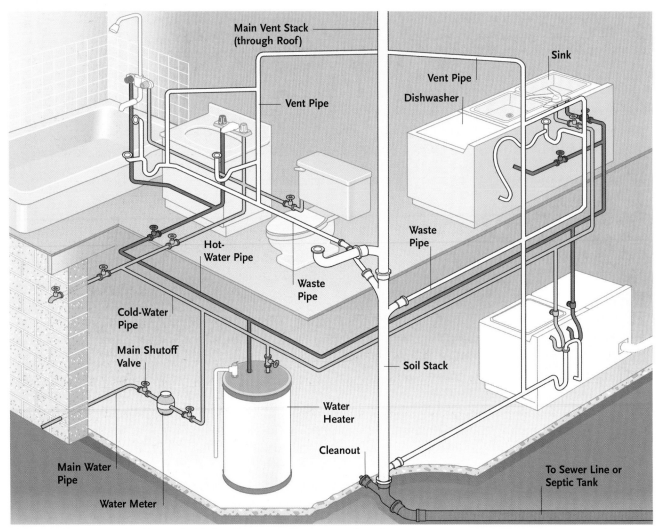

ABOVE Here is a typical household plumbing system. Water arrives from the municipal system or a private well. The cold-water supply lines branch from this main line; hot-water lines are first routed through the water heater. All fixtures receiving water are also connected to drainpipes and vent pipes. All drain and vent lines converge on the soil stack, which extends through the roof.

Tankless Water Heaters

Tankless systems are rather simple devices. When you turn on a hot-water tap or shower, cold source water is run through metal pipes that quickly heat it to the desired temperature. When the water is turned off at the tap or shower, the burner turns off and no reservoir of hot water is stored. Tankless water heaters do not heat water with any more efficiency than tank water heaters, but the off-cycle losses are avoided, and you pay to heat only the water that you use, as you use it.

For the least expensive devices, typical flow rates range up to 2 gallons per minute, but more costly devices can deliver up to 5 gallons per minute. When selecting your tankless unit, consult a salesperson and be prepared to tell them the volume of water you expect to run through the unit and the temperature of the source water. Both will affect burner size. Gas units can deliver the highest volume of hot water, whereas electric units can supply up to around 3 gallons per minute.

Select a demand water heater based on the amount of hot water you'll need at peak demand. Here are some common volume assumptions:

- Faucets flow at a rate of 0.75 gallons (2.84 liters) to 2.5 gallons (9.46 liters) per minute.
- Old-fashioned showerheads flow at 2.5 gallons (9.46 liters) to 3.5 gallons (13.25 liters) per minute.
- Low-flow showerheads flow at 1.2 gallons (4.54 liters) to 2 gallons (7.57 liters) per minute.
- Clothes washers and dishwashers consume hot water at 1 gallon (3.79 liters) to 2 gallons (7.57 liters) per minute.

Plumbing a tankless water heater is relatively simple, but because the unit must be piped for gas, you will need to bring in a plumber who can work with both water and gas.

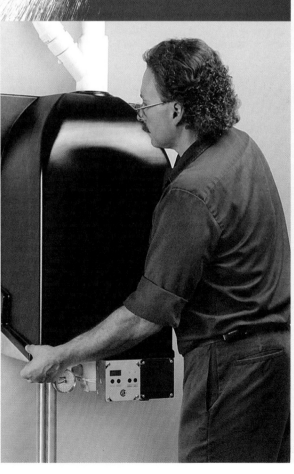

To cut down on the amount of hot water required for showering, a low-flow showerhead will use just 1.2 gallons per minute.

cutting and joining plastic pipe

There is little green about plastic pipe, but it is one of few alternatives for home plumbing systems, and learning how to install it makes sense. The good thing is that it lasts, so if you install it correctly, you won't need to replace it for some time. Old plastic pipe is recyclable. You'll find the pipe, adhesive, and other tools at home centers.

TOOLS & MATERIALS

- ► Plastic pipe ► Backsaw or hacksaw
- ► Miter box ► Work gloves and goggles
- ► Pipe primer ► Pipe
- ► Solvent cement
- ► Compression clamp fittings
  (when working with cast iron)
- ► Utility knife ► Emery cloth

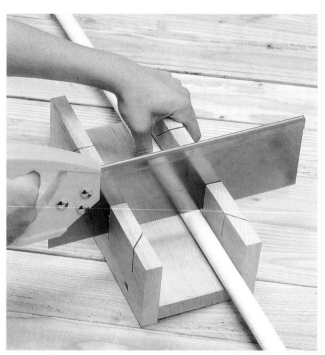

1 A simple wooden miter box is a great tool for making square cuts on plastic pipe. Just place the pipe in the box, and hold it tightly against the side. Then make the cut with a backsaw, and remove the burrs from the cut end using emery cloth.

3 The first step in joining pipe is to clean the end of the pipe and the inside of the fitting with pipe primer. For PVC pipe, this cleaner is usually colored purple.

4 Once the primer is dry, apply a liberal coat of solvent cement to the end of the pipe and the inside of the fitting. Open the windows and use an exhaust fan to remove the cement fumes from the room.

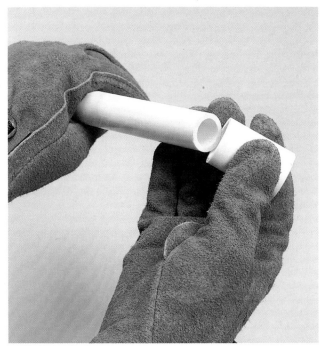

2 Once the pipe is cut, install the appropriate fitting and check to see if the assembly fits where it needs to go. If things look good, join the two.

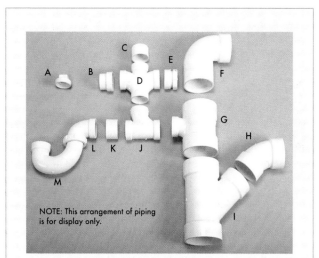

NOTE: This arrangement of piping is for display only.

BASIC PLASTIC DRAINAGE PIPING

Plastic drainage piping includes the following: (A) clean-out plug, (B) threaded adapter, (C) coupling, (D) cross, (E) ground-joint adapter, (F) street 90-deg. elbow, (G) 3 x 1½-in. T-fitting, (H) 45-deg. elbow, (I) 3 x 2-in. Y-fitting, (J) sanitary T-fitting, (K) coupling, (L) trap arm, (M) trap.

WHICH PIPE?

WHICH TYPE OF PIPE you can use for projects depends on your local code. Here are some pipes you may find installed in your house:

- Copper (rigid and flexible): hot- and cold-water supply pipes
- Galvanized steel: hot- and cold-water supply pipes; drainpipes
- Cast iron: main supply and drain and vent pipes
- PB (polybutylene): hot- and cold-water supply pipes
- ABS (acrylonitrile butadiene styrene): drain and vent pipes, drain traps
- CPVC (chlorinated polyvinyl chloride): hot- and cold-water supply pipes
- PVC (polyvinyl chloride): drain and vent pipes, drain traps

Rigid Copper

Galvanized Steel

Cast Iron

PVC

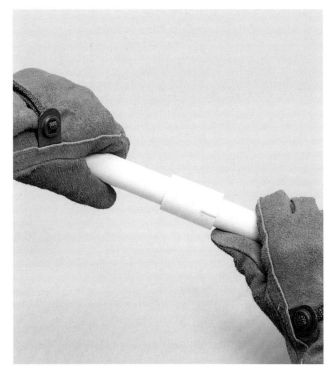

5 Immediately after applying the cement, push the two parts together; turn them about ¼ turn; and hold them for 10 seconds. This fuses the assembly so the pieces can't be taken apart.

Water Filtration:

Whole-House & Point-of-Use Filtering Systems

Even potable municipal water can stand a little cleaning up. Chlorine, chloramines, and VOCs are common in treated water. On the other hand, for those who use well water, it often contains chemicals that you would be well-advised to remove before you drink it. For this purpose, there are two general classes of water filters for your home: point-of-use (POU) filters that attach at the sink and whole-house water filtration systems, also referred to as point-of-entry (POE) water filters.

When deciding which type of filter makes sense for you, try to determine where contaminants may be coming from. For instance, a POE water-filtration system might take the contaminants out of the water as it enters your home, but if you live in an old house that has lead pipes or lead in the material that joins the pipes, water will pick up new contaminants "down stream" between the street and the tap, so a POU filter may be required.

POU water filters are not that expensive, and for purifying drinking water, they are an excellent option. Costs run upwards of $150 for good units, with replacement filters running as much as $50. POE water-filtration systems are costly, with unit and installation costs easily totaling more than $5,000, especially when you add in the cost of the filters. For both POE and POU systems, there is often a prefilter to take sand and sediment out of the water before it gets to the more sensitive water filter.

No matter what type of system you use, there are a number of different types of water filters. Here is an overview.

Activated Carbon. Carbon can be treated with heat to activate it. That means that the carbon, which is very porous naturally, will have an electrical charge as well. The charge can help absorb contaminants. The more surface area of carbon that is exposed to the water, the cleaner the water will get. If you want to remove VOCs, including chlorine/trihalomethane (THM), which are a class of VOCs, and radon, carbon filters are a good choice. But if you want to filter heavy metals, arsenic, or biological contaminants, you will need another kind of filter.

Kinetic Degradation Fluxion. Kinetic Degradation Fluxion (KDF) employs oxidation/reduction (a chemical process known as redox) to remove chlorine, lead, mercury, iron, and hydrogen sulfide from water. These filters are actually a formulation of high-purity copper and zinc that not only bring purification to the water-filtering process but have a mild antibacterial, algicidal, and fungicidal effect as well. Because of its effectiveness with hot water, this filtration method can be used to remove chlorine and other contaminants from flowing hot water, like that found in showers.

KDF comes in two forms: KDF 55 granules are most effective at removing chlorine and water-soluble heavy metals; KDF 85 granules effectively reduce iron and hydrogen sulfide.

Reverse Osmosis. Reverse osmosis (RO) filters use a filter membrane with tiny pores (0.0005 micron) to purify water. RO is very effective at removing asbestos, salts, metals, lead, and nitrate. But RO systems need a prefilter because sediment will clog the system and chlorine will damage it. For prefilters, carbon is a good choice. When an RO system is in place and working, it can offer very pure water, if you can stand to wait for it—RO systems typically purify just one gallon a minute. Most RO systems are designed for under-sink applications.

Hollow Fiber Ultrafiltration. Hollow Fiber Ultrafiltration (HF UF) systems force water through straws that have billions of tiny pores that are each 0.05 to 0.02 micron wide. With pores that small, the filters can remove bacteria, viruses, and parasites. HF UF systems can purify about ten times as much water as RO systems in the same amount of time, and they waste only about 3 percent of the water.

Ultraviolet Light. Ultraviolet (UV) light purifies water, it doesn't filter it. But UV is a very effective method: as water passes by, UV will destroy all but 1 percent of bacteria, viruses, molds, and cysts. That said, UV works best when combined with a filtration system that removes sediment, VOCs, and other unwanted material.

When buying filters, look for certifying labels from Underwriters Laboratories (UL), National Sanitation Foundation (NSF), or Water Quality Association. These labels will identify which contaminants the filters are capable of removing. (See "Installing a Water Filter," page 170.)

Programmable Lawn Watering

American households can easily use 400 gallons of water each day, and around 120 gallons of that is used outdoors—60 gallons, on average, going to watering lawns and gardens. Across the United States, landscape irrigation accounts for nearly 30 percent of all residential water use. That adds up to around 7 billion gallons of water per day. Water experts believe that half of irrigation water use goes to waste due to evaporation, wind, or improper system design. In fact, many people simply overwater their lawns, putting water in them too often and for too long.

Weather-based irrigation controllers are systems that provide water only when it is required, based on soil conditions and recent and current weather conditions. These controllers can reduce water use by 20 percent compared with conventional equipment, with a potential savings of 24 billion gallons per year across the United States. That's equal to more than 7,000 hoses running nonstop for a year.

In weather-based irrigation controllers, soil moisture sensors determine the amount of water in the ground that is available to plants. These sensors have to be professionally installed, but they can save a household more than 11,000 gallons of water each year.

Look for a WaterSense rating on your device.

COPPER FITTINGS

You can join both rigid and flexible copper tubing with soldered joints and fittings, including couplings, which join pipes in a straight line; reducers; 45- and 90-degree elbows to make bends; and reducer fittings, which join pipes of different diameters.

Coupling
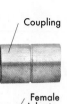

Female Adapter

Compression fittings are often found on water-supply tubes and shutoff valves for fixtures. This is because, unlike soldered joints, compression fittings can be taken apart easily. They can also be used in spots where it's impractical or dangerous to solder, such as in an unventilated crawl space. These couplings become watertight when you tighten the threaded nut, drawing a flange against the end of the pipe. Couplings are available with threaded nuts on both ends or with one end threaded and the other straight, for soldering.

Male Adapter

¾ x ½ x ½ T-Fitting

¾ x ¾ x ½ T-Fitting
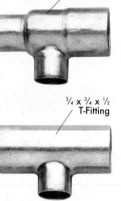

Flared fittings are usually only permitted for flexible copper pipe (Type L) used on gas lines, but some local codes may permit them in areas where soldering is not safe, as long as the pipes are not behind finished walls. Two tools are required for flared fittings: the flaring tools and the flaring set. The base part of the flaring tool clamps around the end of one of the pipes being joined, and the top of the flaring set forces the lip of the pipe against the clamp. This creates a bell-shaped flare. A flaring nut placed on one side of the joint threads into a flaring union on the other.

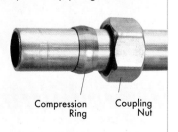

Compression Ring   **Coupling Nut**

cutting copper pipe

Copper is used primarily in water-supply lines. Learning how to cut and solder it correctly will prevent costly water leaks later. It comes in 20-foot lengths, which means that you'll have to do some cutting no matter what job you are doing. To make these cuts, use a tubing cutter or a hacksaw. Of course, copper is recyclable.

TOOLS & MATERIALS
► Copper tubing
► Tubing cutter
   or hacksaw & miter box
► Multipurpose plumber's
   tool or wire brush

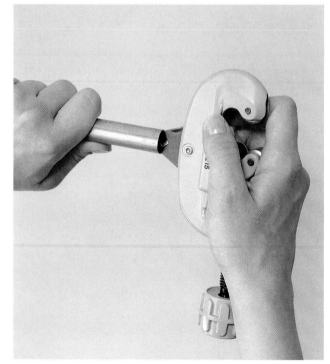

3 Once the cut is made, remove the interior burr using the burr remover that's part of the tubing cutter. You can also remove the burr with a round file.

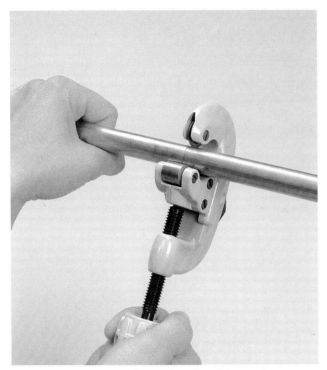

1 A tubing cutter is the preferred tool for cutting copper pipe. Mark the pipe to length; then tighten the cutting wheel against the pipe. Slowly turn the tool around the pipe, tightening the wheel as it cuts.

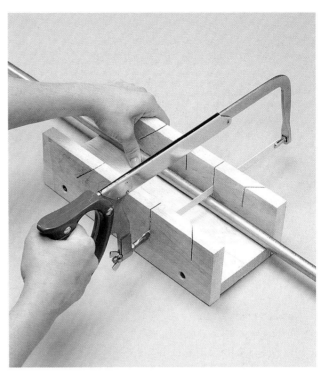

2 If you don't have a tubing cutter, you can make good cuts with a hacksaw. Just be sure to use a miter box for this chore. You can build one by screwing together three scrap boards.

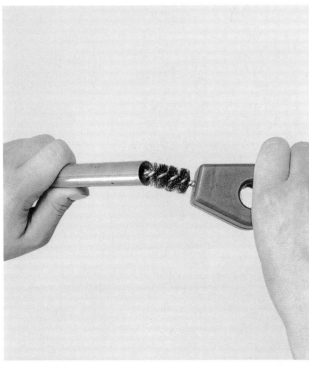

4 A plumber's multipurpose tool can do several pipe prep chores, like deburring pipes (above) and cleaning the inside of copper fittings prior to soldering.

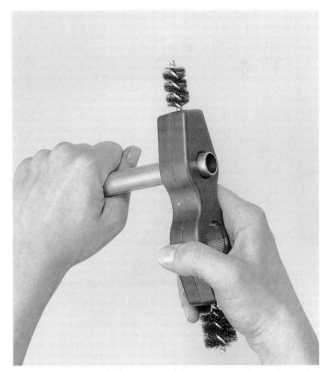

5 Use emery cloth or a multipurpose tool to clean the end of copper pipe before soldering. If dirt or other impurities are left on the pipe, the solder may not bond properly and the joint will leak.

soldering copper pipe

Before soldering copper pipe, make sure to don leather gloves and safety goggles to protect yourself against molten solder burns. Start by applying flux to the parts and pushing them together. Heat the joint, and press the solder onto the pipe. Protect combustible items with a piece of flashing, and wipe the joints clean when they are done.

TOOLS & MATERIALS

- ► Copper pipe
- ► Emery cloth
- ► Bristle brush
- ► Flux (soldering paste)
- ► Solder ► Propane torch
- ► Sparker ► Sheet metal
- ► Work gloves ► Clean rag
- ► Pipe fittings
- ► Safety goggles

don't get a solder burn

IT'S EASY TO BURN YOUR-SELF WHEN SOLDERING PIPE. ALWAYS MAKE SURE THAT YOU TURN OFF YOUR TORCH WHEN IT'S NOT IN USE. REMEMBER ALSO THAT SOLDERED JOINTS ARE VERY HOT; ALWAYS LET THEM COOL BEFORE TOUCHING THE PIPES.

1 The first step in soldering copper pipe is to coat the pipe end and fitting with flux. Use a small brush, and make sure everything is coated liberally.

2 Slide the fitting over the end of the pipe and twist it so that the flux is spread around the entire joint.

INSULATING PIPES

For pipes that will carry hot water, it's smart to save energy (and the associated costs) by using pipe insulation. Fit preformed polystyrene insulation tubes around hot-water pipes, and tape them in place. You can also wrap the pipes in strips cut from fiberglass batts.

Either system will not only reduce heat loss but also prevent cold-water pipe sweating in the summertime. If you have pipes running through an unheated crawl space, insulate (or protect with a heating cable) both hot- and cold-water pipes to keep them from freezing.

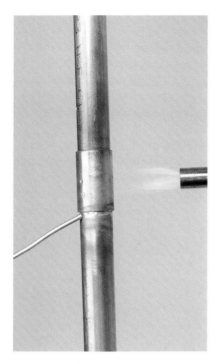

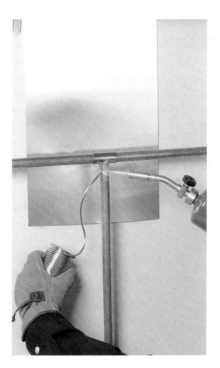

3 Push the other pipe into the coupling, and heat the fitting with a torch. Press the solder against the joint until the joint is filled.

4 When soldering joints close to combustible materials, use a piece of flashing to protect these areas. Generally, just fasten the flashing using a piece of duct tape.

5 Once both sides of a joint are filled with solder, remove the torch and wipe the joint clean with a rag. Wear sturdy leather gloves to protect your hands from burns. Test your work by turning the water back on. If the joint leaks, heat the joint to melt the solder and start again.

SHUT OFF THE WATER BEFORE GETTING STARTED

Before you begin work on a section of pipe, you'll need to shut off the water supply to that part of your plumbing system. The main shutoff valve for your house's system (right) will be near the spot where the municipal pipe enters your home or, if you have well water, near the storage tank. Other shutoff valves farther along allow you to turn off just part of the water system, such as to one bathroom, while still allowing you to have water in the rest of the house. Most fixtures, such as sinks and toilets, should have their own shutoff valves (left), usually located right where the supply lines come through the wall or floor.

PLUMBING & LIGHTING OPTIONS

Green products can be glamorous, even beautiful, as shown in the energy-saving washer and dryer, opposite, low-flow fixtures, above and left, and the LED fixture, far left. Though green products are increasingly manufactured from recycled materials or from environmentally safe components, they don't have to look bland and utilitarian. Manufacturers are producing fashionable green plumbing and lighting products for every home.

heating, ventilation & air-conditioning

Heating and cooling systems have undergone a revolution in the past few years, and a wide variety of green choices are now available. Most of the improvements in heating and cooling equipment center around making the units much more efficient than earlier models. So replacing an old boiler, furnace, or air conditioner with a new model will most likely help reduce your carbon footprint and save money on fuel costs in the bargain. However, it is important to remember that efficient equipment works in tandem with other measures, such as insulation, energy-efficient windows, and stopping air infiltration. Buying Energy Star products means you are selecting from the most efficient units available. But all heaters and air conditioners are sold with energy labels that estimate fuel usage for the individual units. This chapter covers the basics of heating and cooling equipment, including gas and oil systems, and heat pumps—as well as ways to purify the indoor air. There is also a section on geothermal heat pumps, which is technology that uses the temperature of the earth to heat and cool homes.

COMPARING HEATING SYSTEMS

YOU CAN COMPARE PRICES AMONG GAS, OIL, OR ELECTRIC FURNACES, or even wood stoves, but when thinking about upgrading your home's heating system, don't forget to factor in installation costs. Switching to gas could mean that you'll have to pay to run a supply line into the house. Sticking with oil could mean replacing a rusting storage tank. Electric heat may cost more per month but save you thousands on installation compared with alternative systems. Ask heating contractors for installation estimates and fuel suppliers for approximate operating costs.

Because all heat output is measured in British thermal units (Btu), you'll have a common denominator to make comparisons.

Replacing or upgrading an existing system is a major project; it's important to find out how efficient the new system will be compared to the old one. For a well-maintained existing system, you can subtract half the unit's age from the original efficiency rating. For example, a 20-year-old oil-burning furnace that was 65 percent efficient rates at 55 percent. Of course, if you pay a contractor to make combustion-efficiency tests, you'll get a more accurate rating. Once you know the increase in efficiency with a new system, you can estimate how much less fuel you'll use every year, how much money this will save each year, and how many years of savings it will take to recover your investment in the new equipment.

System Expansion

Installing a furnace or an entire network of HVAC ducts or heating pipes are not do-it-yourself projects—these must be put in by professional contractors. However, when you've added new living space to your home—whether by finishing an attic or garage, enclosing a porch, or building an addition—you will need to provide heat for the space. You have the option of extending your home's existing system into those spaces or installing individual electronic heaters or portable space heaters.

HOT-WATER SYSTEMS

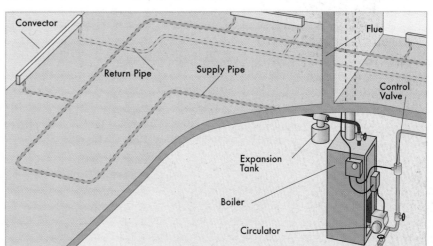

Hot-water (or hydronic) systems use a pump, called a circulator, to force heated water from a boiler through a network of pipes. Heat transfers from the pipes to the air at radiators or baseboard convectors and continues back to the boiler for reheating. Older homes have one large pipe loop. Newer homes have two or more loops, each with its own thermostat, to heat different zones of the house more efficiently.

HOT-AIR SYSTEMS

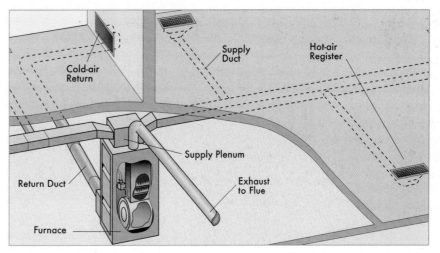

Hot-air systems use a blower to force heated air through a large supply plenum and into a system of ducts. The ducts lead to registers in the floor and walls of your living spaces. Cold-air registers and return ducts take cooled air back to the furnace for reheating. These systems require dust filters. Because they provide dry, hot air, a furnace-mounted humidifier is often needed to maintain indoor comfort.

Hot-Air Systems

New runs of ducts can be extended from the furnace's plenum or from a main duct in an extended-plenum system. Cut a hole in the plenum or main duct using sheet-metal snips; the hole should exactly fit a metal collar, either straight, to run sideways from the plenum, or takeoff, to run upward from a main duct.

Round metal ducts are then snapped or hammered together, depending on the type of duct, and attached to the system. There are T- and Y-fittings to make branches; for turns, use 45- and 90-degree-angle pieces or sections of flexible duct. Each new run must also have a damper, to shut off heat to that duct run and balance the system if needed. The final joint in a run of ducts should be attached with a drawband—a steel collar that is tightened with bolts (like a band clamp).

Use flexible metal straps, called hangers, to attach new ducts to basement ceiling joists. You can easily heat the first floor by placing heat registers (grilles with movable vents) in holes cut into the floor and running the ducts to the registers with transition fittings called boots. To bring heat to the second floor, you'll need to run the ducts up the wall or through closets, and box them in using studs and drywall.

Hot-Water Systems

Hot-water heating pipes run in a circuit around the house. Usually, you won't need to add new pipes to the

FURNACE TYPES

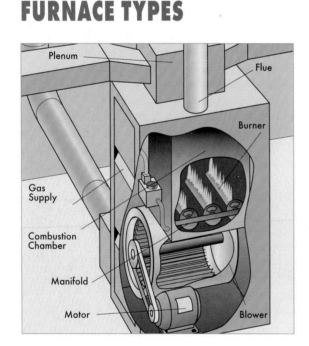

GAS-FIRED

Gas-fired furnaces burn natural gas or liquefied petroleum (LP) gas to heat either air that is blown through a system of ducts or water that is circulated to radiators or baseboard convectors through pipes. Older gas-fired appliances have pilot lights that burn all the time. Improved modern systems have electronic igniters to light the flame as the gas starts to flow. Gas furnaces burn cleanly and convert up to 95 percent of the fuel into heat.

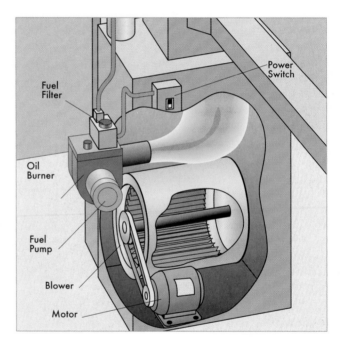

OIL-FIRED

A high-pressure oil burner, mounted either outside or inside the furnace, pumps a fine mist of oil and air into a combustion chamber, where it is ignited by an electric spark. This in turn heats a heat exchanger that passes the temperature onto air or water that circulates throughout the house. Unlike natural gas, which is fed from a gas main to provide a constant supply of fuel for gas systems, oil must be delivered. Oil burns less efficiently than gas, with furnace efficiencies under 90 percent.

Rooftop Solar Energy

Solar systems have been around for some time. And while the technology has been improving, it is still an expensive proposition for most homeowners. The most promising systems use photovoltaic cells to convert sunlight directly into electricity. You can have a contractor install a system that provides all of your energy needs, but don't disconnect from the grid, as you will probably need utility power to supplement your solar energy. This is not only true for locations where the sun doesn't provide enough energy, but also true when heavy duty appliances draw more than 30 amps in startup mode. There are many state and federal incentives for installing solar. A basic whole-house system will run you more than $20,000. That's around $10 per watt for a typical 2kW rooftop system. If your electric bill is $100 per month, and even that is high for many people, it will take you more than 15 years to pay off the solar installation.

Installing solar power systems is not a do-it-your-self project. Look for a contractor who is a member of the Solar Energy Industries Association (seia.org).

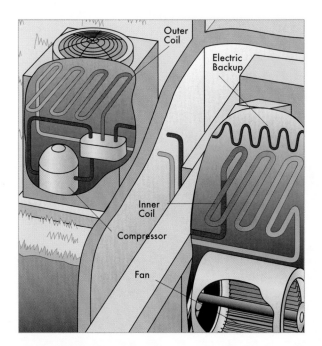

HEAT PUMPS

In summer, heat pumps run like air conditioners. In winter, the system reverses, extracting heat energy from the air (or from the ground, in the case of ground-source heat pumps) to warm air in the house. But when the outdoor temperature drops to about 35°F, a backup system takes over, and the system loses fuel efficiency. The units are most cost-effective in regions with roughly equal heating and cooling demand. (See "Geothermal Ground-Source Heat Pumps," page 149.)

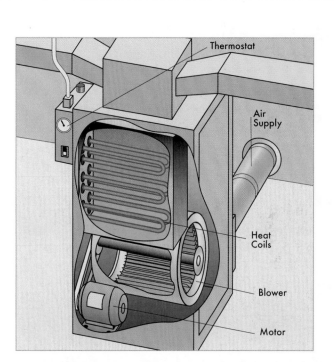

ELECTRIC

Electric furnaces can heat air or water by passing current through heavy-duty heating coils. Electric heat elements also are included in heat pumps that provide both heating and cooling. Electricity can power central systems and is used to heat individual baseboard convectors. Electric systems require almost no maintenance because they generate heat without combustion. They are 100 percent efficient in your house, but not at the utility plant where power is generated.

system to install a new convector but instead can tap into existing lines. Most systems have the excess capacity to handle one or two additional convectors.

There are three common layouts for hot-water systems. A series loop has the convectors as part of the circuit; hot water enters each unit through a supply riser and exits through a return riser, it then moves on to the next convector in the loop. One-pipe systems have supply and return branch lines that feed each convector from a main supply loop. Two-pipe systems have entirely separate circuits for supply and return. You need to know what kind of system you have before you start cutting pipe.

Electric Systems

It may not be practical to extend your home's heating system into a finished garage or attic. Your other heating options include installing a wood stove, space heater, or electric convector. Although electric heaters aren't as efficient as gas or oil systems, a single room unit is still far cheaper and easier to install than extending ducts or pipes. Wall-mounted baseboard convectors run along the bottom of the wall like hot-water convectors; recessed models are installed through the exterior wall. They are available in both 120- and 240-volt models.

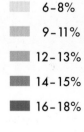

YOUR GREEN CHOICES

Lowering the Thermostat

HEATING SAVINGS

▮ 6–8%	
▮ 9–11%	
▮ 12–13%	
▮ 14–15%	
▮ 16–18%	

SAVINGS FOR ONE EIGHT-HOUR DECREASE OF 10°F (5°C) PER DAY

Savings on your energy bill depend on home size and actual heat loss or gain, geographic location, frequency of temperature changes, and range in degrees of change.

Source: *Honeywell Inc.*

baseboard convectors

Baseboards are an efficient and comfortable way to deliver heat, but remember to securely attach them to cut down on the noise created by hot water rushing through them.

TOOLS & MATERIALS
- ► Screwdriver ► Power drill/driver
- ► Clamps ► Propane torch
- ► Pipe cutter or hacksaw ► Work gloves
- ► Baseboard convector
- ► Pipe & fittings ► Bleeder valve ► Solder
- ► Flux ► Scrap Type X drywall & foil

4 Remove the valve, and drill a hole through the floor. The hole and valve will be hidden by the convector end cap.

8 Use a wire-brush tool or sandpaper to brighten the mating edges (inside and out) of the old pipe and the new fitting.

1 Locate the new baseboard unit over a supply pipe in the floor below. Start by installing the reflector panel on the wall.

2 Position the convector element on brackets attached to the reflector panel. Be careful not to bend the heat-dispersing fins.

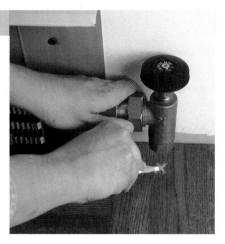

3 Temporarily fit the cutoff valve onto the end of the convector pipe, and mark the floor below where the supply pipe will rise.

5 After drilling a hole for the return pipe at the other end of the convector, solder on a bleeder valve. Protect the wall from flame.

6 Test-fit pipes and fittings to reach from the convector valves to the hot-water supply pipe below the floor.

7 Cut off the water supply, and use a pipe cutter to cut away a section of the supply pipe to install a T-fitting.

9 To draw solder fully into the joint and prevent pinhole leaks, paint the connecting pipe parts with flux.

10 Take care to protect surrounding wood from flames. A clamp holds this piece of nonburning drywall covered with foil.

11 Once the pipe joints are soldered, slide on the adjustable heat-control flap and the front cover of the convector.

Humidifiers

To add moisture to dry winter air and create an indoor environment that's comfortable for you and good for your house as well, improving indoor air quality, you can use a variety of portable or central humidifier systems. Here is a look at some of the options.

Portable and Central Systems

Portable, or console, humidifiers are concealed in small cabinets. They are helpful if one room is particularly dry or if you have a heating system without an air-distribution system, such as electric baseboards, that isn't suited to a central humidifier system. The drawback is that you have to add water to console storage tanks periodically. Also, they require maintenance much more often than central systems.

Central humidifiers are attached to the home heating system, normally at the plenum, where heated air is distributed to the ducts. The advantage is that the appliance is part of the house; you don't have to plug it in or add water. But an automatically replenished water supply can become a breeding ground for pollutants that are spread through the ducts and into living areas. Treating the water and doing seasonal maintenance can reduce this problem.

Types of Appliances

If you are shopping for a humidifier, bear in mind that two of the four basic types, just by their design, are more likely to disperse microorganisms. Ultrasonic humidifiers, which use high-frequency sound waves to generate a cool mist, and impeller humidifiers, which

Humidifiers can prevent a range of problems, such as mold growth, and help maintain a home's humidity at a comfortable level. As they tend to run unseen in the background, be sure the plumbing is checked and double-checked.

TOOLS & MATERIALS

- ► Level tape ► Marker ► Metal shears
- ► Screwdriver ► Adjustable wrench
- ► Needle-nose pliers ► Pipe clamp
- ► Work gloves ► Humidifier ► Humidistat
- ► Duct (flexible or metal) ► Mounting collar
- ► Saddle valve

5 Use flexible duct or a length of standard metal duct and an elbow fitting to connect the humidifier to the supply plenum.

6 A typical humidifier has a solenoid valve to control water flow. This small pipe runs from the valve to the distribution tray.

HUMIDIFIER TYPES

Heat from your furnace warms the air in your house and dries it out, too. Forced-hot-air systems in particular can lower indoor humidity to the point at which people feel uncomfortable. You can add moisture to the air with portable humidifiers, although the most economical systems connect to the furnace. These have a moisture control, called a humidistat, and feed moisture directly into the warm air flow.

PORTABLES
Grille
Humidistat
Fan
Air Filter
Reservoir

1 In a typical installation, you mount a paper template for the humidifier on the main return plenum above the furnace.

2 After marking the main supply plenum for the humidifier duct, cut the template through the sheet metal with metal shears.

3 It's important to level the humidifier for even water distribution. This unit has a small bubble level built into the water tray.

4 Cut through the main supply plenum to make a hole for the humidifier supply duct. This kit comes with a mounting collar.

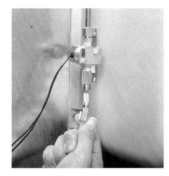

7 To bring water from your supply piping to the unit, most humidifiers supply either flexible copper pipe or hard plastic tubing.

8 Install a saddle valve (if permitted by code) on the supply pipe. Clamp it to the line, and turn the handle to pierce the pipe.

9 Central-system humidifiers typically have a catch basin that recirculates water, or an overflow drain-pipe like this one.

10 Install the humidistat, which allows you to regulate indoor humidity, on the plenum or by the existing thermostat.

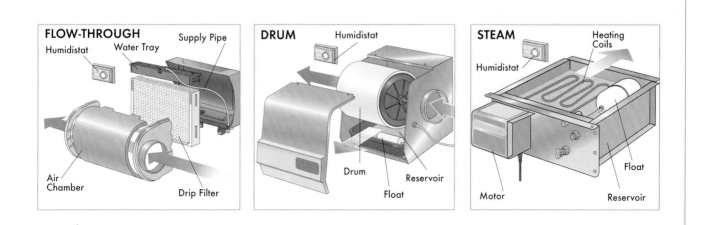

FLOW-THROUGH
Humidistat · Water Tray · Supply Pipe · Air Chamber · Drip Filter

DRUM
Humidistat · Drum · Float · Reservoir

STEAM
Humidistat · Heating Coils · Motor · Float · Reservoir

make a mist with a high-speed rotating disk, produce the greatest dispersions of microorganisms and minerals. Breathing misted air containing microscopic dust mites, mold, bacteria, and other pollutants can cause respiratory problems and allergic reactions.

The other two types of humidifiers generally disperse fewer pollutants. Evaporative units pick up water from a holding tank with a belt, sponge pad, or wick that is exposed to the airflow from the furnace. Warm-mist or similar steam-vaporizer humidifiers can completely eliminate pollution problems. A heating element boils the standing water before it is dispersed as mist into the air flow, which distills the minerals and kills bacteria and mold.

Cooling Systems

The time to collect your thoughts about keeping cool this summer is before the weather gets too hot and humid. By planning early, you'll avoid making a rash decision or being stuck with what's left at the home center. Before buying an air conditioner, ask some basic questions: Will it fit in the window? Will it keep the room cool? Is it so noisy that you won't sleep?

Capacity

The cooling power of an air conditioner is measured in units of heat energy called British thermal units (Btu). An air conditioner's Btu per hour (Btuh) rating indicates how much heat energy it can remove from the air in an hour. Some larger units are rated in tons, which measure the energy it takes to melt one ton of ice in a day. A ton is equal to 12,000 Btuh. As a general rule, 5,000 Btuh are needed to cool a 150- square-foot room. Add 1,000 Btu for every additional 50 square feet.

Central Air vs. Room Units

Central air-conditioning is an attractive feature in the resale market, but it's costly and difficult to install in many homes. A contractor may be able to set up machinery and ducts in an unused attic or use forced-air heating ducts, but in a two-story house, you may have to give up some cabinet or closet space to install ducts on the first floor. In most homes, one or two window or in-wall units can keep crucial rooms comfortable and spill out enough cool, dry air to reduce heat and humidity in adjacent areas.

Duct Sealants and Ducts in Conditioned Spaces

If you are using ducts to heat and cool your home, your two main goals should be to (1) carefully seal the seams of the ducts so that they do not leak air and (2) run the ducts through conditioned (insulated) space as straight as you can.

As for sealing ducts, even common sense will tell you that if you are blowing air under pressure into a duct system that leaks like a sieve, you are going to lose conditioned air into nonliving spaces, which will dramatically drive down the efficiency of your HVAC system. After achieving a mechanical connection between ducts, seal them with an acrylic- or butyl-based specialty tape, or a duct-sealing mastic. Don't use duct tape, which has a rubberized adhesive and dries out over time.

If ducts must be run in unconditioned spaces, they must be insulated to retain the relatively hot or cold air contained within.

As for where to run ducts, here too, common sense will tell you that if you blow heated air into a duct system that runs through ice cold—or nonconditioned—space, you will see a dramatic drop in the HVAC system's efficiency. The same is true for an air-conditioning system that blows cold air into ducts that run through hot attic space. Ideally, you want to run ducts through conditioned space. Even if the temperature of the conditioned space is not the same as the living space, your aim is to lower the degree differential between the air temperature inside the duct and the temperature of the air that the duct is running through.

TYPES OF AC UNITS

CENTRAL AC: Central AC systems consist of an outside unit with a compressor, condenser coil, and fan, and an interior evaporator coil installed in the supply duct of a warm-air furnace. Indoor heat is picked up and carried through pipes by a refrigerant to the condenser coil outside. Central air is expensive to install if your home lacks heating ducts but may still be cheaper (and quieter) than an array of room units. Modern, high-pressure lines can work with small-diameter hoses that are easy to install in existing spaces.

WINDOW UNITS: If you need to keep one room or area cool in the summertime, the easiest solution is to install a window unit. You don't have to make a hole in your house or install extensive ductwork, and most units can be plugged in and working an hour after you open the box. The best location is a double-hung window with a wall outlet nearby. The weight of the unit is carried on the sill and held in position with brackets at a slight downward slope for proper drainage of condensation. Extensions on each side of the unit slide out to seal the opening.

HEAT PUMPS: Heat pumps can heat and cool your home. They have an outdoor coil and compressor and an indoor coil and fan. (There are also self-contained through-the-wall units.) In hot weather, the heat pump acts like a conventional air conditioner. In cold weather, the cooling cycle of refrigerant is reversed to create a heat gain inside the house. But as the temperature outside drops, heat pumps lose efficiency, and an electric backup heater kicks in. The units are most economical in areas with roughly equal heating and cooling demand.

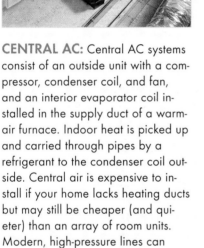

IN-WALL UNITS: Individual room units can be installed through the wall to avoid blocking the view through a window or having to remove the unit when it's cold. Like window units, in-wall units have two coils made of copper tubing and aluminum fins, one facing inside and one facing outside. These machines work like central systems, but all the components are built into one box. Most room units can be plugged into a standard 120-volt outlet, but some require 240 volts. You should be sure that the unit does not overload the circuit.

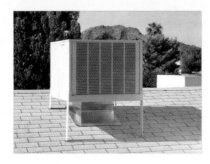

CHILLERS: Evaporative chillers (sometimes called evaporative coolers) are typically used to cool the air in commercial buildings or large homes in the Southwest. Chiller units can deliver from 10 to 500 tons of cooling. Modern chillers with heat exchangers and high-efficiency motors can use as little energy as 0.5 kilowatt per ton of cooling. Chillers usually flow water through evaporator and condenser tubes surrounded by refrigerant. Hot refrigerant is then condensed back into liquid in a cooling tower.

Air Quality

Modern houses and apartments are built to be airtight for greater heating and cooling efficiency. They're so airtight, however, that new air circulates back into the house very slowly—it may take hours for the air in a new house to recycle itself. This creates not only stale air but a buildup of indoor pollutants. These pollutants include irritants, such as dust, smoke, mold spores, pollen, and animal dander—which not only bother your lungs but clog up heating and cooling systems, computers, and other electronic equipment—but also more serious environmental hazards, such as the outgassing of formaldehyde from construction materials.

Several devices are available to clean the air of a tightly sealed house. Forced-air cooling and heating systems can have electronic filters installed right inside the HVAC ducts. If you don't have these systems, buy a portable air cleaner with a HEPA filter. Developed by the U.S. Atomic Energy Commission to remove almost all airborne particles, HEPA (high-efficiency particle accumulator) filters are widely used in hospitals and labs where clean rooms are needed. A true HEPA filter removes 99.97 percent of particles as small as 0.3 micron. (A micron is one-millionth of a meter; the period at the end of this sentence is several hundred microns across.) An ultra HEPA, or ULPA, filter removes particles as small as 0.1 micron. HEPA filters need to be replaced periodically, typically every one to three years.

YOUR GREEN CHOICES

HVAC Systems: Three Types, One Green

HVAC stands for heating, ventilation, and air-conditioning. But too often, remodelers and homeowners install only heating and air-conditioning and forget the ventilation aspect of a system. Do not underestimate the importance of ventilation, especially in a home that aspires to be green. A properly ventilated home can save a small fortune in heating costs, especially if fuel is saved when a ventilation system conditions incoming fresh air with the heat or relative coolness contained in the "exhaust" air before it exits the home.

There are three types of ventilation systems, and you probably have an example of one of these in your home today: supply-only systems, exhaust-only systems, and balanced systems.

Supply-Only Systems just supply outside air to the home; they do not do anything to condition it with the energy contained in the exhaust air. When the HVAC system turns on, cool (in winter) or hot (in summer) outdoor air simply pours into the ducts from the outside and it needs to be conditioned (heated or cooled) before it gets to your rooms. If it is zero degrees outside, and you have your thermostat set at 70°F, you have to pay to heat that air.

Exhaust-Only Systems simply pump air out of a room. These fans are commonly found in bathrooms and kitchens. Exhaust-only systems require close watching because even small fans can depressurize a room and draw fumes back into the house (backdrafting) from flue pipes on heating and cooling appliances. If your gas furnace has an air-intake pipe for supplying combustion air directly to the furnace (a sealed-combustion unit), you lower the backdraft risk.

Balanced Systems bring in fresh air while they exhaust the air from inside the home that is being replenished. Through a heat exchange system, the balanced system uses the energy contained in the outgoing air to condition the incoming air. Yet these systems do not let the air actually mingle. A balanced system is your greenest choice because it saves you the energy you would otherwise expend to heat up or cool down the outdoor air to the desired temperature for use in your home. But balanced systems are not easy to install because they are complicated and require a trained technician. Ask your HVAC contractor for advice. Installing a balanced system is not a do-it-yourself task. (See "Air Exchangers," page 148.)

ELECTRONIC CLEANERS

An electronic air cleaner can be mounted anywhere in the ductwork of a forced-air system. Generally, the most practical location is near the furnace at the end of the return plenum. Before dusty air from the house is sent back into the furnace for reheating, it passes through a prefilter and a row of removable cartridges that contain electronically charged plates. Aside from basic sheet-metal connections, you'll need to provide power for the plates and controls, including a sail switch, located in the return plenum. It activates the cleaner when air flows through the ducts.

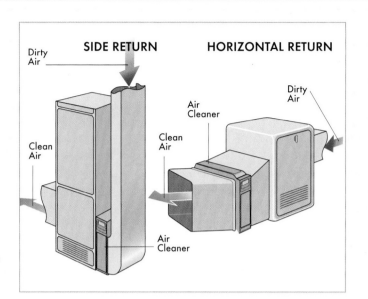

MEDIA CLEANERS

A media air filter performs the same tasks as a standard fiberglass mesh furnace filter. However, it does the job more thoroughly because instead of using loosely woven, flat mesh to trap particles, these filters are made of a tightly interlocking network of microscopic fibers folded like an accordion. The configuration creates a large surface area in a small space. The increased density helps to capture more particles in the airflow than a standard filter. The increased area makes some media filters ten times more effective than a typical disposable filter. Like an electronic unit, most media filters are mounted in the ductwork near your furnace. They are contained in a metal box frame that has an access door so that you can remove the media filter for cleaning or replacement. These filters are passive compared to electronic systems. You need to make the same kind of alterations to existing ductwork to install them, but you do not need to install wiring.

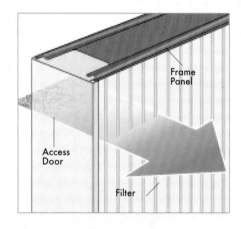

ELECTRONIC AIR FILTERS

Electronic air filters are built into the ducts near your furnace. A unit can be added to existing systems by modifying the ducts. A typical electronic cleaner has a prefilter that is similar to a standard furnace filter. It traps large dust particles and can be removed for cleaning. Next in line is one or two metal boxes (also removable for cleaning) containing thin metal plates. Particles in the airflow, typically in the return duct, are positively charged on their way to the plates. The plates themselves are negatively charged to attract the particles, which are driven against the plate walls as they pass through the system. These appliances can remove over 90 percent of most airborne pollutants, including pollen and smoke particles. The drawback is that larger particles hitting the plates can make an annoying sound—like an outdoor bug-zapper.

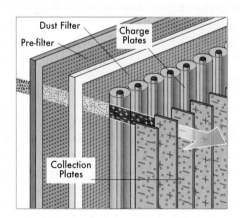

Whole-House Air Filtration

A technical group called the Heating, Refrigeration, and Air-Conditioning Engineers (ASHRAE) has put out a ventilation standard that states homes should have a fresh air flow of 7.5 cubic feet per minute per resident, plus 1 cubic foot per minute for every 100 square feet of living space. As the air is delivered to the home through the HVAC duct system, it can be filtered to improve indoor air quality.

Achieving superior indoor air quality can rarely be done with a standard nuisance-dust filter, but you can use filters that trap particulates as well as bacteria, viruses, and VOCs. Note that these filters often require your HVAC fan to blow harder, which will draw more power and even shorten the life of your blower motor. But for many people, that is a small price to pay for really clean air.

When choosing a filter, look for the "minimum efficiency reporting value" (MERV) scale, which ranges from 1 to 16. The higher the MERV, the tighter the filter, and the more particles the filter can take out of the air. The best nuisance-dust filter has a MERV of 4, whereas HEPA filters can achieve 16. A MERV 4 filter removes 20 percent of the particles in the air, but a MERV 16 filter removes more than 99 percent of particles in the air, down to 0.3 micron in size. Mold spores and pollen are up to microns thick, whereas viruses are less than 0.1 microns thick.

Filter types include mechanical filters, which have to be tossed when clogged; pleated filters, which are slightly more efficient than mechanical filters; HEPA filters, which are effective for trapping pollen and spores; and electrostatic filters, which zap contaminants.

AIR EXCHANGERS

AN AIR EXCHANGER is often added to the ductwork of tightly built houses that have only minimal ventilation. Most are designed around the basic plan of two fan-assisted pipes: one to exhaust stale air and one to bring in fresh air. Where the pipes pass each other, a common wall or other media transfers up to 75 percent of the outgoing temperature to the incoming air supply. This way, you can exchange stale air year round without heating or cooling the fresh supply.

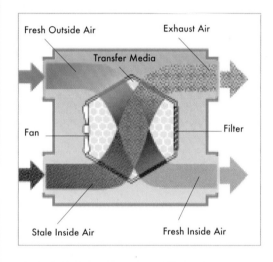

PORTABLE CLEANERS

PORTABLE AIR CLEANERS may have several types of filters. The most basic filters are similar to the ones used in hot-air furnaces to trap dirt. Some have to be replaced, while others can be washed and reused. Some machines also include an ion generator to force particles against surfaces. The most effective filter is a HEPA filter, which removes nearly 100 percent of airborne particles. A portable room air cleaner, such as the one shown,  will provide six air changes per hour in a 15-by-17-foot room. Manufacturer's literature, mainly the material data sheet, should list filter capacity and effectiveness against different pollutants.

Geothermal Ground-Source Heat Pumps

Each year, the average U.S. household produces 60 tons of carbon dioxide (a greenhouse gas) when its HVAC unit fires up to heat and cool the home. The reason for the carbon dioxide production? Your HVAC unit is burning gas or oil. Some innovative companies are now marketing a time-tested device to heat and cool homes that reduces the amount of fuel used. Geothermal ground-source heat pumps require only electrical energy to run their compressors, and they don't consume any oil or gas.

Here's how they work: a ground-source heat pump system depends on the ability of the earth to absorb or give off heat at a predicable rate. That's a fairly safe assumption, given the steady state of the earth's temperature just a few feet below the surface. With ground-source heat pumps, the heat is moved to its desired location by liquid-filled coils that are run through the ground, either vertically or in horizontal trenches. The coils are typically filled with treated water, but some close-loop coils actually contain refrigerant.

The heat pump uses a cycle of evaporation, compression, condensation, and expansion to move heat either into or out of the home. In the summer, the geothermal heat pump concentrates and moves heat from the house into the relative coolness of the earth. In the winter, the geothermal heat pump concentrates and moves the relatively warm heat energy in the earth up into the home.

Air-source heat pumps, the more common type, work on the same principle but are not as efficient as a ground-source units because they use the relative heat contained in the outside air—which ranges widely in temperature—instead of the earth.

A residential geothermal system is costly to install. A compressor and pump system are placed in your home and hooked up to the coil-loop systems. Horizontal ground loops are the most economical to install, because they can be put in trenches just 6 feet deep. Vertical pipes require drilling, which can really run up the installation bill. With either a horizontal or vertical loop system, you need to run about 600 feet of pipe for every ton of heating and cooling load. A ton equals 12,000 Btu per hour, and at peak demand most houses require around 36,000 Btu per hour.

According to the EPA, a ground-source heat pump can reduce heating and cooling energy demands by 40 percent compared with air-source heat pumps and by over 70 percent compared with electric baseboards or standard air-conditioning equipment. Geothermal heat pump units are as much as 50 percent more efficient than efficient gas furnaces. More than 1 million U.S. homes are heated and cooled with ground-source heat pumps and the technology is widely viewed as very reliable.

Though lower gas and oil bills will allow you to save money over the lifetime of the system, you won't see a true return on your investment for over a decade, or longer. That said, the geothermal technology is a viable alternative to burning fossil fuel, and it drives down the carbon footprint of your home to very low levels. Indeed, combined with solar panels, a geothermal system can effectively take the heating and cooling of your home entirely off the grid.

5

trim and finishes

How do you go green when trimming and painting or finishing wood in your home? After all, this is probably the part of remodeling your home that can have the greatest environmental impact, square foot for square foot. That's because trim often uses high-quality lumber, such as clear (knot-free) or No. 2 wood. Both of these lumber grades demand premium parts of the tree. Then you will paint or apply some other type of finish to the wood. So, going green at this stage of the job is a matter of making the right product choices. Third-party-certified lumber or composite-wood substitutes reduce pressure on forests, and a wide range of natural wood finishes are available that bring remarkable results with little impact on the environment. It used to be that natural wood finishes were exotic and hard to find, but with the increased popularity of the green movement, they're now readily available and considered high-performance products. Let's take a closer look.

FINISH WORK

TRIM IS BOTH PRACTICAL AND DECORATIVE. It covers rough edges and seams between different building materials inside and out, and it adds a distinctive touch that gives a house architectural detail and character. Installing trim can be a rewarding job if you master the art of making various kinds of simple miter cuts and getting a tight fit. To cut miters, you need a good miter box and a backsaw with a sufficient number of teeth per inch to make fine cuts without splintering the molding. Power miter saws make quick work of cutting even difficult angles. Trim is sold by the foot, in lengths ranging from 6 to 14 feet. Try to get lengths that will span each wall, corner to corner, to avoid unsightly splices. Keep in mind that many softwood varieties of trim can be either finger-jointed or clear. Finger-jointed is less expensive because it has splices and must be covered with paint. Clear trim can be stained.

Types of Molding

Home centers carry pine, oak, and poplar moldings in a great variety of shapes that are designed for specific locations and uses. The first trimwork to be installed are the casings that go around doorways and windows. Next are base and shoe moldings, which trim the wall at the floor. Cove or crown molding is used along the wall at the ceiling, and corner molding for both inside and outside corners is used to hide seams and protect corners. Because techniques for milling are not perfectly standardized, it's best to buy all the pieces of trim from the same milling lot to avoid fractional differences in size.

Decorating With Trim

Trim does have a functional side—it covers gaps, rough edges, and transitions between building materials. But when skillfully laid out, it can do much more. Wide baseboards, wainscoting along walls, picture molding, crown molding, and false beams on ceilings all add architectural detail and a decorative touch that can't be achieved with paint or wallpaper.

The overall design, type of trim used, and variety of wood you choose will have a lot to do with the results you achieve. (For more details on trim profiles, see page 154.) Clean, tight mitered joints are also important to the overall effect. For that you'll need a good miter-box saw or a power miter saw like the pros use, even if you have to rent it.

Installation Tips

Mark the locations of studs on the floor before the walls are drywalled so that you know where to nail the trim. Also, note the locations of any in-wall braces you may need to secure the trim.

Despite good equipment and careful layout, some trim joints still need a little adjusting. To close up a joint, try a trick called back-cutting. Use a sharp block plane to undercut the back edges on both pieces of trim so the boards won't touch until the visible surfaces meet.

BACK-CUTTING JOINTS

To make tight miter joints, use a sharp saw blade and a miter box or miter cutter to produce a clean angle cut. Test fit the joint, and if it doesn't close tightly, use a block plane to shave a thin amount of wood from the bottom part of the cut. Be careful not to plane along the cut line on the face of the joint. This back-cutting ensures that the two cut faces will touch.

USE A PLANE to back-cut miter edges, shaving with the wood grain.

FOR EXACT 45-degree joints, sharp saw and plane blades are a necessity.

COPING JOINTS

For inside corners, coped joints allow you to match two intricate molding faces. Cut the first piece square, and butt it into the corner. Cut the other piece on a 45-degree angle, leaving the face exposed. Use a pencil to outline the cut edge, and follow this when you make the second cut with a coping saw, back-cutting it slightly so the cut face mates tightly with the corner piece.

CUT A 45-DEG. face onto the intersecting trim; then scribe the cutout.

USE A COPING SAW to back-cut along the scribed line; file the edge if needed.

You can usually nail through trim without splitting the wood, but predrill if you are nailing near the edge, into oak (or other hardwoods), or into very thin or narrow trim.

Installing Crown Molding

To calculate the rough lengths of molding you'll need, start by measuring all the walls about 2 inches below the ceiling. If the adjoining surfaces are true, simply follow the wall and

MOLDING PROFILES

BASE MOLDINGS

Base moldings can be as simple as plain square stock (S4S) or more elaborate with built-up components like shoe and base cap. Colonial base (top) is a more traditional style, while Ranch base (center) is common in today's homes. Contemporary base (bottom) is a stock item or easily made with a router or saw.

CHAIR RAILS

These moldings do what their name implies—protect walls from damage caused by chair backs bumping up against them. They have evolved into purely decorative trim that visually divides open wall space or creates a demarcation between paint, wallpaper, or paneling. There are many styles available that range from simple to sublime.

CROWNS

Aptly named, crown moldings are often the most elaborate and costly moldings in a room; they can add a crowning touch to almost any space. Styles range from simple 7/8-inch-wide coves to custom-made crowns that are up to a foot or more edge to edge. They may be used alone or layered with other moldings for dramatic effect.

CASINGS

Perhaps the most utilitarian molding style, casings serve mainly to cover openings or joints between walls and window or door jambs. Because they must be miter-cut at corners and other intersections, always use pieces from the same stock run to ensure that the molding profiles will match up when installed.

ceiling lines. You can test for bumps and depressions using a long, straight 2x4.

Install the crown with glue and nails driven into wall studs. You can drill pilot holes through the top of the molding and drive 16d finishing nails into the top plate of the wall frame or into the ceiling joists.

If the wall and ceiling aren't true, you can do one of two things. The first is to force the crown into position using a wood block and toenails. This may work when the ceiling is fairly flat with only a few shallow depressions. The molding itself won't be straight, however, which may magnify the problem.

The second thing you can do is to test a scrap piece of molding at several locations to find the lowest point of the ceiling. Then level that low point along the walls where you'll be working, and strike chalk guidelines. Install the molding along the guidelines, and fill any gaps between the top of the molding and the ceiling with joint compound or caulk. This tends to flatten out the crown molding, though.

Installing Corners

In most cases, the best approach is to install all outside corners before inside corners. But you need to plan the installation carefully, and allow at least an inch or so of extra wood in case you make an error and need to recut coped joints at inside corners.

When two outside corners are separated by an inside corner, save the piece coped at both ends for last. In rooms with walls longer than your molding stock, of course, you'll need to piece the lengths together with a scarf joint.

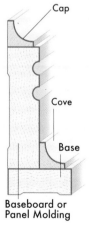

Cap

Cove

Base

Baseboard or Panel Molding

BUILT-UPS

Although there are many ready-made molding profiles, "trimming out" can be a carpentry art form. By combining different types of molding and square stock, you can create unique built-up trim profiles to suit your taste or your home's decor. The illustration at left is just one example, using four basic molding styles.

Natural Wood Finishes

To treat and preserve wood, you do not have to coat it with paint or polyurethane. An earlier chapter covered low-VOC (volatile organic compound) paints, so the green options covered here concern wood finishes. There are a variety of natural wood finishes available today that can offer protection approaching that achieved with nongreen finishes. These finishes may not perform as well as high-VOC polyurethane or oil-based paints, which both flow and settle very well and have good durability; and natural finishes may have to be applied more often than high-VOC finishes, but the environmental rewards are substantial. In fact, these finishes often have natural ingredients, such as linseed oil, orange oil, carnauba wax, rosemary oil, beeswax, pine resin, and shellac. As much as these ingredients sound edible and like something you might put in a fruit smoothie, all things natural are not always safe to touch or eat. So even though these finishes are natural, per se, treat these finishes as you would any paint.

Wood Oil. Wood oil is a term usually used to describe tung oil or linseed oil. Tung oil is not a petroleum product. It comes from the seed of the tung tree, and it can bring a warm finish to wood floors, doors, and trim. Linseed oil (derived from flaxseed) has long been known to bring a lush look to wood, though it will yellow over time when used in its pure form and is best applied when mixed with other oils. Both tung oil and linseed oil perform best when finished with a coating of wax. If you search "natural wood finishes" on the Internet, you will find a wealth of products that include tung oil, linseed oil, and many others. Other natural wood finishes include oils made from natural vegetable oils and waxes, which are also viable as wood finishes.

Note that wood oils are not entirely free of toxic chemicals. Often you need mineral spirits to clean up, especially with tung oil. So unless you are using a disposable brush and avoiding the cleanup phase altogether, you are still ultimately depending on petrochemicals for the wood-treatment process.

Penofin. Penofin is a penetrating oil wood finish and it is made from Brazilian rosewood oil. It is a flexible, water-resistant oil and is ultraviolet resistant. You will need mineral spirits to clean up. Note that used application rags must be soaked in water when you are done, as they may spontaneously combust.

Shellac. This resin can offer a look that ranges from clear to orange, and it is naturally derived from a substance secreted by Asian tree insects. Shellac is alcohol-soluble, which means that it can be "healed" (softened and respread) with alcohol at any time during its service life if you need to recoat or patch it. It is most widely used as a sealer and clear finish for floors. Shellac cleans up with denatured alcohol.

Beeswax. If you are looking for a warm, transparent, antistatic finish, look at various beeswax wood-finish products. Beeswax can be applied to wood, cork, linoleum, and even stone. But beeswax isn't good for areas where there is much traffic as it doesn't wear well, so avoid using it on floors. Like shellac, beeswax can be "healed" with additional coats, and it can be thinned with a citrus solvent. Beeswax won't blister or peel, and it can be brought to a warm shine by buffing.

INSTALLING BASEBOARD

Most baseboards require two nails at each stud location. You can also drive nails into the bottom plate. For built-up baseboards, install the main board first; then add the cap and other accent moldings, nailing them into the main board or wall studs. Nail the base shoe to the floor only so that it can move independently of the baseboard and prevent gapping. For outside corners, make miter cuts to connect the molding; for inside corners, make coped cuts. These types of cuts help keep the molding from showing gaps.

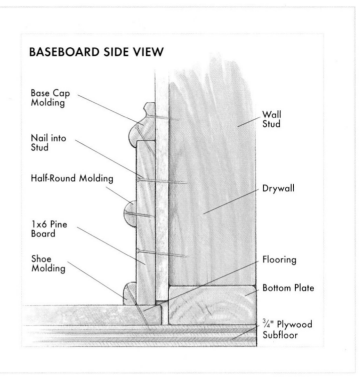

BASEBOARD SIDE VIEW

Base Cap Molding
Nail into Stud
Half-Round Molding
1x6 Pine Board
Shoe Molding
Wall Stud
Drywall
Flooring
Bottom Plate
¾" Plywood Subfloor

BASEBOARD STYLES

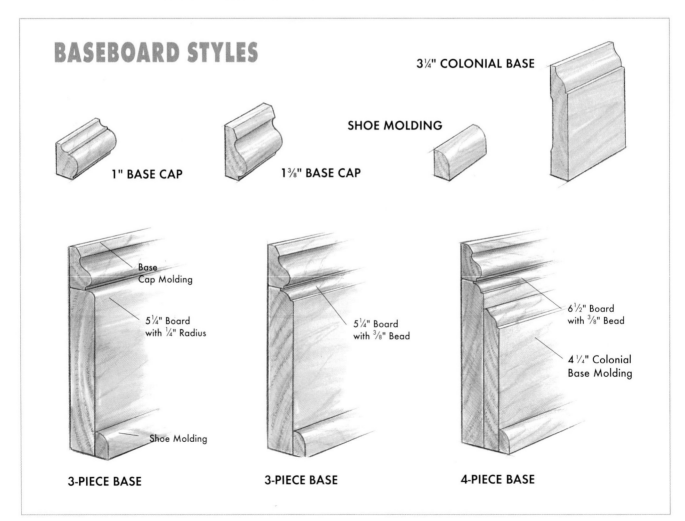

3¼" COLONIAL BASE

SHOE MOLDING

1" BASE CAP

1⅜" BASE CAP

3-PIECE BASE
Base Cap Molding
5¼" Board with ¼" Radius
Shoe Molding

3-PIECE BASE
5¼" Board with ⅜" Bead

4-PIECE BASE
6½" Board with ⅜" Bead
4¼" Colonial Base Molding

MOLDING DETAILS

You can use molding combinations, such as beaded molding and decorative medallion blocks, to create distinctive door trim.

More elaborate door surrounds are available in precut hardwood kits. Period moldings are now also made from foam.

Originally made from plaster, ceiling medallions are now made of light foam glued and joint-compounded in place.

Cornice moldings for ceilings can be built up in stages from stock lumber or ordered in paintable foam sections.

Elaborate cornice moldings can be painted, stained, or treated with a variety of faux-finish surface glazes.

Complex cornices, medallions, mantels, and other special trim pieces are also available in exotic hardwoods.

Once you've cut the cope on inside corners, create a tight fit by adjusting the position of both corner pieces and by sanding or filing the cope as needed. To adjust the tacked-in-place square-cut piece up or down for fitting, tap it with a hammer and block.

Baseboard

Baseboard hides the gap between the wall and floor and for that reason is present in almost every room of the house. It was developed in the eighteenth century, as owners of grand houses began to prefer plaster walls over wood paneling, and today it remains true to its purpose of protecting wall surfaces from shoes, furniture, and other domestic hazards. As an architectural detail, baseboard provides a foundation to a wall, as a base does to a column.

Over the years, baseboard has diminished in stature if not ubiquity. Georgian and Federal homes had substantial base molding, sometimes made of marble, but always with its detailing in keeping with door and window casing. Victorian and Craftsman decorators also preferred deep baseboards, although with simpler profiles, the latter often favoring a wide, flat board with a slightly rounded top edge. Modern homes typically have narrow ranch- or Colonial-style moldings, sometimes with the same type of trim also used for the window and door casing.

When choosing baseboard, it's important to make sure it pairs well with the door and window casing. Hold a piece of baseboard against the casing's edge, in the manner they will be installed, to make sure they meet nicely. Sometimes a poor match can be remedied with

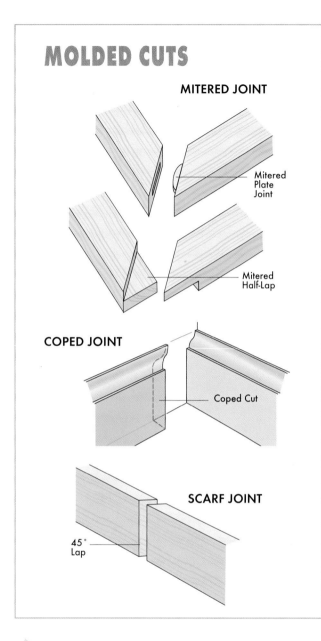

MOLDED CUTS

MITERED JOINT

Mitered Plate Joint

Mitered Half-Lap

COPED JOINT

Coped Cut

SCARF JOINT

45° Lap

plinth blocks installed beneath the casing or with a back-band added to the casing's outer edge. You'll also need to decide whether to install a base shoe—a slender, usually rounded strip of molding installed along the baseboard's bottom edge. Base shoe is flexible and can follow floor contours to hide gaps left by the baseboard.

Door and Window Casings

Casing is the trim that surrounds door and window openings and hides the gap between the wall finish and the jambs of the door or window frame. In most homes, both today and historically, the same casing is used for the doors and windows, although main entry doors often carry different embellishment from internal doors. Casing plays an important and unique decorative role because it frames passages, thereby affecting the view of what lies beyond the passage, just as a picture frame contributes to the visual impact of the painting it contains.

Most casing styles can be grouped into one of two broad categories: tapered and square. Tapered casing is heaviest along its outside edge and tapers toward the edge that contacts the door or window jamb. Because of its taper, this type of casing is almost always installed with mitered corners (like a picture frame). Square casing has the same thickness on both sides and, if not smooth, has symmetrical detailing across its face. Square casing can be mitered at the corners or can be combined with decorative corner blocks and plinth blocks, adding visual weight and substance to the treatment.

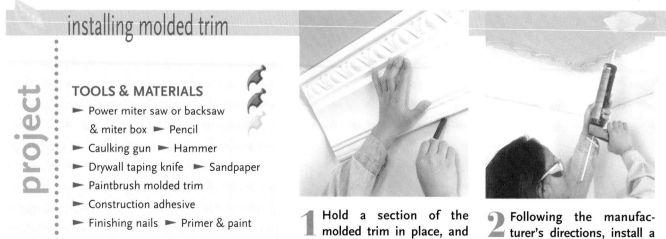

project

installing molded trim

TOOLS & MATERIALS
- ► Power miter saw or backsaw & miter box ► Pencil
- ► Caulking gun ► Hammer
- ► Drywall taping knife ► Sandpaper
- ► Paintbrush molded trim
- ► Construction adhesive
- ► Finishing nails ► Primer & paint

1 Hold a section of the molded trim in place, and mark guidelines along the top and bottom edges with a pencil.

2 Following the manufacturer's directions, install a bead of adhesive just inside your lines on the wall and ceiling.

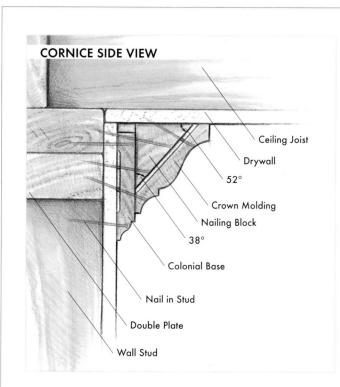

CORNICE SIDE VIEW

- Ceiling Joist
- Drywall
- 52°
- Crown Molding
- Nailing Block
- 38°
- Colonial Base
- Nail in Stud
- Double Plate
- Wall Stud

ATTACHING A CROWN MOLDING

With most molding installations, you can nail into wall studs to make solid connections. On some cornice installations, however, upper nails will reach into ceiling joists every 16 inches only if the joists run perpendicular to the wall. Where joists are parallel with the wall, you need either nailing blocks or a continuous nailer for support. You may want to install the blocks for extra support in any case.

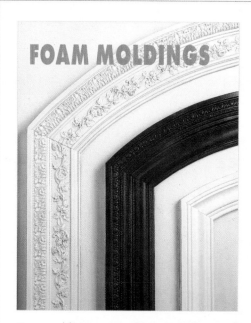

FOAM MOLDINGS

Foam moldings are cast from original, carved-wood trim. The cladding accepts paint.

There are many ways to join wood trim—for example, with miters, half-laps, and biscuits. On some baseboard corners, you may have to make a coped joint. If you have to butt baseboards, cut mating edges at 45 degrees so that if the joint opens slightly, you won't see a gap. With reproduction trim made of rigid polyurethane foam, you can use a utility knife or trim saw to make cuts. Install this trim with adhesive and nails.

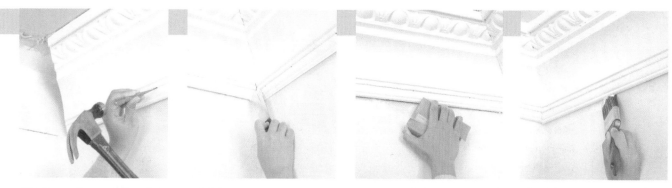

3 Press the molding into the beads of adhesive, and fasten the lightweight sections with finishing nails.

4 Where molding sections meet, and along the top and bottom edges, use drywall compound to fill seams and gaps.

5 Spread the compound smoothly, and when it dries, lightly sand the wall and ceiling seams with fine sandpaper.

6 Wipe away sanding dust; cover the fresh compound with a prime coat of paint; and finish with a full-strength coat.

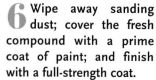

installing crown molding

TOOLS & MATERIALS

- ► Chalk-line box and measuring tape
- ► Crown molding and nailing blocks
- ► Power miter saw and coping saw
- ► Files
- ► Hammer
- ► Power drill and bits
- ► Finishing nails
- ► Nail set
- ► Wood glue
- ► Caulk and caulking gun

1 Once you've established your guideline location, snap a chalk line for the molding.

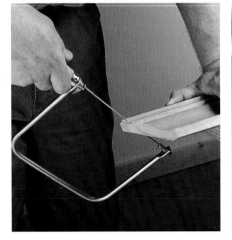

6 Use a coping saw to start the profile cut. Angle the saw to back-cut the coped piece.

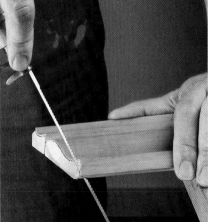

7 Rotate the saw as needed to maneuver the thin blade along the profile of the miter.

8 Use an oval-shaped file (or a round file in tight spots) to clean up curved sections of the profile.

INSTALLING DOOR & WINDOW CASING

The first step to installing casing is establishing the reveal: the narrow strip of jamb that is left exposed when the casing is installed. Without a reveal, it will look as if you're trying to make the jamb and casing appear as one piece, but unsuccessfully. Most reveals are about $1/8$ inch. When you decide what looks best, make light pencil marks representing the reveal on each jamb at the corners of the opening; use these marks for your measurements. To install mitered casing, cut the casing pieces and temporarily tack them in place, then make sure the joints fit tightly before permanently attaching the casing. Nail the casing to the jamb edges with small (4d or so) finishing nails; then nail through the outer edges of the casing into the wall framing, using 6d finishing nails. If you're using corner and plinth blocks, install them first, then cut the casing to fit in between. It usually looks best if the casing is slightly narrower than the blocks, creating reveals on those pieces as well as along the jambs.

2 Nail or screw the support blocks to wall studs and the wall top plate every 16 inches.

3 Install the full-length square-cut cornice, fitting it to the corner. Don't nail within 3 or 4 ft. of the corner.

4 Measure out from the corner (plus an extra couple of inches) to find the rough length of the coped molding.

5 Cut the coping miter on another board, and transfer the dimension from Step 4, measuring from the miter tip.

9 Use a flat rasp as needed to clean up the upper section of the coped cut or to increase the back-cut angle.

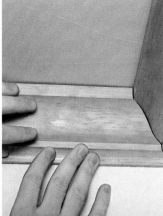

10 Test fit the coped piece in place, supporting the other end to be sure the board is level.

11 Adjust and fit pieces, support coped piece in place, and drill near the coped end to prevent splitting.

12 To finish, drive and set finishing nails to secure the corners; then sand or caulk the joint as needed.

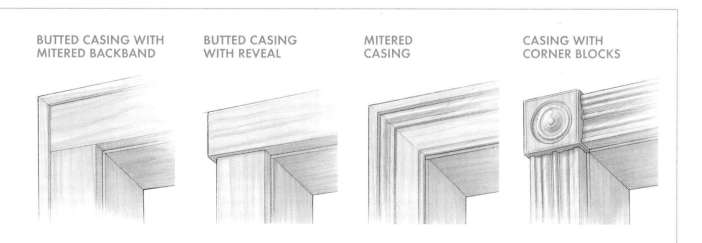

BUTTED CASING WITH MITERED BACKBAND

BUTTED CASING WITH REVEAL

MITERED CASING

CASING WITH CORNER BLOCKS

making scarf joints

On straight runs in large rooms, you may not be able to buy stock molding long enough to reach wall to wall in one piece. In this case you have to join the lengths, creating additional joints. The best approach is to cut an overlap between the pieces, called a scarf joint. Simply slice 45-degree cuts through the thickness of both pieces so that the surface of one covers the cut section of the other.

TOOLS & MATERIALS

► Power miter ► Clamps ► Baseboard
► Shoe molding ► Wood glue and filler
► Power drill and bits ► Hammer ► Nail set
► Sanding block ► Sandpaper

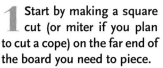

1 Start by making a square cut (or miter if you plan to cut a cope) on the far end of the board you need to piece.

2 Cut both the 45-deg. miters that will form the scarf joint. (Locate the scarf over a wall stud.)

3 Test fit the scarf joint (without glue), and predrill through both pieces at the joint.

4 Apply would glue to both sides of the joint. You will need to wipe off some excess after nailing.

5 Drive finishing nails through the predrilled holes, and set the heads just below the wood surface.

6 Fill nailholes with wood filler. You may need to wait and fill the holes again: fillers can shrink as they set.

7 Clean up any traces of glue and filler around the joint with sandpaper before finishing the wood.

8 To further disguise the joint, consider nailing a shoe molding to the bottom of the baseboard.

Polyurethane

Polyurethane is a polymer that can be manufactured for a wide range of end uses that include the cushions in your furniture, the insulating foam in your walls, and the clear finish on your floor and trim. A versatile chemical, it can be chemically configured for high durability. Though there are natural floor and trim finishes available today, they would have to be applied and reapplied to match the durability of even a single application of any polyurethane. So, how do you go green while obtaining the desired durability and workability of oil-based polyurethane, which is the gold standard for performance? A balanced choice is to select a low-VOC, water-based polyurethane. Today's low-VOC polyurethanes offer good workability, fast dry times (three hours), and low odor.

Pros and Cons. Note that water-based polyurethane does not have the same durability of old-fashioned, high-VOC polyurethane. That's because most water-based polyurethanes contain just 30 to 35 percent solids, compared with as much as 50 percent solids for oil-based products. It is the solids that actually form the finish. So, if you want to use a water-based polyurethane and achieve the same durability of an oil-based product—especially in floor applications with high traffic—you may have to coat the surface four times, instead of two times, and then coat it again every two years. However, water-based polyurethane cleans up with water, a real advantage over oil-based products.

Water-based products stay blond and don't mellow to the golden hue of oil-based polyurethane products. The advantage to a water-based urethane that doesn't change color is that it can be repaired with a patch, so you can avoid having to recoat the entire floor, door, or trim if just a part of it is damaged. Finally, even water-based polyurethane contains solvent. Typically this is ethylene glycol or propylene glycol. So, even the greenest polyurethane must be treated with care.

project

assembling a jamb

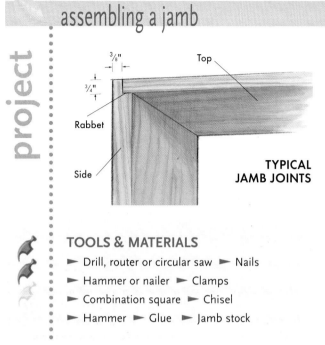

3/8"
3/4"

Top
Rabbet
Side

TYPICAL JAMB JOINTS

TOOLS & MATERIALS

- ► Drill, router or circular saw ► Nails
- ► Hammer or nailer ► Clamps
- ► Combination square ► Chisel
- ► Hammer ► Glue ► Jamb stock

1 Cut the head jamb to length, and mark the joint outline with a square for a ¾-in. jamb leg.

2 Set the blade depth on a circular saw to reach halfway (⅜ in.) through the thickness of the board.

3 To control the rabbet cut, firmly clamp a guide board and the jamb to a stable bench.

4 Make the innermost cut with the saw along the guide. Make multiple passes to kerf the remaining wood.

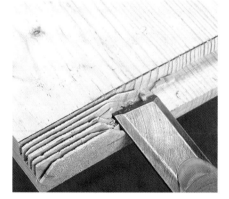

5 You can use the saw to remove all the wood, or clean up the thin strips between kerfs with a sharp chisel.

6 When the rabbet is cleaned up and ready for assembly, mark a nailing line on the outside of the joint.

7 Add carpenter's glue to the mating surfaces of the jamb parts just prior to assembling them with nails.

8 Square up the jamb frame before fastening. Set the pieces around a square block for support.

installing simple colonial casing

Once the jamb is in place, you can install casing around the opening. The technique shown here is for colonial casing with products available from home centers and lumber yards. The mitered joints will ensure a continuous seamless border of molding around the opening. When installed, you have the option of applying a clear finish or painting the trimwork.

TOOLS & MATERIALS

► Hammer   ► Combination square
► Miter saw   ► Nail set
► Clamshell or ranch casing
► finishing nails   ► Wood glue

1 Mark the reveal by sliding the blade on the combination square. Cut a miter on one end of the casing.

2 Align the short side of the miter with one reveal mark; transfer the opposite mark to the casing.

3 Use 4d finishing nails to tack the head casing to the head jamb of the door. Leave the nailheads exposed.

4 Cut a miter on a piece of side casing. Rest the miter on the floor or spacer (for carpet or finished floor).

5 Mark the length of the side casing pieces by running a pencil along the top edge of the head casing.

6 Apply a small bead of glue to both miter surfaces. Nail the side casing to the jamb and wall framing.

7 Drive a 4d finishing nail through the edge of the casing to lock the miter joint together.

8 Use a nail set to recess the nailheads about 1/8 in. below the wood surface.

6

kitchens & baths

The kitchen and the bathroom are two locations where you can apply a great deal of the information you have learned from other chapters in this book, ranging from green insulation in walls to daylighting strategies that bring natural light in from outside. Low-flow fixtures and point-of-use water filters that we covered earlier can serve both the kitchen and bath, and in both of these rooms the importance of venting moist air is crucial. Knowledge of the green chemistry of paints, adhesives, carpets, and finishes will also serve you well as you specify your green materials and building practices. But we're not done yet! In this chapter, "Your Green Choices" coverage will offer crucial information on energy-efficient appliances, green countertops, and green substrates used in cabinetry. In addition, there is some of the basic how-to information you'll need to tackle common kitchen and bath projects. 🍃

installing base cabinets

Base cabinets are difficult to install because both the floor and the wall surface can be out of level or plumb. To correct any problems, make liberal use of cedar shimming shingles.

Start by installing the corner cabinet. Add the next cabinet in line, and shim it in place using wood shims. Be sure to check for level as you work. Screw the cabinet to the wall, and continue installing the rest of the cabinets along the wall. Finish up by installing the toe-kick boards next to the floor.

TOOLS & MATERIALS
- ► Stud finder (or nail)
- ► Cabinets and hardware
- ► 48-in. level
- ► Measuring tape
- ► Pencil
- ► Wood shims
- ► Utility knife
- ► 2½-, 3-, and 3½-in. wood screws
- ► Handsaw
- ► Power drill/driver with assorted bits
- ► C-clamps
- ► Screwdrivers
- ► Vinyl or wood kickplates
- ► 1x3 ledger board
- ► Quarter-round molding

drilling holes for plumbing lines

DRILL HOLES FOR PLUMBING AND WASTE LINES BEFORE INSTALLING THE CABINETS. IT IS EASIER TO WORK WHEN THE CABINETS ARE OUT IN THE MIDDLE OF THE FLOOR. JUST TAKE CAREFUL MEASUREMENTS OF WHERE THE SUPPLY AND DRAIN LINES ARE, AND TRANSFER THESE TO THE CABINET BACK.

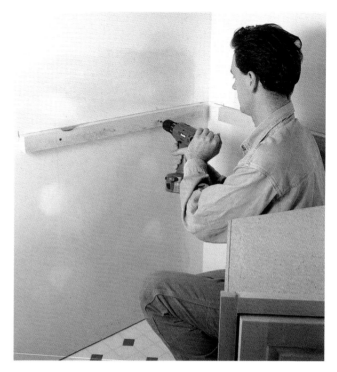

1 Measure the height of base cabinets, and transfer this dimension to the walls. Mark a level line on the wall where the cabinets fall. Then screw ledger strips behind any corner cabinets to support the back of the countertop.

4 The next step is to screw the back of the cabinet to the wall. Just locate the wall studs, and drive screws through the back cleat and into the studs. Make sure to check level between cabinets.

2 After installing the corner cabinets, start adding the adjacent units. Make sure these are aligned square to the wall and are level and plumb. To raise the cabinet, slide wood shims underneath the sides.

3 Also use shims between cabinets to maintain proper alignment. First, clamp the cabinet stiles together. Then install the shims, and when the fit is right, drive screws to join the stiles. Remove the clamps.

5 Once all the cabinets are installed, attach the toe-kick boards at the bottom of the cabinets. These boards will hide any gaps between the bottom of the cabinets and the floor.

TOE-KICK HEATERS

Toe-kick heaters have a short profile designed to slide into the normally empty space under kitchen cabinets. They are a good solution for providing auxiliary heat when needed or to provide spot heat on particularly cold days. To install one, you will need to bring power from an existing junction box to a new switch and pull cable from the switch to the heater—similar to the method used for installing under-cabinet lighting. Cut out the opening in the toe-kick space; then pull the cable into the room. Make the necessary electrical connections, and slide the heater into position.

installing a water filter

There are many different water-treatment systems. The best one for you depends on what's in your water. So, your first step is to have your water tested. There are simple do-it-yourself test kits available. But you'll get a more thorough analysis if you send your sample to a testing laboratory. Once you get your results back, shop for a filter that will remove the impurities you have. (See page 126.)

TOOLS & MATERIALS

- ► Filtration system
- ► Installation kit (saddle valve, water lines with compression fittings if not included with the system)
- ► Adjustable wrench or appropriate open-end wrenches
- ► Pliers
- ► Screwdriver

1 The carbon filter unit is designed to mount under the kitchen sink. Clear a space near the cold-water supply pipe, and mount the canister on the side of the cabinet. Some units simply hang on a couple of screws, like this one. Others are installed on a simple bracket.

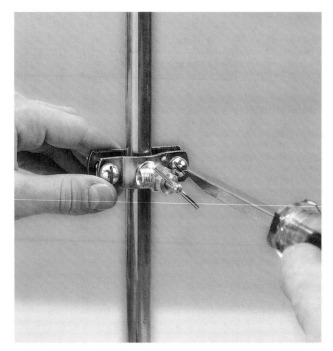

4 Make the water connection to the cold-water pipe using a simple saddle valve that comes with the filter kit. Back out the tapping pin on the valve; then hold the plates against the pipe and alternately tighten the bolts a little at a time until the assembly is tight. Turn the tapping pin clockwise until it pierces the pipe.

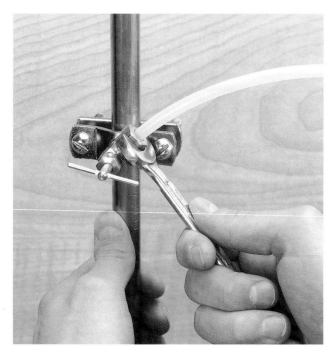

5 Join the filter unit to the saddle valve using a plastic hose and a compression fitting. Then run hose between the filter and the faucet, again using compression fittings. Turn on the water supply, and check the installation for any leaks. If you find any, try tightening the compression nuts.

2 If your sink has a knockout plug for a sprayer or hot-water dispenser, this is the perfect spot for the filter faucet. Just remove the knockout using a flat-blade screwdriver. If you don't have a hole, you can drill one through the sink or the countertop next to the sink to provide easy access.

3 Lower the filter faucet into the hole; then tighten it in place by installing a mounting nut from below the sink. Have someone above hold the faucet so that it points in the preferred direction while you tighten it from below.

YOUR GREEN CHOICES

Countertops

Some countertops, especially laminate countertops, aren't very green for any of three simple reasons: (1) the adhesives that hold the countertop material to the substrate may off-gas harmful fumes; (2) the binders that hold the particleboard or plywood substrate together can off-gas harmful fumes or formaldehyde; and (3) the countertop materials themselves may be unsustainable to harvest and manufacture.

An immediate solution is to look for countertops made from recycled-wood-fiber particleboard or plywood substrates that are made with formaldehyde- and VOC-free adhesives and binders. But a number of other green countertop solutions have come on the market recently, and these include:

■ Countertops created from paper products made water- and stain-resistant with natural resins. They are not as porous as concrete countertops and can be remarkably chip- and scratch-resistant.

■ Terrazzo, a smooth, multicolored countertop made of marble or stone chips embedded in a cement binder; and terrazzo-style counters, which can be made of recycled glass and cement; both can be polished to a high gloss.

■ Natural stone countertops that have had their raw materials extracted in a sustainable way or that use natural stone that was quarried long ago and recycled from other uses.

■ Quartz countertops that are nonporous and stain resistant offer a green surface, if the materials that make up the countertops come from postconsumer and postindustrial recycled material.

■ Bamboo countertops. When bamboo is used for countertops, bands of it are glued together—similar to a very large cutting board.

installing a dishwasher

project

The typical kitchen dishwasher can be a great energy- and labor-saving device. You should run a dishwasher only when it is full. To save energy, look for an Energy Star model. If you are replacing an existing unit, chances are your plumbing hookups are already in place. Just place the new appliance in the opening and make the necessary connections.

TOOLS & MATERIALS

- ► Dishwasher ► Compression T-fitting
- ► Compression shutoff valve
- ► Copper tubing (⅜ in. or larger)
- ► Adjustable wrench ► Bucket
- ► Rubber or plastic drain line ► Hose clamps
- ► Backflow preventer ► Wire connectors
- ► 12-gauge electrical cable
- ► Basic electrical tools ► 1-in. wood screws

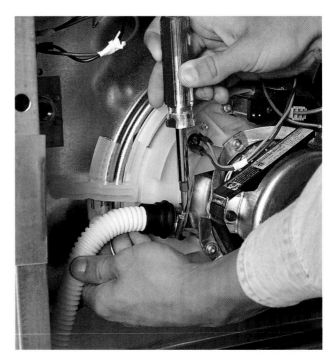

1 The first step in installing a dishwasher is to attach the discharge hose that takes the wastewater to the waste-disposal unit port. Tip the dishwasher on its back to gain easy access to the underside. Then attach the discharge hose to the unit's pump using a hose clamp.

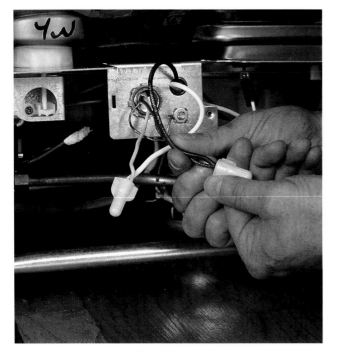

3 Run 12-gauge cable into the electrical box, and tighten the cable clamp. Connect like-colored wires using wire connectors; then attach the ground wire to the grounding screw.

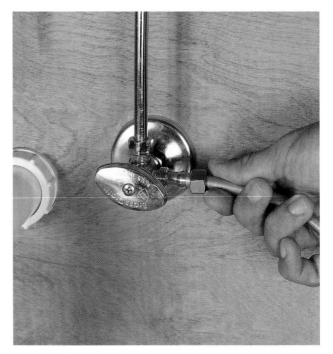

4 Attach the existing hot-water supply tube to the top of a dual-stop shutoff valve. Then slide a compression nut and ferrule over the end of the dishwasher tubing, and connect this tubing to the side of the valve. If this joint leaks once the dishwasher is running, use pipe-sealing tape to seal the threads.

2 Use ⅜-in.-dia. flexible copper tubing to connect the shutoff valve under the sink to the bottom of the dishwasher. Connect the two using a compression nut and ferrule.

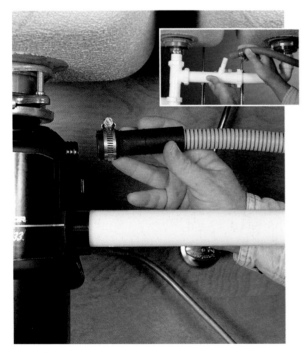

5 There are two ways to connect the dishwasher drain hose. If you have a waste-disposal unit, connect the hose to the dishwasher port on the side of the unit. If you don't have a disposal unit, attach the hose to a T-fitting installed in the connecting pipe between the sink drains (inset).

YOUR GREEN CHOICES

Energy-Efficient Appliances

The average U.S. household spends around $1,900 per year on energy. Whatever your motivation—from the satisfaction of not paying the utilities to reducing greenhouse gas emissions created by electricity generation—you can save a fair amount of energy each year by buying energy-efficient appliances. The best way to determine if an appliance is energy efficient is to look for an Energy Star label. Appliances that comply with Energy Star guidelines use 10 to 50 percent less energy and water than models that are not Energy Star rated.

When shopping for appliances, note that even seemingly insignificant choices can have a big impact. The EPA points out that if just one in ten homes used Energy Star appliances, the change would be like planting 1.7 million acres of trees.

Energy Star rates all of the appliances that go into your home, from refrigerators and dishwashers to water heaters, and even lightbulbs. Here is some appliance-specific information.

Dishwashers. Replacing a dishwasher manufactured before 1994 with an Energy Star dishwasher can save you more than $30 a year in utility costs. Because the average life of a dishwasher is 12 years, that's $360 dollars in savings. Energy Star dishwashers use at least 41 percent less energy than the federal minimum standard for energy consumption, and they optimize the use of water, too.

Refrigerators and Freezers. Energy Star-qualified refrigerators require about half as much energy as models manufactured before 1993. They also use at least 15 percent less energy than required by current federal standards. Energy Star freezers use at least 10 percent less energy than required by current federal standards.

Water Heaters. Heating water represents 15 percent of your home's overall energy consumption. Energy Star-rated water heaters use 10 to 50 percent less energy than standard models. The water heater's efficiency is measured as an Energy Factor (EF), which is usually listed beside the Energy Guide label. The higher the number, the more energy efficient the water heater.

173

installing a sink in a vanity

Most bathroom sinks are either self-rimming or metal-rimmed models. The basic difference between the two is how each is attached to the vanity top. Self-rimming units rest on top of the counter and are kept from moving by metal clips that are installed from underneath or by a generous bead of adhesive caulk. Metal-rimmed units, on the other hand, are attached to the underside of a metal rim, and the metal rim is attached to the counter. The drawings below show the difference between the two.

These days the self-rimming type is more common. It is the type installed here. In many contemporary bathrooms, the sink of choice is more often an above-counter model, which works as well as the other sinks, but has a much more distinctive look.

TOOLS & MATERIALS

- ► Saber saw ► Adjustable wrench
- ► Screwdriver ► Utility knife
- ► Power drill/driver with $^3/_8$-inch bit
- ► Silicone caulk and caulking gun
- ► 2x4s for bracing ► 8d finishing nails
- ► Colored wood filler ► Hammer ► Nail set
- ► Sink and laminate countertop

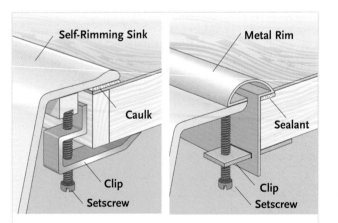

SELF-RIMMING SINKS are set in caulk and held with clips. Rimmed sinks, on the other hand, are supported by metal rims that are set in sealant. The sink is pushed up against the rim from below and is held by a clip.

1 Mark the centerline of the sink location on the vanity top. Then mark the centerline of the sink on the underside of its rim. Turn the sink over, and place it on the countertop so that the two marks line up. Then trace around the perimeter of the sink.

3 Cut the sink opening using a saber saw. Make sure to use a sharp blade and hold the saw firmly against the vanity top. If the saw bounces up and down when you are cutting, this can mar the surface. If you can't keep the base from bouncing, cover it with duct tape to prevent any damage.

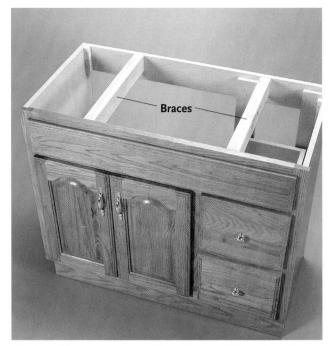

2 Provide extra support for a heavy sink by installing a 2x4 brace on both sides on the sink opening. Attach them using screws driven through the cabinet framing and into the ends of the braces. On the finished side of the cabinet, use finishing nails; set their heads; and fill the holes with colored wood filler.

Braces

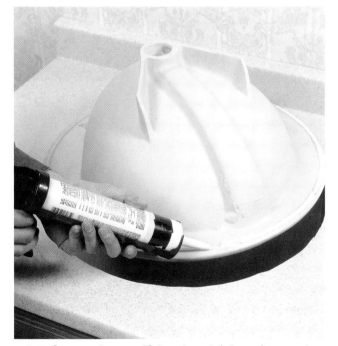

4 Before putting a self-rimming sink into the opening, apply a generous bead of silicone caulk to the underside of the sink rim. Then turn the sink over and lower it into place. If the sink needs clips, install them now. Let the caulk dry, and clean up any excess caulk.

Cabinetry

Most cabinetry isn't very green for some simple reasons. If the cabinets are not solid-wood cabinets, the substrate is made of particleboard, and the particleboard is likely held together with an adhesive that contains formaldehyde. Secondary contributors to nongreen cabinets are the harvesting techniques used to obtain the wood veneers that face cabinets and the adhesives that hold the veneers in place.

Finding green cabinets is relatively easy. Look for cabinets that use formaldehyde-free MDF, wheatboard, or formaldehyde-free plywood. Additionally, look for FSC- or SFI-certified solid woods, or cabinets that use recycled or reclaimed woods.

installing a toilet

There are two basic types of toilets: two-piece units, which have a base and a tank, and single-piece units in which the tank is part of the base. The single-piece models are less complicated to install because you don't have to deal with mounting the tank. But these units are heavier and harder to move around. The two-piece units are generally less expensive.

TOOLS & MATERIALS
► Adjustable wrench
► Spirit level
► Silicone caulk & caulking gun
► New toilet ► Wax ring seal
► Plumber's putty ► Spud washer
► Washers & nuts
► Braided stainless-steel riser or chromed copper riser

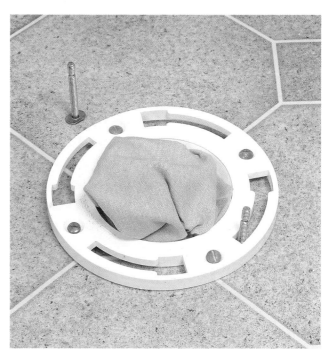

1 Begin installing a new toilet by gluing a toilet flange into the waste line. Make sure that the flange is aligned so the bolts that hold the toilet are on the sides of the flange. Screw the flange tightly to the floor. Push a rag into the hole to keep sewer gas from entering the room.

3 Lower the toilet onto the flange so the holes in the base of the toilet fall directly over the flange bolts. Gently rock the toilet from side to side and front to back until it sits firmly on the floor. Install washers over the bolts, and tighten the bolt nuts against these washers.

4 If your toilet has a separate tank, like this unit, first install a spud washer on the top of the base to act as a seal between the base and the tank. Then lower the tank into place, and fasten it to the base by tightening nuts on the tank bolts.

2 The toilet is sealed to the waste system with a wax ring mounted on a plastic cone. To install it, remove the rag and lower the ring onto the toilet flange. The cone goes directly in the flange hole, and the flange bolts push through the wax.

5 Connect the water supply line to the tank, and test the toilet by flushing it a few times. Look for leaks around the supply line, around the base, and between the tank and base. If everything is dry, finish up by applying a bead of silicone caulk where the base meets the floor.

INSTALLING A WAX-FREE GASKET

Traditional wax gaskets have worked well for years, but they have some drawbacks. They are not easy to use in temperature extremes, and they are not forgiving when you need to deal with unusual floor heights

during installation: alone, they can be too small; stacked they may be too big. Fluidmaster's new wax-free bowl gasket makes life a little easier. You can install it in any temperature without having to worry about cracked or soft, sticky wax, and it is adjustable during installation.

The gasket assembly fits inside 3-inch-diameter drainpipes (plastic, copper, or cast iron) and comes with a sleeve that fits 4-inch drainpipes, so you're ready for any situation. O-rings ensure a tight seal in the drainpipes.

Before you install the gasket assembly, insert the 3-inch-diameter gasket into the drainpipe. If it is too loose, you'll need to use the 4-inch sleeve. You will also find two O-rings, a thick one and a thin one, one of which goes at the bottom of the gasket or sleeve. Use whichever one gives you the best fit.

To install the gasket, just barely insert it into the drainpipe. Then wrap the square cardboard spacer that comes with the unit (not shown in the photo) around the gasket, and secure it at the two cut corners. Push the gasket down into the pipe until it touches the spacer or is 1 inch above the floor, whichever comes first.

Slip the supplied floor bolts into the toilet flange's mounting adjustment slots, and attach the supplied plastic retainer nuts to hold the bolts steady. Line up the holes in the toilet base with the bolts, and lower the toilet. Apply weight to the toilet to allow it to rest on the floor. The gasket will engage the toilet's horn, and the cardboard spacer will collapse and will not interfere with the gasket. Secure the toilet to the flange, and you're done.

7

exteriors

The exterior of your home calls upon so many different building components, from housewrap and termiticides to shingles and gutters, that you have many options for going green. Your home's exterior is exposed to the weather, yet it is also part of the thermal envelope. So it's crucial to pick products that are green, durable, and can be integrated into the home's structure. Life-cycle analysis will surely come into play as you weigh the pros and cons of products in light of the environmental costs of their manufacture compared with their durability and performance over their entire service lives. Whether you are choosing siding, decking, or roof shingles, carefully consider how the product will perform in three, six, and ten years—and beyond. Wood siding may seem like a green choice today because it comes from a renewable source. But over time, will the care and maintenance of that siding have a greater environmental cost than, say, using siding made of cement, even though cement may not be the greenest product to manufacture? This chapter offers you some guidance on product choices, as well as some basic how-to instruction for common building activities.

SIDING CHOICES

SIDING PROBLEMS CAN USUALLY BE FIXED BY MAKING SPOT REPAIRS—such as replacing a rotted clapboard or cutting out a cracked piece of vinyl siding. But when it comes to completely residing the house, you'll have to decide whether to use vinyl, aluminum, wood, or masonry veneer. Every material has its proponents, but it's important to remember that the siding you finally pick will change the look of your home for years to come and may require alterations in trim details that can loom as large as the residing job itself. Many people think vinyl siding looks synthetic, even when it is embossed with a simulated wood grain. But vinyl is usually the least expensive option because it is so easy to install. Aluminum siding tends to look more like painted wood clapboards, but the patter of rainfall takes on a metallic tone and a wayward baseball can leave a dent—a repair you should need to make on cars but not houses. Wood siding looks like wood, and for many homeowners holds a special appeal. But it needs regular repainting or restaining—a big job that has convinced a lot of people to switch from wood to vinyl or aluminum.

Getting to the Top

Tackling siding jobs means spending time on ladders and scaffolds, so it's worth going over some basic safety tips. For starters, you need a Type I extension ladder, rated to carry up to 250 pounds per rung. Set the ladder's bottom feet far enough out from the wall so that it won't tip backward, but not too far out—about a quarter of the ladder height is a good rule of thumb. Put pieces of wood under the feet if the ground is soft or uneven. When you're on the ladder, wear shoes or boots with heels for the best grip, and don't overreach—leaning over to the side can tip a ladder.

For more ambitious siding jobs that cover more than one story, you'll want to use scaffolding. You can rent ladder jacks that hold a scaffold plank, pump jacks that rise vertically, or pipe scaffolding equipment. Pipe systems provide the most stable work surface, but it takes time to set up the pipe framework and wooden decks. Scaffolding higher than 12 feet should be anchored to the wall for stability.

Housewraps

Building wrap, or housewrap, is an improvement on the felt paper that was once commonly installed over wood sheathing. It is designed to be a one-way material, somewhat like the fabric used on rainwear and parkas called Gore-Tex. It is woven tightly enough to prevent air infiltration, which improves energy efficiency and comfort by cutting drafts at leak-prone seams in corners and around windows and doors. But the fabric will allow interior moisture to escape, something that tar paper does not do. This is an important distinction, because if interior moisture is trapped in the wall, it can soak insulation, reducing its

thermal value and causing rot in the plywood sheathing and framing. Run wide rolls of housewrap horizontally to cover one story at a time, with edges tucked into the openings.

SCAFFOLDING

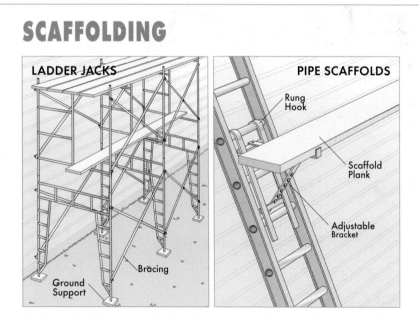

LADDER JACKS

Bracing

Ground Support

PIPE SCAFFOLDS

Rung Hook

Scaffold Plank

Adjustable Bracket

IF YOU HAVE TWO LADDERS, the most economical and versatile scaffolding is an adjustable ladder jack for each one and a scaffold plank. Scaffolding made of interconnected pipe sections can stack on each other as work proceeds.

Nonwood Siding

Though wood is your greenest choice for the building's structural frame and sheathing, it may not be the best green choice for your siding. Wood siding requires a great deal of care, often in 5- to 7-year cycles, when the siding needs to be repainted or restained and perhaps even treated with insecticides or chemicals that inhibit mold. Though wood siding can last dozens of years or longer when properly cared for, you may want to side your home with a nonwood product. A popular choice is cementitious siding, also called fiber-cement siding. It's true that the manufacture of cement siding is a carbon- and energy-intensive process, but the life span on the finished cementitious siding—a low-maintenance product—can far outweigh the environmental costs of the maintenance required for wood siding. In a life-cycle analysis, which takes into account all of the environmental costs of producing paint and wood treatments for wood siding—including the possible harvest of trees to entirely replace wood siding—cementitious siding may be the prudent green choice.

Here are some other features of cementitious siding: it never rots, even when wet; it can resist the affects of salt spray, a desirable thing for coastal installation; termites and mold don't recognize cementitious siding as food; and the fiber-cement siding products available today are largely unaffected by ultraviolet (UV) rays. To address the carbon-intensive manufacturing process, some newer lines of cementitious siding use additives of recycled fly ash to reduce the amount of Portland cement in the siding. Always look for siding that has been painted at the factory and that has a Class 1(A) fire rating and a warranty in excess of 20 years. You'll be pleased to find that this type of siding comes in various profiles and not just plain planks.

Panel Advantages

Because labor accounts for so much of the final bill in a residing job, plywood panels can be an attractive, cost-saving alternative. Typically, just two workers can panel an average-size house in about a weekend, and the skill needed is within the range of many do-it-yourselfers. Also, panels are often available in 4 x 9- and 4 x 10-foot sheets that reach from foundation to roof edge.

Many lumberyards carry one of the most popular plywood panels, called Texture 1-11. These sheets have grooves cut into the face 4, 8, or 12 inches apart to simulate separate planks. But many other styles and surface treatments are available, although not all plywood can be used for siding—only sheets rated for exterior use, assembled with special glue that can withstand the exposure.

While the panel surface will be coated with stain or paint for appearance and protection against the weather, panel edges often are not coated. They are the weak links, because layers of thin plywood laminations are exposed along the edges. If they soak up water, the panel is likely to delaminate, which can pop nails and create an array of repair problems. You can protect against this deterioration by brushing a primer coat on the edges prior to installation or by concealing the edges with trim, such as vertical corner boards. It's also important to caulk or flash seams around windows and doors and on two-story projects where one sheet rests on top of another.

SIDING MATERIALS

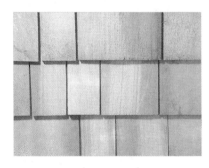

WOOD SHINGLES AND SHAKES are easy to work with because the joints don't fit tightly like cabinetwork, and the layout does not have to be precise. The main drawback is that the installation is labor-intensive, which can drive up a contractor's price. But repair is easy—split damaged shingles into small pieces for removal, and weave replacement shakes into the wall so there is no noticeable line around the repair.

SOLID WOOD SIDING can be installed vertically, horizontally, and even on an angle. Cost ranges from moderate to very expensive, depending, of course, on the wood species you use. Although wood siding will need periodic restaining or repainting, it's difficult to match its natural beauty. Stagger joints by at least one stud course to course and when you make repairs. Cut out a damaged section between studs, and conceal the new piece using paint or stain.

PANEL SIDING can be made from hardboard or plywood. It's usually less expensive than other types of siding and easy to install (at least on the first floor) because each sheet covers so much area. Some panels are made to resemble materials ranging from shingles to stucco, while others are available in a variety of finishes, including smooth surfaced, rough-sawn, and with grooves every 4 or 8 in. to resemble planks.

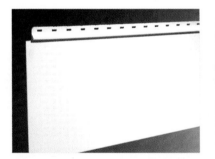

ALUMINUM SIDING is moderately expensive and somewhat difficult to install. It is a lot stiffer than vinyl, the number-one choice today, but any scratches that expose base metal through the finish are noticeable. Metal also dents, a problem that generally requires replacement instead of repair. But from a distance, aluminum looks more like painted wood clapboards than many vinyl products and, unlike wood, does not need repainting every few years.

VINYL SIDING is typically less expensive than aluminum or wood, is easy to install, and requires little to no maintenance. The trade-off can be a synthetic look and a plastic-like shine in the sun, even when the vinyl is embossed with a wood-grain finish. Vinyl siding is more likely than aluminum to fade in sunlight or crack in cold weather. But damaged vinyl can be patched; you have to unlock the interconnected pieces and make a visible lap joint where the replacement meets undamaged material.

BRICK AND STONE facing materials are both beautiful and durable, but they cost more than other siding materials, mainly because of the time and skills needed for installation. Standard sizes of bricks are easier to install than irregular stone. Arranging an attractive and functional collection of rocks borders on being an art and requires difficult cutting and shaping. But modern face stone—cast masonry that is colored and textured to look like rocks—makes the job easier.

MATERIAL OPTIONS & CORNER DESIGN

MITERED SIDING

Sheathing · Housewrap · Siding

OUTSIDE CORNER BOARDS

Housewrap · Sheathing · Siding

INSIDE CORNER BOARDS

Sheathing · Housewrap · Siding

CORNER BOARDS protect leak-prone siding joints at the corners of a house. Mitered joints look neat and elegant but aren't as durable as other options, and the technique requires laborious hand-fitting. Butted outside corner boards are easier to install—you nail them in place, then cut the siding to butt squarely against them. Also, at inside corners, you can butt clapboards or simply nail trim boards in place on flat siding.

 **PLAIN BEVEL** (clapboard) siding is used for horizontal applications. It comes in clear and knotty grades for a more rustic look. The boards are thick along the bottom and taper toward the top.

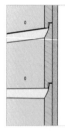 **SHIPLAP SIDING** provides the weatherproof security of a lap, and a decorative bend that looks like quarter-round molding below each seam. Overlaps can absorb movement of the house frame without opening.

 **RABBETED BEVEL** siding (Dolly Varden) is used only in horizontal installations. It is thicker than beveled siding and has a rabbeted overlap. It comes with a smooth or saw-textured face.

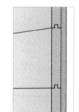 **TONGUE AND GROOVE** siding is available in a variety of patterns and sizes from 1x4 to 1x10. Some versions have a chamfer or bead along the edge to create a more finished appearance.

installing clapboard

TOOLS & MATERIALS

- ► Circular saw
- ► Drill ► Spacing jig
- ► Ladder ► 4-ft. level
- ► Hammer ► Building wrap
- ► Measuring tape ► Work gloves
- ► Clapboard ► Corner boards
- ► Nails

1 Install prefinished inside and outside corner boards to provide square edges against which the siding can butt.

2 Snap a level line for the base course, and nail a starter strip of lath along the bottom edge of the sheathing.

Plank Siding

Clapboard or plank siding is well suited to a wide range of architectural styles. Real wood offers flexibility and an attractive look—so much so that there are many imitations available in vinyl, aluminum, and other synthetics. The biggest disadvantage of wood siding is that it must be repainted about every 7 years or restained every 3 to 5 years, depending on conditions at your site.

Cedar and redwood are preferred woods for siding, but Douglas fir, larch, ponderosa pine, and local species are also used. You will pay more for cedar and redwood, but these two are naturally more resistant to decay than most other woods and are available in prime-quality grades that look good enough to protect with a clear sealer, instead of coats of paint or stain.

Like panel siding, plank siding can also be made of hardboard. It's cheaper than solid wood but less durable. You also must be careful during installation to prevent damaging moisture from getting in. Hardboard plank siding is generally available in two forms. One has splines that hook over the course below and allows blind nailing. The other is rabbeted along the bottom edge.

Level and Plumb

Though plank siding usually is installed horizontally, it can be applied vertically or diagonally as well. For a good-looking, professional-quality job, horizontal siding must be level, and vertical installations must be plumb.

The layout of the first board is critical, as this board is the base for all successive rows. Even a slight error in measurement during the early stages can lead to notice-

SPACING JIG

You can speed up the installation of clapboard or shakes and increase the overall accuracy of the project by relying on a simple siding jig. (Jigs save time on clapboards, shakes, and any siding installed in horizontal courses.) The idea is to create a moveable measuring tool that duplicates the overlap on each course. Every few rows you still should measure back to the base course, and check the current course for level. But you

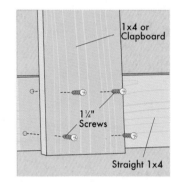

won't have to stop work and check each piece if you use a jig. To construct the jig, screw a small cleat to a rectangular piece of wood in a square T-shape. (1x4s work well.) Use a square to check alignment; then clamp the pieces and screw them together. Be sure to use screws that won't protrude through both pieces and scratch the siding underneath. To use the jig, slide the cleat section along the bottom edge of the last piece of siding you installed, and make a pencil mark, or simply set the next course in position on top of the jig. The long riser of the upside-down T will gauge the amount of exposure on the next piece and keep your clapboard installation uniform.

3 On panels with built-in laps, tack the edge of the last panel; then install the next sheet, and nail through the lapped section.

4 Periodically check the weather exposure at the ends and middle of each row as you progress, even if using a jig.

5 Joints should be staggered at every course. Place joints at random intervals spaced a minimum of 16 in. apart.

6 Cut around obstructions as you go. Always overlap boards and fittings so that rainwater will run off, not in.

able problems after several courses. To keep the installation on track, double-check horizontal installations after every fourth or fifth course—or more often if you haven't installed siding before. Don't measure from course to course, but go all the way back to the first one. After measuring the vertical spacing at the corners, snap a chalk line at the point where the top of the next piece will be installed.

If you find that boards are beginning to run out of level (or plumb on vertical installations), make several small adjustments in the next few courses instead of one big fix that stands out.

Buying Wood Shingles

Wood shingles and shakes are not just for roofs alone—they also make an attractive siding material for many house styles. Although you can buy traditional and fancy-cut wood shingles made especially for siding, it's okay to cover walls with roof shingles and shakes as well. But because weathering on siding is not as severe, you can save by using a lower grade of roof shingle.

Shakes are machine- or hand-split from blocks of wood called bolts. They're thicker than shingles and less

ESTIMATING GUIDE: SQUARE FOOTAGE COVERAGE OF FOUR BUNDLES OF SHINGLES (Single Coursed)

LENGTH	EXPOSURE								
	4"	5"	6"	7"	8"	9"	10"	11"	12"
16-inch	80	100	120	140	—	—	—	—	—
18-inch	72	90	109	127	145	—	—	—	—
24-inch	—	—	80	93	106	120	133	146	—

uniform along the exposed edges, but they last longer. Wood shingles are sawed smooth. Both types come from woods like western red cedar and redwood, and are available with a fire-retardant treatment. It's wise to allow an extra 10 percent for waste.

Choosing an Exposure

The amount of the shingle surface exposed to the weather is called the exposure. Manufacturers should specify the allowable exposure, since it varies depending on the material. But as a general guideline, calculate the maximum exposure by subtracting $\frac{1}{2}$ inch from half the overall length of the shingle. You can reduce the exposure for looks and greater weather protection, but remember that smaller exposures use more shingles. A typical exposure requires about four bundles of shingles per 100 square feet of wall area.

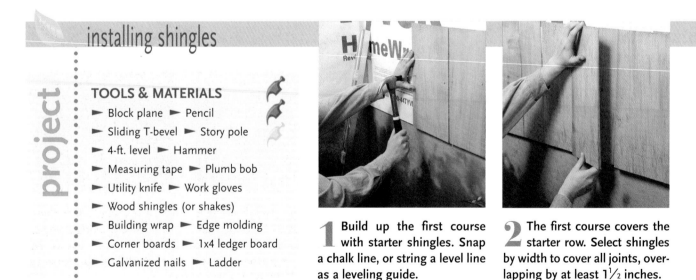

project

installing shingles

TOOLS & MATERIALS
- ► Block plane ► Pencil
- ► Sliding T-bevel ► Story pole
- ► 4-ft. level ► Hammer
- ► Measuring tape ► Plumb bob
- ► Utility knife ► Work gloves
- ► Wood shingles (or shakes)
- ► Building wrap ► Edge molding
- ► Corner boards ► 1x4 ledger board
- ► Galvanized nails ► Ladder

1 Build up the first course with starter shingles. Snap a chalk line, or string a level line as a leveling guide.

2 The first course covers the starter row. Select shingles by width to cover all joints, overlapping by at least $1\frac{1}{2}$ inches.

SHINGLE CORNERS OPTIONS

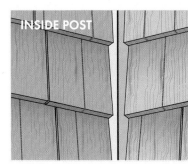
INSIDE POST

OUTSIDE CORNER BOARDS

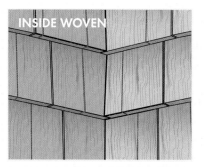
INSIDE WOVEN

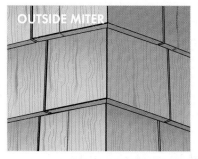
OUTSIDE WOVEN

OUTSIDE MITER

AT CORNERS, you can butt shingles together, or weave them against trim. Mitering looks good, but it's time consuming and doesn't weather well. Woven corners offer better protection but require cutting and fitting. Butted corners offer the most protection.

SHINGLE DESIGN OPTIONS

RANDOM STRAIGHT

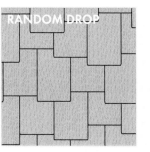
RANDOM DROP

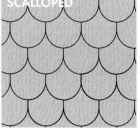
SCALLOPED

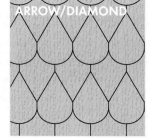
ARROW/DIAMOND

3 Mark the weather exposure at the middle and ends of each finished course; then snap a chalk line to guide your row.

4 To keep the courses level and make the installation easier, install a temporary guide board leveled across the wall.

5 Drive galvanized nails about ¾ in. from shingle edges and 1 in. above weather exposure. Space shingles ⅛ to ¼ in. apart.

6 Use a hand block plane to dress shingle edges for fit. Stagger seams so they don't line up course to course.

Rainwater Capture

Rainwater is free, and it makes a lot of sense to capture and reuse it (especially in arid areas), for drinking, washing, or landscaping. Even in geographic regions where the water supply isn't a problem, rainwater can be captured and stored for watering lawns and trees, which can drink up thousands of gallons each year and run up your bills.

The amount of water you can collect might surprise you. If you receive just 1 inch of rainfall and have a 2,000-square-foot roof, you will collect over 1,200 gallons of water. That water can be "passively" captured or "actively" captured. Passive systems simply catch the rooftop water and pipe it to some place for immediate use, such as a garden or lawn. Active systems capture, store, and filter the water for further use. For active systems, you will need an in-tank electric pump to move the water into your plumbing system. There are a number of rainwater harvest companies that offer capture-and-storage options for both aboveground and below-ground storage. Search "rainwater harvest" on the Internet for options near your home.

If the water is going to be made potable, it can be filtered while still in the storage tank, or it can be filtered on a whole-house basis at the source pipe, or even at point of use. In any case, special attention must be paid to straining out sediment, as that is often a feature of captured rainwater that has run across various outdoor surfaces. Note that if you plan to capture rooftop rainwater a metal roof is ideal. Traditional shingle roofs can contain petroleum residue that may end up in your water. If you have an asphalt shingle roof, have the runoff tested before you drink it.

As you have probably determined by now, installation of an active rainwater harvesting system is a job for specialty contractors. However, at little or no cost, you can easily set up rudimentary passive systems that capture rainwater from gutters and downspouts for landscaping.

Flat Roofs

Flat roofs look good on modern houses in architecture magazines, but they have problems. They would be great in a climate where it rarely rained. And some houses just don't work with a steep gable or Prairie-style hip roof, so they're stuck with a water-collecting top, which is bound to need repairs.

Old-style flat roofs were built up from as many as five layers of asphalt felt paper, each one sandwiched between beds of molten tar, applied with the kind of labor-intensive steps builders don't have the time for today. But if you have an old built-up roof, don't be too eager to tear it off. First, removal of so much heavy material is a major project. Second, if the roof was applied over a solid frame and covered with gravel (called ballast) to keep it flat and shielded from sunlight, the surface could last 40 years or more. Third, most of these flat roofs just don't spring a leak somewhere in the middle of the interlaced layers, where it is difficult to make a long-lasting repair. They normally open up along the edges at seams protected by metal flashing, which are easier to fix.

Fixing Edge Leaks

Along the edge of a flat roof, water enters where metal flashing is raised. Hairline breaks can be sealed with a liberal coat of roof cement and reinforcing fabric. Larger and longer openings need to be reset. After cleaning out any debris, trowel as much tar as you can fit under the raised edge and renail the flashing to the roof. Add a coat of tar on top of the metal and over the new nails, extending it past the flashing onto the roof a few inches. Then embed in the tar a layer of fiberglass roofing tape, and add a final, top coat of tar.

Repairing Newer Flat Roofs

With modern coatings such as modified bitumen, bubbles, punctures, and other openings are easier to fix—with one caution. The rubbery sheets of these roofs are not joined to each other with tar. They are fused by heating the material until it begins to melt, making it easy to add a waterproof cover. The old section can be cleaned, scarified, and then heated to fuse with a patch piece. But because of fire danger, this is best done by a professional roofer.

Permeable Pavers

Impermeable concrete and asphalt do not absorb rainwater runoff or snowmelt, nor do they let it pass through to the soil beneath. So instead of seeping into the ground, the runoff water ends up cascading down the street and directly into rivers, lakes, and aquifers. When that happens, the runoff water is not subjected to the natural purification process offered by common soil. Indeed, water that seeps through soil—even just 4 feet of soil—is naturally cleansed by microbes and straining action. When it is not strained, many of the toxins contained in rainwater runoff, such as fertilizer, insecticide, and petroleum products, are carried directly to the water supply.

You can help purify rainwater runoff by simply allowing it to seep through your driveway and sidewalk. This can be accomplished by avoiding traditional concrete and asphalt and using porous concrete, porous asphalt,

or—much more commonly available—permeable concrete brick pavers.

Permeable pavers are bricks that are made of concrete—sometimes they are called interlocking concrete paver blocks. They are typically installed on a bed of compacted sand. When properly installed, the pavers' shapes and installation pattern create a minimum ¼-inch gap between each block to allow water to pass through. The pavers can also be made of permeable concrete for optimum drainage. Permeable concrete allows water to flow through the block, kind of like a porous filter. Please note that some pavers are available that create gaps between the paver blocks that are too small to be considered permeable. If the gaps are smaller than ¼ inch, or if the pavers are not made of permeable concrete, you do not have a permeable paver surface.

The Interlocking Concrete Pavement Institute (Icpi.org) maintains a Web site that has a remarkable array of excellent resources, installation tips, material sources, and Web-based videos that will teach you everything you could possibly need to know about concrete pavers.

Green Roofing

On a hot, sunny day, put a piece of black cloth on the ground next to a piece of white cloth, and the black cloth will get hotter. Put some wood battens under either piece of cloth, and the air flowing beneath the cloth will cool it down. That's nearly all the building science you need to know about roof temperatures and green roofing.

Why all the fuss about roof temperatures? A hot roof means a hot house and more money spent on cooling the house. EPA figures show that $40 billion is spent each year in the United States to cool buildings. But there is more to the story than your utility bills. Hot roofs actually drive up the amount of pollution created when electricity is generated to power those air-conditioning units. Because 90 percent of the electric energy in the United States is generated by fossil fuels, hot roofs contribute directly to unnecessary pollution.

Fortunately, the color of your roof has a lot to do with the amount of heat if generates. A roof with black shingles reflects back just 5 percent of the sun's heat. A roof with gray shingles, however, reflects back about 20 percent of the sun's heat, and white shingles reflect around 25 percent. As a result, black roofs get as much as 9°F hotter than white roofs, and if the shingles have low solar emittance, the shingles won't radiate that heat back out to the air; instead, the heat gets transferred into the building. The EPA has found that just changing the color of a roof can reduce cooling costs by 10 to 30 percent.

These tiles replicate the look of thick, hand-split cedar shakes, but they are made of recycled EPDM rubber and TPO plastic, the same type of plastic used in car bumpers.

■ **Cool Roofs Shouldn't Be Confused with Green Roofs.** Green roofs usually refer to the process of installing living plants on the rooftop to absorb rain and keep the building cool, an entirely viable technology, especially for flat roofs. But let's take a closer look at cool roofs.

■ **Labels to Look for.** A number of clever roofing manufacturers have come up with lighter-colored shingles and shingle-surface treatments that have the advanced ability to reflect sunlight and emit heat. These shingles are composed of highly reflective granules (with higher solar reflectance) that are also effective at releasing absorbed heat (higher solar emittance). Yet the shingles don't look too light.

■ **Look for Energy Star Ratings on the Shingles.** Energy Star accepts a roofing material that has an "initial" (upon installation) solar reflectance greater than or equal to 0.25, meaning that 25 percent of the sun's heat is reflected. Or look for the Cool Roof Rating Council (CRRC) approval on your roofing products. CRRC tests roofing material and rates the solar reflectance and solar emittance to create a CRRC rating of between 0 and 1. The higher the number, the better.

■ **Check the Solar Reflectance Index.** The Solar Reflectance Index (SRI) is expressed as a number from 0 to 100. The SRI uses solar reflectance and thermal emittance, as defined by the American Society for Testing and Materials (ASTM), a national standards setting agency. For SRI, the higher the number, the better. Any roofing product labeled by CRRC or Energy Star is a safe bet for a cool roof.

Metal Roofs. The use of metal roofs opens up a broad opportunity to treat the metal with factory-applied reflective paints that bring strong, enduring reflectivity and high cool-roof ratings to these materials. In fact, Oak Ridge National Laboratory determined that a reflective metal roof can save homeowners up to 40 percent of summer cooling costs. If you use the Energy Star product listing to research cool-roof options, you'll find that the overwhelming majority of Energy Star roofs are metal roofs. Plus, metal roofs are 100 percent recyclable.

Tile Roofs. Tile roofs are cooled by using age-old technology: lighter-colored tiles and passive airflow beneath the roofing surface. Today's tile roofs are generations beyond natural clay tiles. New tiles are made of composite materials, plastic, rubber, concrete, and fiber cement. These materials are sometimes installed over barrier-and-batten systems that create airflow under the tiles. These roofs have long warranties (50 years is common) and good fire and wind ratings. But they are costly to install and some require beefed-up rafters to support the extra weight.

Synthetic Slate. With synthetic slate, roofing is typically made of recycled industrial rubber and plastic that is injection molded in the shape of a slate tile. The tiles can also replicate the look of thick, hand-split cedar shakes. These are made of recycled EPDM rubber and TPO plastic.

TOP RIGHT Though this roof looks like slate, it is actually a rubber slate tile that is made of recycled industrial rubber and plastic. The tiles are injection molded, and the result is an environmentally friendly, lightweight alternative to slate.

RIGHT Today's new roof tiles are made of composite materials, plastic, rubber, concrete, and fiber cement. These tiles are installed with screws on a barrier-and-batten system that creates airflow under the tiles. These roofs have long warranties and good fire and wind ratings.

Choosing Shingles

Four out of five residential roofs are made of asphalt shingles or continuous sheets of asphalt called roll roofing, which is usually reserved for low-slope roofs not visible from the ground.

You may be asked to chose between regular asphalt shingles or fiberglass, with a bottom mat of fiberglass mesh that is lighter, stronger, and longer-lasting than asphalt. Fiberglass-mat shingles are a good choice for reroofing jobs, as they reduce the load carried by the rafters without giving up durability. About 80 percent of all shingles sold for new homes and reroofing are the fiberglass-mat variety, including almost all the heavyweight, overlay-type shingles.

Shingle Weight

Shingle weight is an important factor on both new roofs and on reroofing jobs because heavier shingles last longer, carry a longer warranty, and generally offer a better fire rating. Of course, they are more expensive than lighter shingles. The weight rating (240 pounds for a standard shingle) denotes the total weight of a square of shingles (enough to cover 100 square feet of roof).

The heavyweight shingles are those over the 240-pound rating—generally 300 pounds per square or more. Individual shingles in this category often are configured in layers—like a shingle on a shingle—that simulate the dense pattern of slate or wood shakes. The heavyweights are a good choice for new homes and additions, but a questionable choice for reroofing jobs, where the weight can overload the roof structure.

Color

You don't often see a bright green, blue, or red roof—even though asphalt shingles are available with granules in those colors—because they can become a bit oppressive after a few seasons. Off-white or light gray shingles make a house look larger, but will mar more easily than dark shingles and show wear sooner—even though they will not wear out any faster than dark shingles. Light colors on the roof can reflect more sunlight than dark, which will keep the house cooler in summer and reduce air-conditioning costs. If gaining heat is more important, a dark shingle would be the most energy-efficient choice.

TOOLS & MATERIALS
► Ladder or scaffolding
► Chalk-line box ► Hammer
► Shears ► Utility knife
► Work gloves
► Metal drip edge
► Shingles
► Roofing nails
► Roofing felt
► Roof cement

3 Roll roofing felt on top of the decking, nailing it every 10 to 12 in., 3 in. from the edge. Overlap rows by several inches.

7 To trim shingles in valleys and other areas, use shears or a utility knife. This is a closed valley with interwoven shingles.

1 Roofers have different techniques, but all start with a sound plywood roof deck where nailheads are driven flush.

2 Nail on a metal drip edge at the edge of the eaves with roofing nails. This protects the fascia boards from rot.

4 For the starter course, snap a chalk line and lay the shingles with the tabs pointing up. Put one nail through each tab.

5 The first course covers the starter course with the tabs pointing down. Each shingle should have at least four nails.

6 Start each new course at a 6-in. offset to stagger the seams in adjacent courses in a water-shedding layout.

8 To shingle around a vent stack, trim to overlap only the upper half of the vent collar, and seal underneath with roof cement.

9 To shingle the ridge, cut single, slightly tapered tabs from whole shingles and wrap them across the ridge, nailing on both sides.

10 To save time, let full shingles extend past the roof overhang, and trim all of them at once using shears.

INSTALLING ASPHALT SHINGLES

WHAT YOU'LL NEED. You need only basic tools to install asphalt shingles. You can cut them with shears or a utility knife, and nail them in place with a standard hammer. For reroofing jobs, a pry bar and flat shovel are handy for removing old shingles.

TYPES OF SHINGLES. Dimensional shingles (bottom) are thicker than regular flat-tab shingles (top) and are not uniform in color, which produces a three-dimensional look similar to slate. Heavier shingles also last longer and have better fire ratings.

METAL EDGING

IN REGIONS WITH A LOT OF SNOW, consider this variation on standing-seam roofs. Instead of covering the entire surface, only the first few courses of shingles along the eaves are clad in metal. The idea is to encourage snow to slide off the roof instead of building up in ice dams at the roof overhangs. The bargain-basement version of this installation is simply a long roll of sheet metal (aluminum flashing material) rolled onto the roof and tucked under a course of shingles. The drawback is that the sheet metal has to be face-nailed, which creates leak-prone holes.

Metal Roofing

The look of corrugated metal covering a Quonset hut at an army barracks is still most people's idea of a metal roof, and few would consider that suitable for their home. Recent advances in sheet metal, however, have turned the metal roof into an attractive option. Check Energy Star ratings for energy-efficient roofing systems.

It costs as much as three times more than composite shingles but can last up to 50 years with almost no maintenance—a longevity surpassed only by slate and tile. Unlike the old galvanized tin roofs, metal roofing today is made of steel with a coating of aluminum or a durable polymer.

Metal Roof Options

Many different profiles are available, but simple standing-seam metal roofing, where overlapping ridges run parallel to the eaves, is the most appropriate for older homes that might have had a tin roof at one time. Standing-seam panels, being a light material (just one pound per square foot), may even be used over three layers of composition shingles (local building codes permitting). For roofs that have irregularities, narrow, textured, and dull-finish panels work best.

Metal roofing (even individual shingles) can also cover low-pitched roofs that have a slope of at least 3-in-12; some metal roof systems can handle slopes as slight as $\frac{1}{4}$-in-12 (usually a job for built-up roofing). The installation process involves laying 12- to 16 $\frac{1}{2}$-inch-wide panels and joining them at the seams, wall flashing, valleys, and ridges. The panels are precut to the exact length ordered, up to 40 feet long—for this reason, horizontal seams are unlikely on most homes. Metal roofing can be applied over plywood decking with an underlayment of 30-pound felt.

Laying and joining the panels is not difficult, but handling eaves edges, rakes, and ridges can be. Most metal roofing manufacturers will provide an installation guide.

Care should also be taken not to walk on the metal roof, as dents, scratches, and depressions can easily occur. Be sure to replace all copper, lead, and other metal roof fittings, which might corrode the metal panels. Metal roofs should also be grounded with lightening rods in the event of an electrical storm.

Dealing with Termites

If termites are determined to consume your home as though it were tasty food served up in an endless free buffet, the greenest thing to do, unfortunately, is to kill the bugs. The trick is to contain the termiticide you use so that it doesn't get into nearby water systems and use termiticides that have the smallest impact on your environment.

If you are building an addition that will require a foundation, you can use preconstruction treatments (called pretreats) that apply termiticide to the soil. As the termites crawl up through the soil, they pick up the termiticide and are poisoned. Another common practice for frustrating termites is to use physical barriers, like specially shaped metal shields that are installed at points of entry to your home, such as where the wood sill bears on a pillar or the top of a foundation wall. These physical blocks keep termites out and also force termites to make mud tunnels in the open where you can easily detect them.

Bait the Bugs. Two other approaches to defeating termites is to use baits that detect the presence of termites, so that a pest control operator can come in and selectively use a poison. But an increasingly common practice is to use wood throughout the house that has been treated at the factory with a termiticide and fungicide. It used to be that pressure-treated lumber was used near the foundation or where wood contacted the ground, but that left the rest of the wood used to frame and sheathe the house untreated. Now you can purchase pretreated dimension framing lumber that can be used anywhere, including your attic rafters.

Pick Your Poison. When choosing a poison for killing termites, it's green to pick one that is a "natural" poison. That is, a chemical that occurs in nature and poisons the insects but that does not have metabolic pathways that can poison humans. Opt for such insecticides as pyrethroids, which repel termites, or use insecticides that contain borate. Though borate has long been known to kill termites, it is water soluble and washed away in the rain. A major problem with any termiticide is that it gets carried by rain runoff into aquifers, rivers, and lakes. Recently, however, formulations of borate have shown good resistance to water, so borate is an effective choice. What's more, borate can kill not only termites but other wood-destroying organisms, like fungi. If you can, avoid synthetic neurotoxins, imidacloprid, and fipronil.

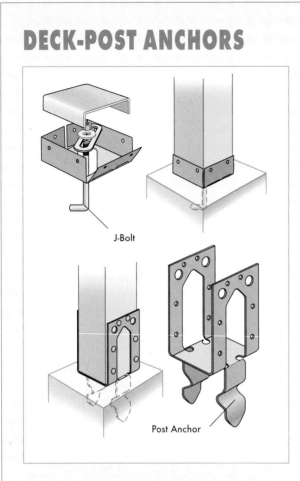

DECK-POST ANCHORS

J-Bolt

Post Anchor

J-BOLTS AND POST ANCHORS are attached to the concrete footing, and the anchor bracing is nailed or screwed to the post. Soak post ends in preservative before attaching.

Deck Framing

House framing can be cratered with misguided hammer blows and studded with bent nails because you won't see the mistakes under siding and drywall. But you will on a deck. Because it is out in the open, you want framing to have both strength and a finish-quality appearance. So consider some of the following tips on both form and function.

Posts on Piers

Keep the support system neat by limiting concrete piers to a couple of inches aboveground—even if the ground is uneven—and make a uniform transition to wood by topping the piers with galvanized post anchors. Often, one end has a pin that embeds in the concrete while it's still wet, and the other has a U-shaped bracket that secures the post.

There are many post-anchor varieties—some that hold 4x6s or 8x8s if your deck needs the support, even some with a threaded rod and nut so you can adjust deck height where a section settles slightly out of level. Although this hardware keeps posts out of the dirt, soak the end grain with wood preservative.

This combination of piers and posts is durable and the easiest way to take up uneven slack between ground and deck. You don't have to establish precise levels and cut posts to exact size ahead of time. You can let them run long and trim to final length when the girder is placed. Posts are more practical than high, aboveground concrete piers and are better-looking, too. While a deck seems perched on top of high concrete piers, posts reaching to grade level seem to anchor it to the site.

installing girders

TOOLS & MATERIALS
- ► Circular saw
- ► C-clamps
- ► 4-ft. level
- ► Hammer
- ► Work gloves
- ► ½-in. pressure-treated plywood
- ► Pressure-treated 2x4s and 2x10s
- ► 3-in. galvanized nails
- ► Wood shims

1 Sight a 2x10 beam for crowning or any arching along the length of the wood. Install the beam with the crown side up, not down, to compensate for stress loads.

2 Double up support beams and increase their width to 3½ in. by adding ½-in. pressure-treated plywood between beams. Beams will sit flush on top of posts.

Extended Posts

If you are taking the time to set posts that rise from the ground to a girder, you may want to get more for your efforts with longer posts that extend past the girder to anchor the railing, too.

In a typical deck plan, posts reach up to a pair of spiked-together 2x10s or 2x12s that carry the joists and decking above. With minor span adjustments (checking your plan with the local building department), you can make way for the post extensions by assembling the girder in two parts—one on each side of the posts, bolted in position. Figure the approximate post height you need to reach the deck floor, plus another 3 feet or so for railing.

This elegant detail provides many options and makes finishing railings easy because there are solid vertical supports in place every few feet along the deck edge before you start adding railings and balusters. And no nailed-on, screwed-on, or even bolted-on railing system applied to the finished deck platform can provide the security of a row of full-height, solid 4x4s.

Dressing Posts

On low decks where supports are recessed, the scruffiest lumber will do as long as it's solid. But on some decks, post supports loom large from the yard. You don't gain anything structurally with a solid 4x4 versus two 2x4s spiked together, but you won't see a seam between boards or nailheads or discolored dings where you swung the hammer and missed.

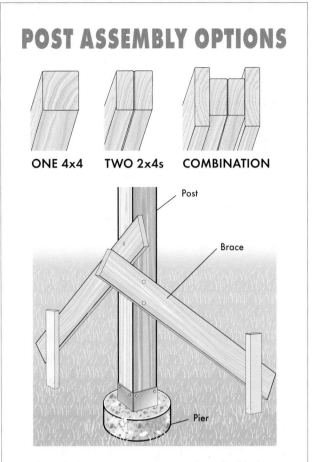

POST ASSEMBLY OPTIONS

ONE 4x4 **TWO 2x4s** **COMBINATION**

Post

Brace

Pier

One 4x4 post is easier to erect than doubled 2x4s, which require assembly and may not cost less in the long run. Using larger posts may save you money, but they should be through-bolted to secure them. Two angle braces will hold each post plumb in both directions.

3 Nail beams together using 3-in. galvanized nails. Set nails 16 in. apart in two separate rows. Make sure both beams are crowned upward and nailed flush.

4 To temporarily position the girder, face-nail a 2x4 to the back of the post, extending up several inches. When you set the girder in place, it will rest against the extended 2x4.

5 To keep the girder from falling while you work on the installation, clamp the face to the 2x4 brace. Another option is to install two braces and set the girder between them.

6 Place a level on top of the beam, and use wood shims on posts to make the beam level. Also, shim any gaps in post-beam joints as needed.

DECK LUMBER OPTIONS

2x4s

2x4s will give a deck a
busy look, due to their
relatively thin widths. If
not pressure-treated,
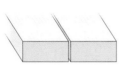
2x4s must be coated with a preservative; they
will also need periodic maintenance. Soak 2x4
ends in preservative before nailing. When you
can, check wood for crowns, cups, and warps
before purchasing.

2x6s

2x6s are a bet-
ter decking
option than
2x4s, as they

require less time to install. These boards can also
be used as joists if the span is short, but check first
with building codes. Use two nails over each joist
to minimize cupping. 2x6s are heavier than 2x4s;
an extra set of hands will help for long boards.

1x4s, ⁵⁄₄x4s, and ⁵⁄₄x6s

1x4s, ⁵⁄₄x4s, and
⁵⁄₄x6s are some of
the more popular
choices for deck-
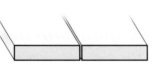
ing. Joists may have to be on 12-inch centers,
depending on wood species and grade. This
decking size is sold in many different grades and
different species. Pressure-treated, cedar, and redwood are the most popular.

Tongue-and-Groove

Tongue-and-
groove boards fit
into each other
for a tight seam.
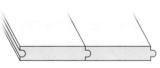
Used mostly on porches with a roof, tongue-and-
groove decks should be pitched to shed water
and waterproofed against the elements to prevent swelling. They are not recommended for use
on open decks where the wood will be exposed
to the elements.

Also, solid posts can be dressed up with nice touches
of carpentry that once were used on exposed beams in
early colonial houses. To make tree-size timbers appear
more finished and graceful, reduce the hard edges with a
chamfer—a 45-degree slice across the corner. Run it
across most of the timber length, and taper it away near
the top and bottom to make the beam square-edged near,
the joints.

Another option is to clad the wood posts with one-by
facing. You can use quality wood to match your siding or
choose a rustic, rough-sawn grade for a contrasting look.
Clad 4x4 posts with 1x6 boards and 6x6 posts with 1x8s.

Choosing Joists

Most deck designs call for 2x8 or 2x10 joists set 16 inches
on center. The length of a joist's span from ledger board
to beam also depends on the species of wood and the
width of the joist. Naturally, thicker boards can span
longer distances and support greater loads than thinner
boards. To find out what the allowable measurement
should be between joists and how far they can span, consult a span table—your local building department should
have them available for your reference.

Wood and Fastener Options

Your deck's joists, beams, and ledger should be made
from pressure-treated wood to stand up to the elements,
particularly any timbers near the ground. But you can also
use standard construction grades if you first coat them
with wood preservative. To build a deck economically
without sacrificing either strength or durability, you might
want to consider using pressure-treated wood for the
joists, ledger, and beams, as these parts of the deck generally are out of sight.

For maximum strength (and to satisfy most local building codes), joists are attached to supporting timbers with
metal brackets called stirrups or joist hangers. These hangers will support more weight than nails can and reduce the
chance of wood splitting at joints. Joists are often doubled
up for extra support or to accommodate designs where
surface boards require increased nailing support. But there
are double-wide hangers to cover those situations—and
hardware designed to reinforce just about every structural
connection you can make on a deck. Even where hardware
isn't required by code, you may find that bridging joints
with metal brackets makes construction easier.

project

J oist hangers need to be installed (some codes require them) with the proper nailing schedule or their holding ability will be compromised. So always check the manufacturer's recommendations and adhere to them, right down to the type of nail required.

TOOLS & MATERIALS
► Joist template ► Combination square
► Hammer ► Marker Joist hangers
► Galvanized nails

1 Make a template to fit just below the flashing; then mark reference lines for plumb and horizontal placement.

2 Size hangers correctly for joists and ledger, and set them plumb to avoid twisted or uneven joists.

3 Use nailing clips stamped into the hanger for position; use galvanized common nails to install it in place.

4 With the hanger fastened to the ledger, set the joist, and nail it in place. Short nails won't protrude.

CANTILEVERS

Cantilevering beams or joists too far can lead to "deflection" (bending), and even outright failure. As a rule of thumb, never cantilever a framing member more than a third of its overall length. For instance, a 6-foot joist should not be cantilevered more than 2 feet.

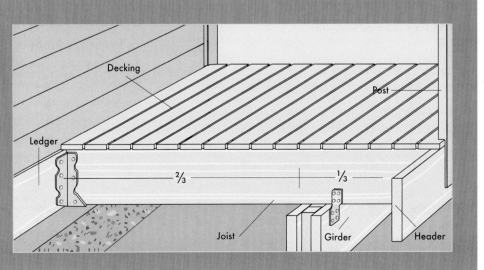

Decking

Post

Ledger

²⁄₃   ¹⁄₃

Joist   Girder   Header

HOUSE-MOUNTED LEDGERS

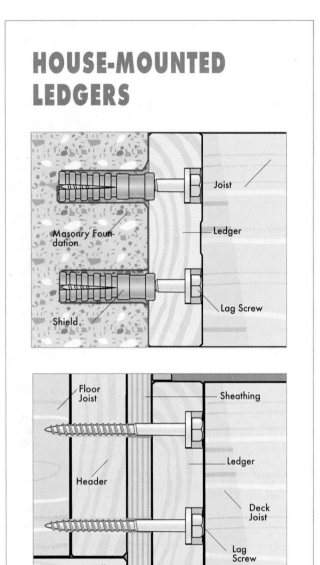

When attaching ledger boards to masonry, predrill the ledger, and use the holes as guides for the masonry holes. Place the board onto the masonry wall; level it; and use a marker to indicate drill points. Then drill and insert shields or anchors. Don't confuse masonry with stucco; ledgers on stucco must be bolted into the house's frame. On other exteriors, strip siding to expose the sheathing; bolt the ledger into the frame. To preserve this crucial timber, use pressure-treated wood and cover the top edge with flashing.

Hanging Joists

One good way to hang joists is to first build the deck's outer perimeter, with outside joists nailed to a belt (also called a header) at the outside of the deck and to a ledger board at the house. Pros who can easily envision the complete layout ahead of time can stack up the components and mark them prior to installation. But for many do-it-yourselfers, it's easier to take one step at a time: build the basic post-and-girder support system, box in the deck space, and then fill in that frame with joists.

As mentioned, most deck designs call for joists on 16-inch centers. But this rule depends on the thickness of your decking material and deck design. If your deck has a herringbone design, for example, which calls for a diagonal pattern of decking boards, the joists may have to be on 12-inch centers. Your plans will only be approved by a building inspector if they specify the placement and thickness of joists.

After you've marked the modular layout of the deck joists on the beam and ledger, check to make sure your frame is square overall by measuring the diagonals from inside corner to inside corner. If the deck is square, the measurements will be equal. You can clamp or temporarily tack the outermost joists in position to complete the deck perimeter. But don't fix them permanently in place until the perimeter is square.

To install the joist hangers, slip one of the brackets around a short section of joist, and set the sample assembly in position. The trick is to position the bracket so that the top of the joist it holds will be flush with the adjacent ledger. If it's not flush, the deck boards—even beefy 2x4s and 2x6s—will ride up and down over their supports. Once you are sure of where the bracket should be, you can use the position of the sample to fix all the brackets in place and attach the joists.

Nail the decking in place. Be sure to leave a space between each board for drainage. Pros let the decking run long at the edges and then trim them all at once using a circular saw.

Nonwood Decking

Nonwood decking has captured a huge market share because it is largely maintenance free; it can be made to look like wood; and it increasingly contains higher and higher percentages of recycled materials. The alternatives to nonwood decking are naturally durable wood products like tropical wood, cedar, and locust, or chemically treated southern yellow pine (ACZA and ACQ), which has its own environmental costs, even in the latest chemical configurations.

A very viable and durable decking product, nonwood decking is usually a composite of plastic resins, wood fiber, and fiberglass, some of which can be from recycled sources. The percent of recycled material in the decking has emerged as the indicator of how green it is, and many decking products that are available today are made with 100 percent recycled products. Frankly, any nonwood decking—made with recycled components or not—has life-cycle benefits because you will not find yourself finishing and replacing the decking every few years. But you can help drive the market for products with recycled components by asking for them where you buy your decking.

Vinyl decking is also available, but it's not very green. The manufacture of vinyl in not an environmentally friendly process, even if the resulting product has a long life cycle. So your best green decking choice is plastic that has a high percentage of recycled content.

This list of manufacturers and associations is meant to be a general guide to additional industry and product-related sources. It is not intended as a listing of products and manufacturers represented by the photographs in this book.

BuildingGreen, Inc.
802-257-7300
www.buildinggreen.com
An independent company that provides accurate, unbiased, and timely information about green design and products.

California Air Resources Board (CARB)
800-242-4450
www.arb.ca.gov
CARB is the California state agency that regulates air quality. Its policies often have national implications.

Carpet and Rug Institute/Green Label
706-278-3176
www.carpet-rug.org
CRI performs independent testing of carpets and rugs to check for chemical emissions.

The Cool Roof Rating Council (CRRC)
866-465-2523
www.coolroofs.org
An independent organization that rates roofing products for their ability to reflect or emit heat.

Department of Energy (DOE)
800-342-5363
www.doe.gov
Promotes America's energy security through reliable, clean, and affordable energy. DOE's website has an expansive offering of free material focused on energy consumption and energy efficiency.

US DOE Energy Efficiency and Renewable Energy (EERE)
877-337-3463
www.eere.energy.gov
Offers authoritative information on energy efficiency and renewable energy.

EarthCraft
404-604-3636
www.earthcrafthouse.com
A residential building guideline, originally focused on homes in the Atlanta region, that serves as a national model for well-built green homes.

Environmental Home Center
206-682-7332
www.environmentalhomecenter.com
A catalog source for green building products.

Environmental Protection Agency (EPA)
www.epa.gov
The website provides a wealth of free information, including lists and sources of products that are in compliance with EPA's various programs.

Forest Stewardship Council (FSC)
202-342-0413
www.fsc.org
An international not-for-profit membership-based organization created to reward good forest management.

Green Building Blocks
www.greenbuildingblocks.com
An online resource for green design and product information.

Green Building Supply
800-405-0222
www.greenbuildingsupply.com
A catalog source for green building products.

Greenguard
800-427-9681
www.greenguard.org
Certifies low-emitting products for indoor air quality.

Green Seal
202-872-6400
www.greenseal.org
Provides environmental testing and certification for arange of materials.

National Association of Home Builders
202-266-8200
www.nahb.org
A national trade association for home builders. Developed the National Green Building Standard.

National Fenestration Rating Council (NFRC)
301-589-1776
www.nfrc.org
An industry group that provides information about window performance.

Oak Ridge National Laboratories
865-574-4160
www.ornl.gov
A science and technology laboratory managed for the DOE.

Southface
404-872-3549
www.southface.org
Promotes sustainable homes through research and and technical assistance.

Sustainable Forest Initiative (SFI)
703-875-9500
www.sfiprogram.org
Conducts site visits and chain-of-custody audits to ensure wood is harvested in an earth-friendly manner.

U.S. Green Building Council
800-795-1747
www.USGBC.org
This organization created and oversees the LEED standard for homes and commercial buildings.

GLOSSARY

Air barrier A physical layer of material designed to restrict air movement through the walls of a building envelope.

Air handler A fan that supplies conditioned air (typically makeup air) to an interior room.

Allergen A substance capable of causing an allergic reaction because of an individual's sensitivity to that substance.

Allergic rhinitis Inflammation of the mucous membranes in the nose that is caused by an allergic reaction.

Antimicrobial An agent that kills microbial growth.

Backsplash The finish material that covers the wall behind a countertop. The backsplash can be attached to the countertop or separate from it.

Base cabinet A cabinet that rests on the floor and supports a countertop.

Bearing wall A wall that supports the structure above it. Joists rest on the top plate of a bearing wall. See *Joist*.

Bio-based product Any product that is made of biological products, especially renewable products, with origins in agricultural and forestry.

Building codes The legal standards and methods that must be followed during any construction project.

Building envelope Elements of the building, including all external building materials, windows, and walls, that enclose the internal space.

Caulking Any one of a number of compounds used to fill cracks and seams.

Chalk line A device used to mark a straight line on a surface. Stretch the chalk-covered cord taut just above the surface. Pull the cord up in the center and release to leave a chalk mark on the surface.

Chair rail A decorative molding midway between the floor and ceiling. Traditionally, chair rails protected walls from damage from chairs.

Circuit The electrical path that connects one or more outlets (receptacles) and/or lighting fixtures to a single circuit breaker or fuse.

Circuit breaker A device that closes an electrical circuit when demand exceeds safe limits.

Conditioned air Air that has been heated, cooled, humidified, or dehumidified to maintain an interior space within the "comfort zone." (Sometimes referred to as "tempered" air.)

Coped joint Two pieces of molding that are joined by cutting the end of one with a coping saw to fit over the contours of the other.

Copper tubing Seamless tubing that is 99.9 percent copper.

Countertop The work surface of a counter, island, or peninsula, usually 36 inches high. Common countertop materials include plastic laminate, ceramic tile, slate, and solid surfacing.

Cove lights Lights that reflect upward, sometimes located on top of wall cabinets.

Crown molding A decorative molding usually installed where the wall and ceiling meet.

Drywall Sheets of gypsum sandwiched between backing paper and a smooth-finish front surface paper. Also called wallboard and, improperly, Sheetrock (a trade name).

Ductwork Sheet-metal passages that carry heated or cooled air, or exhaust air in a ventilation system.

Exhaust fans A fan used in a ventilation system that pulls air from a kitchen.

Exhaust ventilation Mechanical removal of air from a portion of a building— for example, from a piece of equipment, room, or general area.

Floating floor A floor material that is glued together on it's tongue-and-groove edges but is not attached to the subfloor.

Fluorescent lights A type of light containing a phosphor that attracts ultraviolet light and then converts it into visible light.

Frameless cabinets European-style cabinets without a face frame.

Framing The skeleton structure of the studs and joists that support walls, ceilings, and floors. See Joist; Stud.

Fungi Any of a group of parasitic lower plants that lack chlorophyll, including molds and mildews.

Furring Strips of wood attached to a wall to provide support and attachment points for a covering such as hardboard paneling.

General lighting Light that illuminates the entire room.

GFCI Stands for ground-fault circuit interrupter. A type of electrical receptacle that reacts in a fraction of a second to an abnormal condition.

Gray water Wastewater from bathtubs, showers, and washing machines; it does not contain the human waste from a toilet.

Ground-source heat pump A geothermal heating and cooling system that uses the moderating temperature of the earth to condition liquid that is contained in loops of metal or plastic that—through compression cycles— release hot or cold air into a home through air handlers.

Grout A mixture of Portland cement and water, and sometimes sand, used to fill the gaps between ceramic tiles.

Halogen lights High-tech incandescent lights that require special fixtures.

Header A horizontal structural member used to span an opening in the framing, such as for a window or door, and to transfer the structural load across the opening.

Heat pump An appliance that extracts heat from refrigerants that are typically conditioned by outside air.

HEPA High-efficiency particle accumulator (filters).

IAQ Indoor air quality.

Incandescent lights Lights that heat a tungsten filament to incandescence in order to give off light.

Island A base cabinet and countertop unit that stands independent from walls so that there is access from all four sides.

Jamb The vertical (side) and horizontal (top) pieces that cover the wall thickness in a door or window opening.

Joint compound The plaster material used to fill small holes and seams in drywall.

Joint tape Paper or synthetic mesh tape about 3 inches wide that is used to reinforce joint compound applied to the seams between drywall panels.

Joist A floor or ceiling support member that rests on the top plates of bearing walls.

Kitchen fans Fans that remove grease, moisture, smoke, and heat from the kitchen.

Laminate floors Floors whose structural core is covered with a plastic laminate wear layer.

LED lights Abbreviation for light emitting diodes, an extremely efficient way to create light that does not use mercury, as compact fluorescent lights do.

Life-cycle analysis An evaluation of the environmental aspects of a material, from raw material through disposal.

Low-voltage lights Lights that operate on 12 to 50 volts rather than the standard 120 volts.

Non-bearing wall An interior wall that provides no structural support for any portion of the house.

Particleboard A material composed of wood chips and coarse fibers bonded with adhesive into large sheets. It is commonly used as the support for countertops and for cabinet construction.

Partition wall A wall built to separate the rooms of the house—for example, a dining area from the kitchen.

Patching plaster A type of plaster mix used to fill holes and cracks prior to painting.

Plaster A paste-like material used on ceilings and walls that hardens as it dries.

PPM Parts per million.

R-value A unit of measure that expresses how resistant a substance is to the flow of heat. The higher the R-value, the better the insulation qualities.

Radiant heat transfer Radiant heat transfer occurs when there is a large difference between the temperatures of two surfaces that are exposed to each other but are not touching.

Rail A horizontal member that runs between two vertical supports, such as the rails on a cabinet or door.

Range hood A ventilator set above a cooktop or the burners of a range.

Recessed light fixtures Light fixtures that are installed into ceilings, soffits, or cabinets and are flush with the surrounding area.

SEER (Seasonal Energy Efficiency Ratio) Cooling capacity of an AC unit or a heat pump across the time span of one year, expressed as the total Btu in input divided by the watt-hours.

Semicustom cabinets Cabinets that are available in specific sizes but with a wide variety of options.

Sheetrock See *Drywall*.

Shim A thin wedge-like insert used to adjust the spacing between adjacent materials.

Shutoff valves Supply valves that control the flow of water or gas to specific fixtures or appliances.

Sliders Sliding doors are made up of large, framed glass panels. In most cases, one door slides and the other is stationary.

Skylight A roof-mounted window that allows natural light into a building.

Soffit A short wall or filler piece between the top front edge of a wall cabinet and the ceiling above it.

Solid-surface countertop A countertop material made of acrylic plastic and fine-ground synthetic particles, sometimes made to look like natural stone.

Stack effect The overall upward movement of air inside a building that results from heated air rising and escaping through openings in the building superstructure, thus causing an indoor pressure-level drop that can pull outside air into the building.

Stiles The vertical parts of a framework, such as a sash or a door.

Stock cabinets Cabinets that are in stock or available quickly when ordered from a retail outlet.

Stud A vertical framing member of a wall.

Sunroom Also known as a solarium, a sunny room that has many windows or is enclosed by glass panels for maximum sunlight.

Task lighting Light aimed directly onto a work area, such as a sink or a cooktop.

Termite barrier A physical barrier (typically metal) that prevents ground termites from crawling up into a home.

Track lighting Lights that are attached to the ceiling by a track and can be easily moved and adjusted.

Underlayment Sheet material—usually plywood—placed over a subfloor to provide a smooth, even surface for new flooring.

Vapor retarder A material used to prevent water vapor from moving from one area into another or into a building material.

Ventilation The process of removing or supplying air to a certain space.

VOC Abbreviation for a "volatile organic compound"—a potentially harmful chemical that evaporates from liquids or solids at room temperature.

Wainscoting Paneling that extends 36 to 42 inches or so upward from the floor level, over the finished wall surface. It is often finished with a horizontal strip of molding mounted at the proper height and protruding enough to prevent the top of a chair back from touching a wall surface.

Wallboard See *Drywall*.

INDEX

Page 1: iStockphoto.com/Scott Cramer **page 4:** *bottom* John Puleio; *top* courtesy of Ecotimber **page 5:** *top* courtesy of Kohler; *bottom* iStockphoto.com/Jan Pietruszka **page 6:** courtesy of Neil Kelley Cabinets **page 8:** John Puleio **page 9:** courtesy of BluWood **page 10:** courtesy of EnviroGlass **page 11:** *top* courtesy of Delta; *bottom* courtesy of DuPont **page 12:** *top* courtesy of Neil Kelley Cabinets; *bottom* John Puleio **page 13:** courtesy of Demilec LLC **page 14:** courtesy of iLevel **page 15:** courtesy of Contact Industries **page 16:** *left* courtesy of Lennox; *right* courtesy of Milliken **page 17:** courtesy of Whirlpool **page 18:** *left* courtesy of Kohler; *center* courtesy of Demilec LLC; *right* courtesy of DuPont **page 19:** iStockphoto.com/Eric Vega **page 20:** iStockphoto.com/Studio Zipper **page 21:** iStockphoto.com/Jan Pietruszka **page 22:** *top left* courtesy of DuPont; *top right* courtesy of LP; *bottom* courtesy of National Fenestration Rating Council **page 23:** *top* courtesy of iLevel; *bottom right* courtesy of Universal Forest Products; *bottom left* courtesy of Contact Industries **page 24:** *top left* courtesy of Hanson Roof Tile; *top right* courtesy of Monier **page 25:** *left & right* courtesy of Kohler; *bottom* courtesy of Chicago Faucets **page 26:** *top* iStockphoto.com/Stas Perov; *bottom* iStockphoto.com/Richard Walters **page 27:** iStockphoto.com/Natalia Guseva **page 28:** courtesy of ZipWall **page 29:** *top* Environment-i-media; *bottom* Daniel Friedman **page 30:** *top* Eastern Environmental Technologies; *center* courtesy of Johns Manville; *bottom* courtesy of Dumond Chemicals **page 31:** *bottom* iStockphoto.com **page 32:** iStockphoto.com/Michael Braun **page 33:** iStockphoto.com/Kameleon 007 **page 34:** iStockphoto.com/Branko Miokovic **page 35:** *top to bottom* courtesy of Carpet & Rug Institute; courtesy of Greenguard; courtesy of Green Seal; courtesy of Forest Stewardship Council; courtesy of Sustainable Forestry Initiative; courtesy of Rainforest Alliance **page 36:** John Puleio **page 37:** iStockphoto.com/John Tomaselli **page 38:** *top* courtesy of Energy Star; *bottom* courtesy of National Association of Home Builders **page 39:** *left* courtesy of Kohler; *right* courtesy of EarthCraft House **page 40:** *left* iStockphoto.com/DIGIcal; *center* courtesy of Shaw; *right* John Parsekian/CH **page 41:** John Puleio **page 42:** John Puleio **pages 43–46:** *all* John Parsekian/CH **page 47:** *top* iStockphoto.com/David H. Lewis; *center* iStockphoto.com/DIGIcal; *bottom* iStockphoto.com/John Sartin **page 49:** *top & bottom* John Puleio **page 52–53:** *all* courtesy of iLevel **page 54:** iStockphoto.com **page 55:** *left & right* courtesy of iLevel **page 56:** Brian C. Nieves/CH **page 57:** *all* courtesy of Better Barns **page 58:** John Puleio **page 59:** courtesy of iLevel **page 60:** iStockphoto.com/Michael Walker **page 64:** *all* Stephen Munz **page 67:** *both* courtesy of DAP **page 68:** John Parsekian/CH **page 69:** *top right* courtesy of Innovative Insulation; *all others* John Parsekian/CH **page 70:** courtesy of Owens Corning **page 71:** *top* courtesy of Infraspection Institute, Inc.; *bottom both* John Parsekian/CH **pages 72–73:** *all* John Parsekian/CH **page 74:** *all* courtesy of Johns Manville **page 75:** *all* John Parsekian/CH **page 76:** iStockphoto.com/Ron Barnett **page 77:** courtesy of

Georgia Pacific **page 79:** *left* courtesy of USG; *top right* John Parsekian/CH; *top bottom* courtesy of USG **page 80:** *both* Freeze Frame Studios/CH **page 81:** *top right, bottom left & top left* Freeze Frame Studios/CH; *center right* John Parsekian/CH; *bottom right* Clarke Barre/CH **pages 82–83:** *all* Freeze Frame Studios/CH **pages 84–85:** *both* courtesy of Shaw **pages 86–89:** *all* Freeze Frame Studios/CH **page 90:** *top* courtesy of Pure Wool Carpets; *bottom* courtesy of Milliken **page 91:** *top & inset* Paul Weiner; *bottom both* courtesy of Armstrong **page 92:** courtesy of American Olean **page 93:** *all* John Parsekian/CH **pages 94–95:** *all* Freeze Frame Studios/CH **pages 96–97:** *all* Freeze Frame Studios/CH **pages 98–99:** John Parsekian/CH **page 100:** *top* courtesy of Milliken; *bottom* courtesy of EcoTimber **page 101:** *left* courtesy of Shaw; *right* courtesy of EcoTimber **page 102:** iStockphoto.com/ Diane Diederich **page 103:** National Fenestration Resource Council **pages 104–105:** *all* Freeze Frame Studios/CH **page 106:** *all* John Parsekian/CH **page 107:** *right both* Freeze Frame Studios/CH; *top left & bottom left* John Parsekian/CH **page 109:** Freeze Frame Studios/CH **page 110:** courtesy of JELDWEN **page 111:** courtesy of Therma-Tru **page 113:** *all* John Parsekian/CH **page 115:** *all* John Parsekian/CH **page 116:** *left* courtesy of Solatube; *center* courtesy of Kohler; *right* Freeze Frame Studios/CH **page 117:** courtesy of Progress Lighting **page 118:** *both* courtesy of Progress Lighting **page 119:** *all* courtesy of Solatube **page 120–121:** *both* courtesy of Kohler **page 123:** *top* courtesy of Delta; *bottom* courtesy of Rheem **page 124:** *all* Freeze Frame Studios/CH **page 125:** *top right & left both* Freeze Frame Studios/CH; *bottom right all* Brian C. Nieves/CH **page 126:** courtesy of Aquasana **page 127:** *left* courtesy of Aquasana; *right* courtesy of Weathertrak **pages 128–131:** *all* Freeze Frame Studios/CH **page 132:** courtesy of Progress Lighting **page 133:** *top & bottom right* courtesy of Kohler; *bottom left* courtesy of Progress Lighting **page 134:** *left* iStockphoto.com/Francis Twitty; *center* courtesy of WaterFurnace; *right* courtesy of Honeywell **page 135:** iStockphoto.com/David Ross **page 136:** iStockphoto.com/Francis Twitty **pages 140–141:** *all* Brian C. Nieves/CH **pages 142–143:** *all* John Parsekian/CH **page 144:** courtesy of Carrier **page 145:** *top right & top left* courtesy of Carrier Corp.; *bottom left* courtesy of Adobe Air Inc.; *left center & top center* John Parsekian/CH **page 148:** *top & bottom* courtesy of Partnership for Advanced Training in Housing **page 149:** courtesy of WaterFurnace **page 150:** *left* courtesy of White River Hardwoods/Woodworks; *center* John Parsekian/CH; *right* iStockphoto.com/Okana Struk **page 151:** iStockphoto.com/Stu Salmon Page **page 153:** *all* John Parsekian/CH **page 155:** iStockphoto.com/Janice Richard **page 157:** *top left* courtesy of Focal Points Architectural Products; *bottom right, bottom center & top center* courtesy of White River Hardwood/Woodworks; *bottom left* courtesy of Georgia-Pacific; *top left* courtesy of Elite **page 158:** *both* John Parsekian/CH **page 159:** *top right* courtesy of White River Hardwoods/Woodworks; *bottom row* John

Parsekian/CH **pages 160–162:** *all* John Parsekian/CH **page 163:** iStockphoto.com/Oskana Struk **page 164:** *all* John Parsekian/CH **page 165:** *all* Neal Barrett/CH **page 166:** *left* courtesy of IceStone; *center* Freeze Frame Studios/CH; *right* iStockphoto.com/M. Eric Honeycutt **page 168:** *both* Freeze Frame Studios/CH **page 169:** *bottom right* iStockphoto.com/M. Eric Honeycutt; *top right, bottom left & top left* Freeze Frame Studios/CH **pages 170–173:** *all* Freeze Frame Studios/CH **page 174:** *both* Freeze Frame Studios/CH **page 175:** *left both* Freeze Frame Studios/CH; *bottom* courtesy of IceStone **page 176:** Freeze Frame Studios/CH **page 177:** *left both* Freeze Frame Studios/CH; *right* Merle Henkenius **page 178:** *left* courtesy of CertainTeed; *center* courtesy of UniGroup; *right* John Parsekian/CH **page 179–180:** *both* courtesy of CertainTeed **page 181:** courtesy of Celotex **page 182:** courtesy of CertainTeed **page 183:** *bottom right* Brian C. Nieves/CH; *all others* Robert Anderson **pages 184–187:** *all* John Parsekian/CH **page 189:** courtesy of UniGroup **page 190:** courtesy of EcoStar **page 191:** *top* courtesy of Monier; *bottom* courtesy of EcoStar **pages 192–194:** *all* John Parsekian/CH **page 195:** *top* iStockphoto.com/Michael Pettigrew; *bottom* Grady Glenn **pages 196–197:** *all* John Parsekian/CH **page 199:** *all* John Parsekian/CH **page 200:** Fiber Composites LLC **page 201:** Fiber Composites LLC **page 207:** iStockphoto.com/David Ross

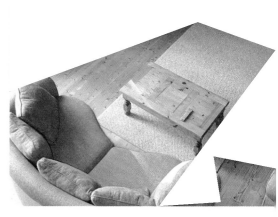

Have a home improvement, decorating, or gardening project? Look for these and other fine Creative Homeowner books wherever books are sold.

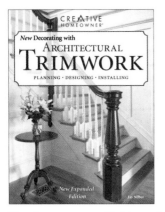

Transform a room with trimwork. Over 550 color photos and illustrations. 240 pp.; $8^1/_2$" × $10^7/_8$"
BOOK #: 277500

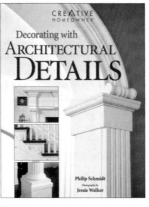

Covers design treatments such as moldings and window seats. 300+ color photos. 224 pp.; $8^1/_2$" × $10^7/_8$"
BOOK #: 278225

A complete guide covering all aspects of drywall. Over 450 color photos 160 pp.; $8^1/_2$" × $10^7/_8$"
BOOK #: 278320

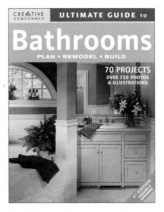

Includes step-by-step projects and over 630 photos. 272 pp.; $8^1/_2$" × $10^7/_8$"
BOOK#: 278632

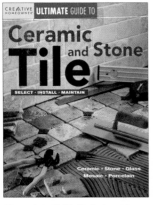

Complete DIY tile instruction. Over 550 color photos and illustrations. 224 pp.; $8^1/_2$" × $10^7/_8$"
BOOK #: 27753

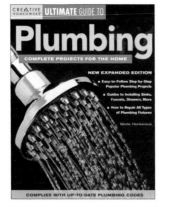

The complete manual for plumbing. Over 750 color photos and illustrations. 288 pp.; $8^1/_2$" × $10^7/_8$"
BOOK#: 278200

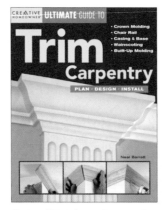

Best-selling trimwork manual. Over 500 color photos and illustrations. 208 pp.; $8^1/_2$" × $10^7/_8$"
BOOK#: 277516

The ultimate home-improvement reference manual. Over 300 step-by-step projects. 608 pp.; 9" × $10^7/_8$"
BOOK#: 267870

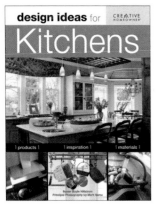

Design inspiration for creating a new kitchen. Over 500 color photographs. 224 pp.; $8^1/_2$" × $10^7/_8$"
BOOK #: 279415

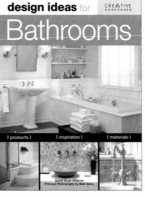

Design inspiration for creating a new bathroom. Over 500 color photos. 224 pp.; $8^1/_2$" × $10^7/_8$"
BOOK #:   3 1901 04367 1801

Techniques and recipes that will save time, money, and the earth. Over 200 photos. 240 pp.; $7^1/_{16}$" × $9^1/_8$"
77838

An impressive guide to garden design and plant selection. 950 color photos and illustrations. 384 pp.; 9" × 10"
BOOK #: 274610

For more information and to order direct, visit our Web site at www.creativehomeowner.com